Mark Twain: Selected Criticism

Mark Twain

SELECTED CRITICISM

Edited with an
Introduction by

ARTHUR L. SCOTT

REVISED EDITION

SOUTHERN METHODIST UNIVERSITY PRESS
Dallas

© 1955, 1967 : SOUTHERN METHODIST UNIVERSITY PRESS : DALLAS

LIBRARY OF CONGRESS CATALOG CARD NUMBER 66-29657

To

MY WIFE

for incalculable services in proofreading and encouragement

PREFACE TO THE SECOND EDITION

WHEN THIS BOOK was first published in the hardbound edition of 1955, it stood alone in the field. Since then it has been joined by over half a dozen paperbacks. *Mark Twain's Wound,* ed. Lewis Leary, 1962, is an excellent casebook of material concerned with the clashing theories of Van Wyck Brooks and Bernard DeVoto. A shorter volume is Henry Nash Smith's *Mark Twain: A Collection of Critical Essays,* 1963, emphasizing Mark Twain's six most important books. Both works are valuable in bringing together critical studies written since 1920.

Because *Huckleberry Finn* is so widely studied, several publishers now offer collections of essays about this novel alone. Ten essays — again starting with Van Wyck Brooks in 1920 — are found in Barry A. Marks, ed., *Mark Twain's Huckleberry Finn,* 1959. About the same number of essays are available in Kenneth S. Lynn, ed., *Huckleberry Finn: Text, Sources, and Criticism,* 1961, which includes three ante-Brooks pieces of criticism. The Norton Critical Edition of *Huckleberry Finn,* ed. Bradley, Beatty, and Long, is extremely useful not only for its annotated text, but also for its rich collection of sources and critiques. Only two of its twenty-three critical pieces, however, antedate Brooks. Almost the same is true of Macmillan's *Huck Finn and His Critics,* ed. Lettis, McDonnell, and Morris, 1962; three of its critical selections were written before 1920.

Discussions of Mark Twain, ed. Guy A. Cardwell, 1963, is broader in scope but quite short. The stress is not upon the in-fighting among the scholars and nearly half of these selections focus upon no particular novel. But once more the period before 1920 is represented by only four essays.

Further proof of Mark Twain's acceptance into academic circles is the number of handbooks which have been published about him for the first time during the past ten years. By far the fullest and most useful of these is E. Hudson Long, *Mark Twain Handbook,* 1958, complete with chronological table, footnotes, and index, plus valuable bibliographies for each chapter. Thin paperback handbooks include Lewis Leary, *Mark Twain,* 1960, Frank Baldanza, *Mark Twain,* 1961 (the longest and best), Douglas Grant, *Mark Twain,* 1962, and Darrel Abel, *A Simplified Approach to Twain,* 1964.

To enumerate the dissertations and scholarly books written about Mark Twain since 1955 would be pointless. Let it suffice to say that interest in Mark Twain is still on the rise in academic circles. The annual bibliographies of *PMLA* for the five years 1955-59 report about 160 Mark Twain items, whereas there are listed about 290 items for the following lustrum 1960-64.

Where does the present volume fit into this scheme of things? It makes available for the first time in paperback the original and still the fullest collection of Mark Twain criticism. Second, unlike most of the new books, it does not stress *Huckleberry Finn* or the quarreling among the critics, nor does it restrict itself almost entirely to criticism written since 1920. Of the thirty-four pieces contained here, twenty were written before that date and some of these are hard to come by elsewhere. In short, we have here a full historical survey of Mark Twain criticism from the very beginning.

There are only a few changes from the first edition. Four of the least informative modern pieces have been dropped in order to make room for the *Saturday Review* essay of 1870, the G. K. Chesterton appraisal of 1910, and two splendid articles — new and hitherto un-reprinted — by John C. Gerber and Hamlin Hill.

ARTHUR L. SCOTT

Urbana, Illinois
September 6, 1966

FOREWORD

THIS VOLUME PRESENTS the cream of Mark Twain criticism from its start in 1867 down to the present. Obscure essays are not reprinted by mere virtue of their obscurity, nor are famous critiques ignored on the grounds of their accessibility or familiarity. Quality and compass are the only guides. For the sake of balance, the years before 1910 are generously represented and care is taken not to overstress particular subjects such as *Huckleberry Finn* or Twain's late pessimism. The selections support no special attitude toward Mark Twain. Some are friendly, some hostile. Some are general evaluations of Twain's work; some are Freudian analyses of his character; some are close inspections of his literary practices.

For the sake of historical perspective, the selections are arranged chronologically. Critical standards are never sacrificed in a desire to represent big-name critics. Always the spotlight is kept upon Mark Twain, not upon his commentators. Certain distinguished Twainians are not represented here because their interests were mainly biographical, editorial, or bibliographical. As for foreign-language criticism, this has been left for a separate project best pursued abroad.*

Gratitude is here extended to the following libraries for making available to me many books and articles not owned by the University of Illinois: The Newberry Library, Library of Congress, Chicago Public Library, Bryn Mawr Library, and the libraries of the universities of Chicago, Missouri, Michigan, Cincinnati, Tennessee, Louisiana, Pennsylvania, Texas, Wisconsin, Princeton, Harvard, and Stanford. Special thanks are also due to Thomas E. Ratcliffe, Jr. and his associates in the Reference Department of the General Library at the University of Illinois for their cheerful aid in locating and borrowing

---

*This foreign-language criticism is of low merit, says Roger Asselineau, who has compiled an annotated bibliography of Twain criticism from 1910 to 1950, not only in the United States and Great Britain, but also in France, Germany, Italy, Spain, and Latin America. See *The Literary Reputation of Mark Twain from 1910-1950, A Critical Essay and Bibliography,* Publications de la Faculté des Lettres de l'Université de Clermont (Paris: Librairie Marcel Didier, 1954). Two other doctoral dissertations treat this same general subject: Arthur L. Vogelback, *The Literary Reputation of Mark Twain in America 1869-1885* (University of Chicago, 1939) and Robert M. Rodney, *Mark Twain in England: A Study of the English Criticism of and Attitude towards Mark Twain, 1867-1940* (University of Wisconsin, 1946).

these scarce items, and in tracing copyrights. I am particularly grateful to Doris M. Frantz, Barbara B. Coburn, Wilma F. Smith, and Hugh F. Pritchard for labors which proved a personal interest in my project. And to Eva Faye Benton in the English Library I express my gratitude for a continued co-operation without which a great deal of my research would have been most troublesome.

ARTHUR L. SCOTT

Urbana, Illinois
August 4, 1955

CONTENTS

Mark Twain: Selected Criticism

INTRODUCTION

FOR THE STUDENT of letters a survey of almost ninety years of Mark Twain criticism holds many rewards, and a few surprises. The familiar pattern is revealed—commencing with book reviews, then a surge of curiosity about the new writer himself and his domestic life, and concluding in the 1950's with academic inspections of the minutiae of his life and work. Perhaps the chief surprise is the discovery that in his own day Mark Twain was *not* regarded universally as an *enfant terrible*—a buffoon who mocked at everything too fine for him to appreciate. Instead, we discover that intelligence and discernment animate much of the earliest criticism. The shrewdest of Twain's contemporaries, indeed, anticipated most of the judgments passed by succeeding generations.

To begin at the beginning, we should remember that in 1867 Charles Henry Webb, in introducing Twain's first book of sketches, insisted that the author was primarily a *moralist* and only secondarily a humorist. Well known is William Dean Howells' praise of *The Innocents Abroad* two years later, but few people recall that Bret Harte, in a long review, extolled this same book not only for its power, originality, and humor, but also for its "really admirable rhetoric, vigorous and picturesque." It is no recent discovery, we find, that Mark Twain perfected "one of the great styles of English" —to quote Bernard DeVoto. Examination of other favorable reviews, too, makes us dismiss the old notion that with *The Innocents* Mark Twain embarked on his career with a popular success but a critical failure.

During the next twenty-five years Mark Twain grew so world-famous as a personality that critics like Howells, Richard Watson Gilder, Brander Matthews, George T. Ferris, H. R. Haweis, Andrew Lang, Henry C. Vedder, and Frank Stockton found it necessary to remind the delighted public, at frequent intervals, that he was far more than a clown. As early as 1874 Ferris prophesied a great future for Mark Twain—paying special tribute to his Americanism, his fresh spontaneity, his breadth and ease, his graphic descriptions, and, above all, "the intense humanity and lifelikeness" of his humor.

That most reviewers in 1876 overlooked the mythical magic of *Tom Sawyer* must be acknowledged. Still worse, the uneven and rather conventional *The Prince and the Pauper* (1881) received more plaudits from the genteel press than did *Huckleberry Finn* (1885), whose disreputable hero distressed many people. Brander Matthews—anonymously at the start—was the first to champion the book. He was soon supported strongly by Andrew Lang in England, who boldly called *Huck* "the great American novel . . . a nearly flawless gem of romance and of humour." The erudite Lang also had some caustic words for the so-called Culture which refused to recognize Mark Twain as being "one among the greatest contemporary makers of fiction." Before he died, Twain rejoiced to hear Sir Walter Besant, William Lyon Phelps, and others also give first place to *Huckleberry Finn,* for he himself had finally come to judge it the best of his novels. Twain's masterpiece, we see, unlike Melville's, was not required to languish three score years awaiting recognition.

There were also, of course, skeptics and detractors. As early as 1882, for example, John Nichol—who admitted that Twain could write magnificently—complained that Twain was suffering the plight of the professional humorist, "who has lost the power of seeing the beauty of the universe, because he has come to regard it as a mere text-book for his sadly incessant and ultimately wearisome jests." Somewhat later, D. F. Hannigan sarcastically termed Twain's comic diatribe on Fenimore Cooper "a literary *delirium tremens."* Meanwhile, critics like William P. Trent and Charles Miner Thompson charged that Twain was singularly devoid of taste and of technical aptitudes, but neither critic was willing to deny his greatness. Trent was forced to conclude that, despite his deficiencies, like Balzac Twain was a "great writer" by virtue of his deep knowledge of the human heart. And Thompson, who asserted that Twain had not created even one living character (Huck "is simply the usual vagabond boy"), ended by admitting that Twain was great, because he had interpreted the national character and taught "the virtues of common sense and honest manliness. If it comes to a choice, these are better than refinement."

By 1896 Mark Twain was probably the most colorful and beloved figure in the entire world. The near-legendary character of his fame resulted in a spate of personal reminiscences which are of possible value only to biographers and historians. Relatives, business associates, old and new friends, and even casual acquaintances filled the family magazines with anecdotal recollections of America's favorite writer. Mark Twain's domestic privacy, moreover, was invaded by reporters eager to tell the world about his cats, his furniture, his household readings, his billiards, and the lines on his left palm. Concomitant with these folksy trifles, however, in the best periodicals there began to appear serious studies with such titles as "Mark Twain's Place in Literature," "Mark Twain—His Work," "Mark Twain as a Prospective Classic," "American Humor: Mark Twain," and "Mark Twain as a Critic." The crowds may have attended Twain's lectures simply to laugh, but these serious articles of the nineties show a remarkable consensus among literary people that the popular idol was more than a mere funny-fellow and that his reputation would endure. "It is like the fun of a circus-clown taking the money at the door," wrote Frank Stockton in 1893; "he may be a queer fellow, but he means business." Stockton was also among the first to point out that "The figure with the tragic mask stalks through much of Mark Twain's work."

Whereas Mark Twain lived abroad during the nineties, the final decade of his life found him back home in America, filling the twin roles of national monument and oracle. But he published few books. Amidst the myriad bagatelles during this decade, there appeared further attempts to evaluate Twain's writings. Undoubtedly the most penetrating attempt was made by Howells in 1901. Explaining Mark Twain's service in liberating America from its deference to Europe, Howells also proved that some things in Twain "wound our conventions rather than our convictions." For the *litterateur* Howells then demonstrated Twain's mastery of style and characterization. And for young readers he issued a prescient warning about Twain's late seriousness: "It would be well for his younger following to beware of reversing the error of the elder, and taking everything in earnest, as these once took nothing in earnest from him."

Andrew Lang and Brander Matthews continued to extol their favorite author during this period, and were supported by such critics as Henry M. Alden, Clarence H. Gaines, Henry Dwight Sedgwick, Thomas M. Parrott, and Hamilton W. Mabie—all striving to keep Twain, the writer, before the eyes of a world dazzled by Twain, the personality. The ablest recruits to Twain's cause were Archibald Henderson and William Lyon Phelps. The former praised, in particular, the cosmopolitanism of Mark Twain and prophesied that ultimately he would be regarded as "America's greatest sociologist in letters." The latter, while not denying the universality of Twain's appeal, insisted also that he embodied "the American spirit" even more than did Whitman. "If there be a living American writer touched with true genius, whose books glow with divine fire," concluded Phelps, "it is he."

The most devastating attack on Mark Twain during these years came from Scotland, where Charles Whibley deplored Twain's "flippant impertinence" and "imbecile lack of taste." *A Connecticut Yankee* he condemned as "a masterpiece of vulgarity." Yet, in the final analysis, Whibley seemed more sad than angry: "Had he never cut a joke, had he refrained from always grinning at grave and beautiful things, how brilliant a fame would have been his!"

Mark Twain's death in 1910 brought a flood of tributes. Memorial poems, eulogies, pictorial displays, editorials, and personal recollections filled the press. It was scarcely a time for considered comment. Henry Thurston Peck in New York and Barry Pain in London raised nearly lone voices against the worshiping acclaim. Within the year, biographies began to appear—Howells' and Henderson's—to be followed in 1912 by the elaborate and somewhat idealized official biography by Albert Bigelow Paine, the companion and literary executor of Mark Twain. For students and collectors there was also Merle Johnson's bibliography of the writings *of* Mark Twain, as well as Henderson's bibliography of writings *about* him. The pattern was being followed.

When the air cleared of tributes, it was discovered that Mark Twain did not require the magic of his living personality to keep his name alive. His death, indeed, gave his writings a stature they had not enjoyed before. To be sure, several critics did maintain that his humor was fading now that it was no longer enhanced by his personal charm, but only William B. Cairns dared to claim that his serious work and his novels lacked permanency. Gradually, the literary historians began to include the name of Mark Twain among the American masters of the nineteenth century. William Marshall Urban, in a perceptive study in 1913, pointed out that posterity would remember not the complacencies of Mark Twain, but his indignations. And in the same year John Macy honored Twain with the most extensive critical treatment he had yet received in a survey of American literature. From this time onward increasing attention was paid by literary historians to Twain's work, particularly after it was dignified by Stuart Sherman's careful inspection in the 1921 *Cambridge History of American Literature.* And immediately after World War I, when American literature became a recognized field of academic study, it is significant that Harper's introduced its famous "Modern Classics" series with *Huckleberry Finn.*

National magazines, moreover, began to accept semischolarly articles on Twain, such as Edith Wyatt's "An Inspired Critic" and H. Houston Peckham's "The Literary Status of Mark Twain, 1877-1890." Probably the most important of these articles was published in *Harper's* by Twain's old friend, Brander Matthews. "Mark Twain and the Art of Writing" now served as the ultimate rebuff to those who still believed in the crudity of Twain's literary style. With professorial thoroughness, Matthews demonstrated (with many quotations) the beauty and power of Mark Twain's language—"as pure as it is nervous and direct and uncompromising." Fault continues to be found with other aspects of Twain's work, but since 1920 almost no one has cared to speak against his literary style. Such studies as these presaged the scholarly research papers (e.g., O. H. Moore's "Mark Twain and Don Quixote," 1922) which now began to appear in academic journals like *PMLA, Education,* and the *Classical Journal.* The family magazines of the twenties continued to carry charming essays on Twain by popular figures such as John Erskine and Helen Keller, but scholarship for the first time was making a serious bid to rescue Mark Twain from the fate of the merely popular writer.

Meanwhile, posthumous publication of some of Twain's literary dynamite (*The Mysterious Stranger,* 1916, and *What Is Man?,* 1917) caused churchmen and psychologists to join scholars in revising certain concepts of Mark Twain. "The Misanthropy of Mark Twain," "The Tragedy of Mark Twain," "The Pessimism of Mark Twain" —such were the studies of this newly revealed facet of his character. Because scholarship thrives on discussion, this evidence that Twain was not just a simple, happy man proved of incalculable benefit to his critical repute. At last there was revealed, for all to see, a complexity—a Mark Twain "problem."

Waldo Frank in 1919 was the first to state this problem and to suggest a solution. Frank envisioned Mark Twain as a tender, dreaming, avid spirit born in the ranks of a hurling and sweating and money-worshiping army with which he forced himself to keep pace. "For this betrayal of his soul," mourned Frank, "his soul brought him bitterness, and the mass of his works are failures." Only in *Huckleberry Finn* did Frank believe that the "great soul" of Mark Twain "burst its bonds of false instruction and false ideal."

The following year, Van Wyck Brooks fabricated an interesting Freudian theory which has been frequently scouted but seldom ignored. To Brooks, Mark Twain was a God-made satirist who was "fairly shanghaied into the business man's paradise" by his wife, who also re-established over him "that old Calvinistic spell of his mother's." Twain, in brief, was a "shorn Samson led about by a little child," who was interested only in making him over into "a candidate for gentility." In 1921 Harvey O'Higgins and Edward H. Reeder supported this view of Mark Twain as a stultified Rabelais or Swift. In a strong Freudian analysis they pictured him as a "biological failure" torn by hidden fears, frustrations, and an inferiority complex —all dating from birth.

Lewis Mumford, meanwhile, followed Frank in bewailing Twain's acceptance of comfort as "the chief art of his period." Mumford felt that Mark Twain deliberately stifled his natural impulses toward beauty and, instead, "accepted the values that surrounded him, and since they were not central human values—he was too honest not to realize this—he stored up, secretly, the bile of despair." Even Fred Lewis Pattee, who ridiculed Brooks's theory, also saw Twain as "a thwarted creator like Melville"—thwarted especially by his own temperament which kept him "dancing in cap and bells for money." Lucy Lockwood Hazard agreed that the trouble lay in the dichotomy of Twain himself, but critics like Carl Van Doren and Vernon L. Parrington refused to see him as a frustrated genius. They saw him, instead, as "the very embodiment of the turbulent frontier" and consequently studied him as an immensely significant American document. Even his "slow drift" from humor to satire and into pessimism they felt reflected the authentic spirit of the age. Carl Van Doren summed it up by asserting: "Mark Twain loafed through the world something like a comic Whitman."

The twenties also found Gamaliel Bradford studying Twain from the vantage point of an older reader who was once charmed by his books—only to discover belatedly that they have made him a worse man. In the end, Bradford saw Twain as a man groping in the dark, laughing inanely. His final impression of him, consequently, was "devastating."

The 1930's produced more volumes about Mark Twain than had appeared in all the years before. They ranged from a scholarly lexicon to the shadowy reminiscences of ninety-year-old Billy Gillis, in whose cabin Twain spent five months back in the Jumping Frog days. Without doubt the most influential volume was Bernard DeVoto's *Mark Twain's America,* 1932. DeVoto carefully examined Twain's cultural background in Hannibal, Missouri, as well as the matrix of his humor in the folk art and the newspaper funny-men of the day. Furthermore, so violently did DeVoto attack the interpretations of Van Wyck Brooks that many critics, even today, find it hard to remain neutral regarding the bitter controversy which ensued. Other significant books during the thirties were Minnie M. Brashear's study of Twain's boyhood in *Mark Twain, Son of Missouri,* Edward Wagenknecht's *Mark Twain, the Man and His Work,* and Ivan Benson's *Mark Twain's Western Years.* Clara Clemens, in *My Father, Mark Twain,* did disclose some new material and give new insights, but the other biographies added little to the body of Twainiana except bulk.

Because 1935 was the centennial of Twain's birth, these years evoked dozens of short evaluations of his writings. Some critics such as Granville Hicks and Newton Arvin joined the Brooks forces, while others extended the DeVoto view. Hicks argued that, since Mark Twain was "too submissive for his own good," he became a mere entertainer, when he might have grown into "a great social novelist." Arvin went still farther. He argued bitterly that Mark Twain is popular simply "because he co-operates with the desire to play hooky." Even the best of Twain's books, said Arvin, are filled with "the slag of buffoonery and false sentiment," inanities, and tired nonsense.

Constance Rourke, V. F. Calverton, Ludwig Lewisohn, Mark Van Doren, and others, however, along with DeVoto refused to believe that Twain ever "sold out" to the upper classes of the East.

Lewisohn even called him our national bard, in the blood-line of Homer.

These were all attempts at general appraisal. More helpful to scholarship were studies by Walter Blair and DeLancey Ferguson. Like DeVoto, Blair sought to orient Mark Twain in his era by demonstrating his debt to the methods of early comedians, especially those of the Southwest and Down East. Ferguson opened up a whole new field with his study of the original manuscript of *Huckleberry Finn*. Comparing this manuscript with the book, Ferguson showed that the revisions were "the work of a skilled craftsman." "Of the thwarted Swift invented by Mr. Brooks and his followers," Ferguson concluded, "there is not a trace." Since 1940 DeVoto and Leon T. Dickinson, among others, have plowed in this field of textual comparison with rich results.

More meaningful than the space devoted to Mark Twain by the general magazines during the centennial decade was the increase in the number of academic articles and doctoral dissertations on special aspects of his thought or work. Theodore Dreiser, for example, not only graced *Esquire* with anecdotes about Mark Twain, but also contributed to the *English Journal* a serious study of the Twain problem. Critically speaking, Mark Twain's reputation finally came of age during the thirties.

Although the years since 1940 have so far produced but one significant biography—that by DeLancey Ferguson—they have seen the publication of numerous other volumes about Mark Twain. Walter Frear has traced the footsteps and pen of Twain during his four months in Hawaii in 1866; and Dixon Wecter, before his untimely death, completed a definitive examination of Twain's ancestral background and boyhood. The other books of recent years almost all reveal their origins in postgraduate research. They are, in consequence, of less general interest, though of great professional value. Such volumes are Gladys Bellamy's *Mark Twain as a Literary Artist*, Edgar M. Branch's *The Literary Apprenticeship of Mark Twain*, and Kenneth Andrews' *Nook Farm: Mark Twain's Hartford Circle*—all published by university presses.

Today Mark Twain is firmly entrenched in our literature along with Hawthorne, Melville, Whitman, and the other "classics." Encouraged by editors, young scholars no longer feel embarrassed to examine such relatively minor aspects of Twain's life and work as his interest in music, his attitude toward the Jews, the receptions accorded his speeches or books, the background of his vocabulary, the origins of his short-lived Anglophobia, his early muckraking, his use of symbolism, his revisions of various texts, and his associations with people or places he hardly knew. If a new letter or sketch by Mark Twain is discovered, it is broadcast with the speed of scandal— subject only to certain restrictions imposed by the Mark Twain Estate. The bimonthly *Twainian* serves as a sort of clearinghouse of information for collectors and students; and the *Mark Twain Quarterly* occasionally carries some brief comments or appreciations. Obliged, like most research, to deal more and more with less and less, Twain criticism is still of value in correcting, supplementing, and revaluating our fund of knowledge. But amid this mass of criticism, an odd new danger has appeared in recent years. Leo Marx recognized it recently when he said of *Huckleberry Finn:* "Today the problem of evaluating the book is as much obscured by unqualified praise as it once was by parochial hostility." No one could appreciate this irony of time more than Mark Twain himself.

1955

1867

CHARLES HENRY WEBB

"MARK TWAIN" is too well known to the public to require a formal introduction at my hands. By his story of the Frog, he scaled the heights of popularity at a single jump, and won for himself the *sobriquet* of The Wild Humorist of the Pacific Slope. He is also known to fame as The Moralist of the Main: and it is not unlikely that as such he will go down to posterity. It is in his secondary character, as humorist, however, rather than in his primal one of moralist, that I aim to present him in the present volume. And here a ready explanation will be found for the somewhat fragmentary character of many of these sketches; for it was necessary to snatch threads of humor wherever they could be found — very often detaching them from serious articles and moral essays with which they were woven and entangled. Originally written for newspaper publication, many of the articles referred to events of the day, the interest of which has now passed away, and contained local allusions which the general reader would fail to understand; in such cases excision became imperative. Further than this, remark or comment is unnecessary. Mark Twain never resorts to tricks of spelling nor rhetorical buffoonery for the purpose of provoking a laugh; the vein of his humor runs too rich and deep to make surface-gilding necessary. But there are few who can resist the quaint similes, keen satire, and hard good sense which form the staple of his writings.

"Advertisement" in Mark Twain's first book, The Celebrated Jumping Frog of Calaveras County, and Other Sketches, *published by C. H. Webb, New York, 1867.*

1870

BRET HARTE

SIX HUNDRED AND FIFTY PAGES of open and declared fun—very strongly accented with wood-cuts at that—might go far toward frightening the fastidious reader. But the Hartford publishers, we imagine, do not print for the fastidious reader, nor do traveling book agents sell much to that rarely occurring man, who prefers to find books rather than let them find *him.* So that, unless he has already made "Mark Twain's" acquaintance through the press, he will not probably meet him until, belated in the rural districts, he takes from the parlor table of a country farm-house an illustrated Bible, Greeley's *American Conflict,* Mr. Parton's apocryphal *Biographies,* successively and listessly, and so comes at last upon "Mark Twain's" *Innocents* like a joyous revelation—an Indian spring in an alkaline literary desert. For the book has that intrinsic worth of bigness and durability which commends itself to the rural economist, who likes to get a material return for his money. It is about the size of *The Family Physician,* for which it will doubtless be often mistaken—with great advantage to the patient.

The entire six hundred and fifty pages are devoted to an account of the "steamship *Quaker City's* excursion to Europe and the Holy Land," with a description of certain famous localities of which a great many six hundred and fifty pages have been at various times written by various tourists. Yet there is hardly a line of Mr. Clemens'

Review of The Innocents Abroad *in the* Overland Monthly, *IV o.s. (January, 1870), 100-101.*

account that is not readable; and none the less, certainly, from the fact that he pokes fun at other tourists, and that the reader becomes dimly conscious that Mr. Clemens' fellow-passengers would have probably estopped this gentle satirist from going with them could they have forecast his book. The very title—*The Innocents Abroad*—is a suggestive hint of the lawlessness and audacity in which the trip is treated. We shall not stop to question the propriety of this feature; it is only just to Mr. Clemens to say, that the best satirists have generally found their quarry in the circle in which they moved, and among their best friends; but we contend that if he has, by this act, choked off and prevented the enthusiastic chronicling of the voyage by any of his fellow-passengers, who may have been sentimentally inclined, he is entitled to the consideration of a suffering world; and it shall stand in extenuation of some mannerism that is only slang, some skepticism that lacks the cultivation which only makes skepticism tolerable, and some sentiment that is only rhetoric.

And so, with an irreverence for his fellow pilgrims which was equaled only by his scorn for what they admired, this hilarious image-breaker started upon his mission. The situation was felicitous, the condition perfect for the indulgence of an humor that seems to have had very little moral or aesthetic limitation. The whole affair was a huge practical joke, of which not the least amusing feature was the fact that "Mark Twain" had embarked in it. Before the *Quaker City* reached Fayal, the first stopping-place, he had worked himself into a grotesque rage at everything and everybody. In this mock assumption of a righteous indignation lies, we think, the real power of the book, and the decided originality of Mr. Clemens' humor. It enables him to say his most deliberately funny things with all the haste and exaggeration of rage; it gives him an opportunity to invent such epithets as "animated outrage," and "spider-legged gorilla," and apply them, with no sense of personal responsibility on the part of reader or writer. And the rage is always ludicrously disproportionate to the cause. It is "Mr. Boythorn," without his politeness, or his cheerful intervals. For, when "Mark Twain" is not simulating indignation, he is *really* sentimental. He shows it in fine writing—in really admirable rhetoric, vigorous and picturesque—but too apt, at times, to suggest the lecturing attitude, or the reporter's flourish. Yet it is so much better than what one had any right to expect, and is such an agreeable relief to long passages of extravagant humor, that the reader is very apt to overlook the real fact, that it is often quite as extravagant.

Yet, with all his independence, "Mark Twain" seems to have followed his guide and guide-books with a simple, unconscious fidelity. He was quite content to see only that which everybody else sees, even if he was not content to see it with the same eyes. His record contains no new facts or features of the countries visited. He has always his own criticism, his own comments, his own protests, but always concerning the same old facts. Either from lack of time or desire, he never stepped out of the tread-mill round of "sights." His remarks might have been penciled on the margins of *Murray*. This is undoubtedly a good way to correct the enthusiasm or misstatements of other tourists; but is, perhaps, hardly the best method of getting at the truth for one's self. As a conscientious, painstaking traveler, "Mark Twain," we fear, is not to be commended. But that his book would have been as amusing, if he had been, is a matter of doubt.

Most of the criticism is just in spirit, although extravagant, and often too positive in style. But it should be remembered that the style itself is a professional exaggeration, and that the irascible pilgrim, "Mark Twain," is a very eccentric creation of Mr. Clemens'. We can, perhaps, no more fairly hold Mr. Clemens responsible for "Mark Twain's" irreverence than we could have held the late Mr. Charles F. Browne to account for "Artemus Ward's" meanness and humbuggery. There may be a question of taste in Mr. Clemens permitting such a man as "Mark Twain" to go to the Holy Land at all; but we contend that such a traveler would be more likely to report its external aspect truthfully than a man of larger reverence. And are there not Lamartines, Primes, and unnumbered sentimental and pious pilgrims to offset these losel skeptics—or, as our author would say, such "animated outrages"—as Ross Browne, Swift, "Mark Twain," *et al.*

To subject Mr. Clemens to any of those delicate tests by which we are supposed to detect the true humorist, might not be either fair or convincing. He has caught, with great appreciation and skill, that ungathered humor and extravagance which belong to pioneer communities—which have been current in bar-rooms, on railways, and in stages—and which sometimes get crudely into literature, as "a fellow out West says." A good deal of this is that picturesque Western talk which we call "slang," in default of a better term for inchoate epigram. His characters speak naturally, and in their own tongue. If he has not that balance of pathos which we deem essential to complete humor, he has something very like it in that serious eloquence to which we have before alluded. Like all materialists, he is an honest hater of all cant—except, of course, the cant of materialism—which, it is presumed, is perfectly right and proper. To conclude: after a perusal of this volume, we see no reason for withholding the opinion we entertained before taking it up, that Mr. Clemens deserves to rank foremost among Western humorists; and, in California, above his only rival, "John Phoenix," whose fun, though more cultivated and spontaneous, lacked the sincere purpose and larger intent of "Mark Twain's."

1870

[UNSIGNED REVIEW]

EVERY TRAVELLER on the Continent has met the American tourist, and formed some opinion of his merits. We do not speak of that variety of American who comes over to spend five or six years in Europe, and finds himself rather more at home on the Parisian boulevards than on the New York Broadway. Nor do we refer to the Americans who have been too highly cultivated to obtrude their national peculiarities upon us in any disagreeable form. There is no pleasanter acquaintance than the gentleman, or still more the lady, of this class who has just enough American flavour to be amusingly original. But, besides these types, the United States are kind enough to provide us with a vast number of travellers corresponding in refinement and intelligence to Mr. Cook's tourists. They are the people who do Europe in six weeks, and throw in the Holy Land and Egypt to fill up their spare time. They are gloriously ignorant of any language but their own, supremely contemptuous of every country that had no interest in the Declaration of Independence, and occasionally, it must be admitted, as offensive as the worst kind of Cockney tourist, whilst even less inclined to hide their light under a bushel. Comparing them with the most nearly analogous class of British travellers, it is rather hard to determine which should have the preference. The American is generally the noisier and more actively disagreeable, but, on the other hand, he often partly redeems his absurdity by a certain

"The Innocents Abroad," from Saturday Review *(London), XXX (October 8, 1870), 467-68.*

naïveté and half-conscious humour. He is often laughing in his sleeve at his own preposterous brags, and does not take himself quite so seriously as his British rival. He is vulgar, and even ostentatiously and atrociously vulgar; but the vulgarity is mixed with a real shrewdness which rescues it from simple insipidity. We laugh at him, and we would rather not have too much of his company; but we do not feel altogether safe in despising him.

We may save ourselves the trouble of any further attempts at description by quoting a few illustrative passages from the book before us. Mr. Mark Twain, the author chooses to call himself, is a Californian humorist after the fashion of Artemus Ward. He came to Europe on a grand excursion trip, and describes his impressions of France and Italy in the true tourist style. He parades his utter ignorance of Continental languages and manners, and expresses his very original judgments on various wonders of art and nature with a praiseworthy frankness. We are sometimes left in doubt whether he is speaking in all sincerity, or whether he is having a sly laugh at himself and his readers. To do him justice, however, we must observe that he has a strong tinge of the peculiar national humour; and, though not equal to the best performers on the same instrument, manages to be an amusing representative of his class. The dry joke, which apes seriousness, is a favorite device of his countrymen; and Mr. Mark Twain is of course not as simple as he affects to be. We merely say this to guard ourselves against the imputation of taking a professional jester seriously; but, whether he speaks in downright earnest or with a half-concealed twinkle of the eye, his remarks will serve equally well as an illustration of the genuine unmistakable convictions of many of his countrymen.

Without further preface we will quote some of Mr. Twain's remarks upon foreign countries. And, first of all, he exhibits that charming ignorance of all languages but English which is so common amongst his fellows. French newspapers, he tells us, "have a strange fashion of telling a perfectly straight story till you get to the 'nub' of it, and then a word drops in that no man can translate, and that story is ruined." He is seriously aggrieved by the names of places, and says that the nearest approach which anybody can make to the true pronunciation of Dijon is "demijohn." The spelling is not much assistance under such circumstances. Speaking of a certain dis-

tinguished artist, he observes, "they spell it Vinci, and pronounce it
Vinchy; foreigners always spell better than they pronounce." Gentlemen who labour under this difficulty of communicating with the
natives naturally fall into the hand of guides, and Mr. Twain and
his friends appear to have suffered terribly from the persons whom
they hired to take them to the sights of foreign towns. Their system
on arriving at any large place was to engage a *valet de place,* whom
they always called "Ferguson," to save the trouble of pronouncing a
new name, and were carried about as helpless victims to such places
as he preferred, besides having to swallow his stories. They took a
characteristic revenge, which appears to have afforded them immense
satisfaction. The way to bully your guide is to affect a profound
ignorance — if you have not got it naturally — and a stony indifference to his information. They therefore told off a gentleman called the
Doctor, to ask questions of the said guide, because he could "look
more like an inspired idiot, and throw more imbecility into the tone
of his voice, than any man that lives. It comes natural to him." Thus,
for example, it was assumed that as Americans they would take a
special interest in an autograph letter of Columbus. The Doctor,
after asking some irrevelant questions, pronounced it the worst specimen of handwriting he ever saw, and added, "If you have got any
specimens of penmanship of real merit, trot them out; and, if you
haven't drive on." The guide, we are told, was "considerably shaken
up."

On the same principle, when shown an Egyptian monument, the
Doctor asked indignantly, "What is the use of imposing your vile
secondhand carcases on us? If you've got a nice fresh corpse, fetch
him out! or, by George, we'll brain you." The most irritating question
you can put to such a guide is to ask concerning any distinguished
character to whom he refers — such, for example, as Columbus or
Michael Angelo — "Is he dead?" And this seems to have met with
such success that Mr. Twain scarcely restrained his companions from
putting the inquiry to a monk in a Capuchin convent, who showed
them some of the personal remains of his predecessors.

We may imagine the temper in which some of the remarkable
sights of the Old World would be contemplated under such circumstances. Mr. Twain, indeed, was much impressed by the cathedral
at Milan. The bill for mere workmanship, he says, "foots up six

hundred and eighty-four millions of francs, thus far (considerably over a hundred millions of dollars), and it is estimated that it will take a hundred and twenty years yet to finish the cathedral." When he gets to St. Peter's, however, he declares that it did not look nearly so large as the capitol at Washington, and certainly not a twentieth part as beautiful from the outside.

Even natural wonders are generally surpassed by their rivals in the United States. The Lake of Como, for example, is pronounced to be very inferior to Lake Tahoe. In clearness it is not to be compared to it. "I speak," he says, "of the north shore of Lake Tahoe, where we can count the scales on a trout at a depth of 180 feet." Mr. Twain, however, feels constrained to add, "I have tried to get this statement off at par here, but with no success; so I have been obliged to negotiate it at fifty per cent discount." Tahoe, we may explain in passing, for the benefit of philological readers, is Indian for grasshopper soup — so, at least, Mr. Twain believes.

The objects, however, against which Mr. Twain feels a special indignation, to which he tells us he is bound to give vent in spite of the remonstrances of his friends, are pictures by the old masters. The old masters irritate him incessantly; and the apparent reason of his objection is characteristic. "Whenever you find a Raphael, a Rubens, a Michael Angelo, etc.," he says, "you find artists copying them, and the copies are always the handsomest. Maybe the originals were handsome when they were new, but they are not now." He "harbours no animosity" against the deluded persons who think otherwise; but he regards them as about as wise as men who should stand opposite a desert of charred stumps and say, What a noble forest! Michael Angelo appears to have been a special annoyance to him. "I never felt so fervently thankful," he exclaims, "so soothed, so tranquil, so filled with a blessed peace, as I did yesterday, when I learnt that Michael Angelo was dead." One would rather like to know how many of Mr. Cook's tourists share this feeling in their hearts, if they only dared to avow their ignorance with an equally touching frankness. Mr. Twain took his revenge by asking the wretched "Ferguson" of the moment, whenever he came to a "statoo brunzo" (Italian for a bronze statue), or an Egyptian obelisk, or the Forum or any other work of art, ancient or modern, whether it too was by Michael Angelo; thus at any rate making somebody else share in his tortures.

In the presence of the ancients he generally indulges in facetiousness of a rather low order. He goes, for example, to some amphitheatre and tries to realize the scene which it once presented. His most vivid picture is that of a Roman youth, who took "some other fellow's young lady" to a gladiatorial show and amused her and himself during the acts by "approaching the cage and stirring up the martyrs with his whalebone cane." But, to say the truth, Mr. Twain here verges upon buffoonery. Once or twice he is driven to what is happily described in the heading of the page as "general execration." Here, for example, is a burst of patriotic eloquence. "O, sons of classic Italy, is the spirit of enterprise, of self-reliance, of noble endeavor utterly dead within ye? Curse your indolent worthlessness, why don't you rob your Church?" And he is very great on occasion in explaining the many advantages of a free and independent Republic as compared with a land groaning under priestly dominion and grovelling superstition. That notion of robbing the Church occurs to him very forcibly at intervals, and he seems to think that, so far as the plan has been carried out, it is the best chance for Italy.

Perhaps we have persuaded our readers by this time that Mr. Twain is a very offensive specimen of the vulgarist kind of Yankee. And yet, to say the truth, we have a kind of liking for him. There is a frankness and originality about his remarks which is pleasanter than the mere repetition of stale raptures; and his fun, if not very refined, is often tolerable in its way. In short, his pages may be turned over with amusement, as exhibiting more or less consciously a very lively portrait of the uncultivated American tourist, who may be more obtrusive and misjudging, but is not quite so stupidly unobservant as our native product. We should not choose either of them for our companions on a visit to a church or a picture-gallery, but we should expect most amusement from the Yankee as long as we could stand him.

1874

GEORGE T. FERRIS

ONE OF THE PLEASANTEST offices of cultivated thought is the study of contrasts in the literatures of different peoples. The trained power of the artist-eye derives no greater pleasure in its discriminating observance of landscapes than that resulting from the arrangement and grouping of the recorded forms of national thought and sentiment, considered purely from the picturesque standpoint.

If this be true of poetry, philosophy, and art in general, it is peculiarly so of national humor. For humor is a direct product from the life-blood. It sucks its ingredients from each hidden taint and essential virtue; from intellectual perversity and moral insight; from external environment and from internal fact.

Other forms of thought are the outcome of single phases, standing together as symmetrical fragments of the individual or the people. Humor comes the nearest to being the one complete revelation, which subtends all the complex secrets of Nature and habit.

The poet sings sweet songs of the world that thrill or soften. But, behind the cloudy forms which his incantations evoke and his genius illumines, the individual fades away. The orator storms, or pleads, or reasons, but the attention slips by the man to fasten on what he says or thinks. The essayist challenges interest for the most part by appeals from the special to the universal.

Not so the humorist, whether the mouthpiece of his age and country, or the mere witness of himself. Harlequin may wear a mask,

---

"Mark Twain," from Appletons' Journal, *XII (July, 1874), 15-18.*

but under the shallow fold the face plays hide-and-seek in vain. The heart beams out in the mirth that quivers on the edge of pathos, or the grotesque laugh, which needs only a little deeper tone to become melancholy. It is the intense humanity and lifelikeness of humor, that set the ultimate stamp on its charm and significance.

Our literary inheritance from the princes of humor is full of finger-marks, index-signs, and marginal notes. We like to query whether Dean Swift, with his terrible scowl and blighting satire, which seem as if inspired from some Dantean depth, where devils mock and laugh, ever had the unctuous enjoyment of roast-beef and mighty ale, that shows in Dick Steele, Charles Lamb, and Charles Dickens? It is pleasant to speculate whether Heine, with his acute French wit sparkling on the current of deep German humor, ever recovered from his infatuation for frisky champagne and Parisian grisettes? Or, if Jean Paul, "the only one," whose imagination pirouetted on earth with as much agility and swiftness as it cleft the upper abysses eagle-winged, never had the vertigo?

Would we not have known exactly how Hogarth looked, his grim features softened by a funny twist of the mouth, even had he never painted himself with an exceeding honest-faced but belligerent-looking bulldog squatted by his side? How we should like to have heard Rabelais, after he had set a nation in a roar of laughter, reading the *Adventures of Pantagruel* to the jolly old abbot!

Or, again, let us overleap the wide abyss of centuries, and stand amid the vast prairies, the gloomy canyons, and the grand forests of the far West. There in mining-camp or squatter settlement we see the figures of Mark Twain, Bret Harte, or John Hay, casting long shadows before them. In the tedious *entr'actes* between fiery whiskey, coffee, and buckwheat "slapjacks," we can hear them make merry over adventures and fancies, which, vitalized by the breath of genius, were soon to ripple the world's face with laughter.

Such whimsical caprices never cease to haunt the students of the humorous in books with a sense of nearness and intimacy in their favorites. We are impertinently curious about them, make them mental bedfellows, as it were, because we love them. The laugh in literature is the "one touch of Nature" (above all others) "which makes the whole world akin."

America has of late years bristled with humorous writers, as does the porcupine with quills. But few of these quills have been pungent in point or well feathered for flight. Yet what persistent jokers! They have sought to offset failures at the lawyer's brief, the doctor's pill-box, the counter-jumper's measuring-tape, the carpenter's plane, or what not. Still, amid a legion of quacks, there are some who have been crowned and anointed with the true "laying-on of hands."

In surveying the distinctive and peculiar American humor, it becomes necessary to banish two highly-gifted men, Holmes and Lowell. The *Hosea Biglow Papers* have all the pungent wit of Pope, the meaty and athletic vigor of Swift. The genial front of the "auto-crat" shines like a fixed star. But their passports are not properly *viséd* by the home stamp. In spite of the use of dialect and other forged ear-marks, with which they would cunningly hoodwink us, we say to these magnificent impostors: "Get you gone, you belong to the world, not to America; you are giants truly, but your national angles, prejudices, and crudities, have been so ground down in the social mill, so polished away in the intellectual workshop, that your humor is that of the cosmopolite. It self-registers as much for any other Anglo-Saxon as for the American."

Mark Twain and Bret Harte may, on the whole, be pronounced our most marked types of humorist. Each one has a noble consti-tuency, but in many respects they are at the antipodes from each other. The latter is impelled to create and idealize, even when most faithful to externals. His plummet feels for the deep heart of hid-den mysteries, and finds love, sweetness, and self-sacrifice, beneath what is odd, grotesque, and barbaric. True, he deals largely with suffering, crime, and misery, in his most vigorous and characteristic sketches, yet is it with that sunny charity, which is the moral equiva-lent of searching insight. He has learned a lesson of the mining-camp, and knows where to look for gold in unsightly places. The essentially dramatic spirit, to which his instincts of form in art lead him, is no doubt partly responsible for the vividness of light and shade which intensifies his stories both in prose and rhyme. Yet, underlying form and method, seems to be a subtile feeling for the truth that good and evil are facts that melt and glide into each other imperceptibly, a recognition of which in painting human life is the tap-root of the soundest philosophy and the deepest humor.

Mark Twain, on the other hand, rarely touches the latent springs of human sentiment, nor is his style more than narrative and descriptive. He strolls in the open, breezy sunshine, happy-go-lucky fashion, yet with a keenness of vision that allows nothing in his horizon to escape him. . . . [A biographical sketch follows.] During the five years which have elapsed since the issue of *The Innocents Abroad,* the aggregate sale of our author's works has reached two hundred and forty-one thousand copies, representing a money-value of nine hundred and fifty thousand dollars. Though a large sale is by no means the only or even the best measure of literary excellence, the above-mentioned fact is so remarkable as to be almost unparalleled.

The differences between wit and humor have been elaborated by numerous essayists. These have said many bright things and many stupid ones on the subject. But, after all, the essence of it eludes definition and analysis. We see the effects, but fail to reach the ultimate force. This, at all events, we know, that wit is purely intellectual, and that humor is deeper and wider in its sources and powers. Wit sparkles in instantaneous gleams. It is the point of collision and also of union between opposites. Thackeray somewhere says that "humor is wit and love;" that "the best humor is that which contains the most humanity; that which is flavored throughout with the most tenderness and kindness."

Of humor in its highest phase, perhaps Bret Harte may be accounted the most puissant master among our contemporary American writers. Of wit, we see next to none. Mark Twain, while lacking the subtilty and pathos of the other, has more breadth, variety, and ease. His sketches of life are arabesque in their strange combinations. Bits of bright, serious description, both of landscape and society, carry us along till suddenly we stumble on some master-stroke of grotesque and irresistible form. He understands the value of repose in art. One tires of a page where every sentence sparkles with points, and the author is constantly attitudinizing for our amusement. We like to be betrayed into laughter as much in books as in real life. It is the unconscious, easy, careless gait of Mark Twain that makes his most potent charm. He seems always to be catering as much to his own enjoyment as to that of the public. He strolls along like a great rollicking schoolboy, bent on having a good time, and determined that his readers shall enjoy it with him.

If Bret Harte has remarkable insight, Mark Twain has no less notable *outsight*. And yet perhaps the great popularity of the latter writer is as much the consequence of his defects as of his powerful gifts. He is representative because he embodies, to a striking extent, in his mode of constructing the forms of humor, the peculiar style of the average American journalist. Journalism on this side of the water has two unique types: the professional funny man, and the police-court reporter. Both these are strongly-marked national characters, and the style in which they serve up dishes for the public breakfast is well known. Hardly a newspaper appears but that it contains a variety of such paragraphs as the following:

John Smith had a beautiful stallion, who was so amiable in his temper that he would always caress the air with an affectionate gesture of his steel-clad hoofs when a stranger approached from behind. Squire Robinson bought the horse. The gorgeous funeral which Deadhead, the undertaker, supplied for the squire a few days after, enabled our respected fellow-citizen, who presides with such dignity in front of the mourners, to fit out his wife and daughter with the latest spring fashions.

It would be unjust to our author to say that he is either one or the other of these types in full flower. And yet how frequently do we see both these gentlemen surreptitiously stealing away out of sight under Mark Twain's coat-tails! Or perhaps it is only a literary illustration of Darwin's doctrine of rudimentary organs and limbs by which he explains changes in structural type. Mark Twain's early literary training was that of a writer for newspapers, where news was scarce and hard to get, and the public demanded their intellectual fare dressed with the hottest, strongest condiments. Is it not natural that we should see distinct and powerful traces of this method in all his later work?

In spite of this fault, our writer is so thoroughly genial, so charged with rich and unctuous humor, that we forget the lack of *finesse* and delicacy in its breadth and strength. Its tap-root takes no deep hold in the subsoil, and we may not always find a subtile and penetrating fragrance in its blooms. But these are so lavish, bright, and variegated, that we should be ungrateful indeed not to appreciate our author's striking gifts at their full worth. *The Innocents Abroad* and *Roughing It* are the most thoroughly enjoyable examples of Mark Twain's humor. While they are not to be altogether admired as intellectual workmanship, the current of humor is so genuine and fresh, so full of rollicking and grotesque fun, that it is more than easy to overlook fault both in style and method. Like most of the American humorists, Mark Twain depends chiefly on exaggeration as the effective element in his art. This has long been acknowledged the peculiar characteristic in our humorous processes. The clean-cut, sinewy force, so common to foreign writers, and no less evident in such men as Holmes and Lowell, is wanting in our distinctive Americans of this guild of literature. Their strength, on the other hand, is large, loose-jointed, and clumsy, the vigor of Nature and free exercise, not that of the gymnasium and fencing-school. It is humor which runs abroad with rambling, careless steps, not the humor which selects deliberately a fixed goal, and disembarrasses itself of every superfluity before commencing the race. What we lose, however, in energy, point, momentum, we gain in freshness and spontaneity.

In using exaggeration as a force in art, Mark Twain exaggerates not characters but circumstances. As a consequence, he is never a caricaturist. We recognize, even in his most extraordinary statements and descriptions, therefore, a flavor of reality, which takes strong hold of the imagination. Many of the unique people, whom he delineates, indeed, in his Western scenes, seem to have stepped right out of life into the printed page, veritable photographs in large and showy settings.

Mark Twain's latest book, *The Gilded Age,* was written in conjunction with Mr. Warner. Our author contributed to this joint production the career of the Hawkins family, and of Colonel Sellers, occupying the first eleven chapters, and twenty-two other chapters, scattered throughout the book. The rest of the composite story must be credited to the accomplished author of *Backlog Studies* and *Saunterings.* We have the word of the authors that there was no intention of making it humorous, the sole purpose being that of bitter satire, true and honest to the core.

Some of the best detached descriptions which have ever emanated from Mark Twain's pen may be found in this book. They show that the author's powers are at their best working capacity, and that the world has a right to look for liberal fruits from them.

1882

JOHN NICHOL

IT IS PROBABLE that, to the lower class of British Philistines, American prose is, at this day, represented not so much by Irving, Emerson, or Hawthorne, as by "Mark Twain," who has done perhaps more than any other living writer to lower the literary tone of English speaking people. The most conspicuous intellectual trait of Mr. Clemens seems to me an almost preternatural shrewdness, thinly veiled under an assumption of simplicity. He knows perfectly what he is about, and is able to turn every incident or circumstance to his advantage. He prefixes a recent paper, "The Idle Excursion," with the remark, "All the journeyings I have done had been purely in the way of business. The pleasant May weather suggested a novelty, a trip for pure recreation, the bread and butter element left out:" but he writes seventy pages about the trip; and so provides for the element ostentatiously neglected. Of the alarming tribe of recent American cynics he is the most genuine. He hates humbug and cant, and nothing delights him more than to run a tilt at copy-book texts. It goes without saying that his "bad little boy" will prosper, and his "good little boy" come to grief; or that he will give an absurd turn to the story of Washington and the cherry-tree. Romance and sentiment, in either continent, fare equally at his hands: "Old masters" at Milan, Florence, and Rome are served in the same manner as the journalists in Tennessee; he writes his text to the sketch of a weazened hag perched on the summit of the Loreley Rock; makes a grimace at the Pyramids; puts

"Mark Twain," *from* American Literature, An Historical Sketch 1620-1880 *(Edinburgh: Adam and Charles Black, 1882), pp. 426-32.*

his finger to his nose among the Alps; and, as it were, turning the statues in the Louvre, the Uffizi, and the Vatican, upside down, inspects their legs. But, if his scepticism is intense, his morality is truculent: he visits the tomb of Abelard, and pronounces a blessing on his semi-assassins; and his blushes are blent with curses over Regent Street.

Mark Twain's attraction is due in great measure to his freshness: he is not an imitator; he does not rely on books—though his writings evince a more than average culture: he is a parodist of his own experience, to which he holds up a mirror, like one of the round balls in German gardens.

> "Life's a jest, and all things show it;
> I thought so once, and now I know it,"

is the refrain of his philosophy. His satire, unlike that of "Billings," is conveyed not so much in dogmatic sentences as in often dramatic narrative, *e.g.* in all that relates to his Western real or imagined adventures, among which "How I Edited an Agricultural Paper" is the most savage attack on newspapers I have anywhere seen. He is, however, capable of condensation, as in the following—one of the keenest of the sarcasms that rely on the favourite Transatlantic figure, hyperbole. It is an editor's "answer to an inquiry from the coming man"—

Young Author.—Yes, Agassiz does recommend authors to eat fish, because the phosphorus in it makes brains. So far you are correct. But I cannot help you to a decision about the amount you need to eat—at least, not with certainty. If the specimen composition you send is about your usual average, I should judge that perhaps a couple of whales would be all you would want for the present. Not the largest kind; but simply good, middling-sized whales.

One of this writer's most successful tricks is to say exactly the opposite of what he means; another is an assumption of modesty, and habit of pretending to laugh at himself. Unsophisticated people are consoled for their own stupidity by the reflection that so brilliant a person had a distant relation who was hanged, and that he himself has been so often duped (*e.g.* by Artemus Ward, by his watchmaker, by the Limerick Indians at Niagara), and has made such a bad map of Paris. The initiated will incline to find a more genuine leaf from the author's autobiography in "My First Literary Venture." Mr. Clemens' satire is often trenchant, seldom fine: it wants the background of good humour which softens that of Mr. Browne. It is more vicious, without any of the grandeur which elevates the malignity of Swift— an author to whom America has produced no proximate parallel. His Western sketches are vivid — we doubt not veracious—and may be useful as deterrents to heedless intending emigrants. His simpler narratives are among his best, and give free play to the remarkable observing powers which stand him in good stead in his records of European travel. Of the two series of those—for *The New Pilgrim's Progress* is but a continuation of *The Innocents Abroad*— the *Tramp Abroad* is in some respects the best. It is more to the point, less ambitious than its predecessors, and its irreverences are less jarring. "Mark Twain," who seems quite out of place in the Desert and on the Sea of Galilee, is at home on the Righi Railroad, as the looker-on at a German students' duel, and a moral lounger at Baden-Baden. The Riffelberg is his altitude; we can scarce imagine him risking the Riffelhorn. The *Tramp* is, on the whole, an excellent guide-book, illustrated by jokes and cuts excluded from the dry dignity of Murray or Baedeker, and with almost as precise practical information as the last. Many travelers from England, as well as America, will be grateful to Mr. Clemens for his thoroughly reliable information as to the *douceurs* legitimately due to the porter, boots, and chambermaid of German hotels, for periods of residence ranging from one day to six months. The most amusing part of this book is in the Appendices, especially those on the use of the Heidelberg Tun, and on "the awful German language." The following gives expression to common griefs:—

I translate this from a conversation in one of the best of the German Sunday-school books: — "*Gretchen.* — Wilhelm, where is the turnip? *Ans.* — She has gone to the kitchen. Where is the accomplished and beautiful English maiden? It has gone to the opera. . . ." There are some exceedingly useful words in this language. . . . The word *Schlag* means blow, stroke, dash, hit, shock, clap, slap, time, bar, coin, stamp, kind, sort, manner, way, apoplexy, wood-cutting, enclosure, field, forest-clearing. This is its simple and *exact* meaning—that is to say, its restricted, its fettered meaning; but there are ways in which you can set it free, so that it can soar away, as on the wings of morning, and never be at rest. You can hang any word you please to its tail, and make it mean anything you want to. You can begin with *Schlag-ader,* which means artery, and you

can hang on the whole dictionary, word by word, clear through the alphabet to *Schlag-wasser,* which means bilge-water, and including *Schlag-
mutter,* which means mother-in-law. Just the same with *Zug.* . . . One
cannot overestimate the usefulness of *Schlag* and *Zug.* Armed just with
these two, and the word *Also,* what cannot the foreigner on German
soil accomplish? . . . In the hospital yesterday a word of thirteen syllables
was successfully removed from a patient—a North German from near
Hamburg; but as most unfortunately the surgeons had opened him in the
wrong place, under the impression that he contained a panorama, he died.
. . . Some German words are so long that they have a perspective. . . .
These are not words, they are alphabetical processions. . . . One can
open a German newspaper any time and see them marching majestically
across the page; and if he has any imagination he can see the banners and
hear the music too. . . . Here are some specimens: *Generalstaatsverordnet-
uebersamerlungen. Wiederherrstellungsbestebungen. Waffenstillstandsunt-
erhandlungen. Kinderbewahrungsaustalten.*

.   .   .   .

In common with graver writers, Mark Twain is in danger of
rapaciously mining out his vein of ore. His last volume might have
marred, but could never have made, a reputation. "The Stolen White
Elephant" is a satire on detectives, in which it is hard to detect a
chance to smile; "Punch, Brothers, Punch" is a joke at which we can
only once laugh; "The Decay of Lying," an evidence of the decay of
invention; "Crime in Connecticut," a lame travesty of Edgar Poe's
"William Wilson." The Nemesis of persistent parody is that, like the
cultivation of the tobacco plant, it exhausts the soil. The successful
writer of burlesques seldom succeeds in anything else. Mr. Clemens'
most ardent admirers cannot read his *Pauper and Prince.* There is
something almost ineffably pathetic in his own half-conscious forecast of his own literary lot in one of the earliest of his books, *The
Mississippi Pilot,* where his keen eye and quick wit, as yet undimmed
by the strain of a professional jester, are displayed to their best
advantage—where the puns spring up naturally as the foam-bells on
the great stream itself. The space given to the following extract is
justified by the fact that it is an unintentional, but weighty apologue
of the whole tribe in whose ranks the author has elected to enlist
himself—as we consider, unhappily, for the passage gives evidence
of far higher capacities. He is speaking of the acquired instincts, the
second nature of the pilot:—

The face of the water, in time, became a wonderful book . . . not to be read once and thrown aside, for it had a new story to tell every day. Throughout the long twelve hundred miles, there was never a page that was void of interest. . . . There never was so wonderful a book written by man . . . the passenger who could not read this book saw nothing but all manner of pretty pictures in it, painted by the sun and shaded by the clouds, whereas to the trained eye these were not pictures at all, but the grimmest and most dead earnest of reading matter.

Now when I had mastered the language of this water, and had come to know every trifling feature that bordered the great river as familiarly as I knew the letters of the alphabet, I had made a valuable acquisition. But . . . I had lost something which could never be restored to me while I lived. All the grace, the beauty, the poetry had gone out of the majestic river! I still keep in mind a certain wonderful sunset which I witnessed when steamboating was new to me. A broad expanse of the river was turned to blood; in the middle distance the red hue brightened into gold, through which a solitary log came floating, black and conspicuous; in one place a long, slanting mark lay sparkling upon the water; in another the surface was broken by boiling, tumbling rings, that were as many-tinted as an opal; where the ruddy flush was faintest, was a smooth spot, that was covered with graceful circles and radiating lines, ever so delicately traced; the shore on our left was densely wooded, and the sombre shadow that fell from this forest was broken in one place by a long, ruffled trail that shone like silver; and high above the forest wall a clean-stemmed dead tree waved a single leafy bough that glowed like a flame in the unobstructed splendor that was flowing from the sun. There were graceful curves, reflected images, woody heights, soft distances; and over the whole scene, far and near, the dissolving lights drifted steadily, enriching it, every passing moment, with new marvels of coloring.

I stood like one bewitched. I drank it in, in a speechless rapture. The world was new to me, and I had never seen anything like this at home. But as I have said, a day came when I began to cease noting the glories and the charms which the moon and the sun and the twilight wrought upon the river's face; another day came when I ceased altogether to note them. Then, if that sunset scene had been repeated, I would have looked upon it without rapture, and would have commented upon it, inwardly, after this fashion: This sun means that we are going to have wind to-morrow; that floating log means that the river is rising, small thanks to it; that slanting mark on the water refers to a bluff reef which is going to kill somebody's steamboat one of these nights, if it keeps on stretching out like that; those tumbling "boils" show a dissolving bar and a changing channel there; the lines and circles in the slick water over yonder are a warning that that execrable place is shoaling up dangerously; that silver streak in the shadow of the forest is the "break" from a new snag, and he has located himself in the very best place he could have found to fish for steamboats; that tall, dead tree, with a single living branch, is not going to last long, and then how is a body ever going to get through this blind place at night without the friendly old landmark?

No, the romance and the beauty were all gone from the river. All the value any feature of it ever had for me now was the amount of usefulness it could furnish toward compassing the safe piloting of a steamboat. Since those days, I have pitied doctors from my heart. What does the lovely flush in a beauty's cheek mean to the doctor but a "break" that ripples above some deadly disease? Are not all her visible charms sown thick with what are to him the signs and symbols of hidden decay? Does he ever see her beauty at all, or doesn't he simply view her professionally, and comment upon her unwholesome condition all to himself? And doesn't he sometimes wonder whether he has gained most or lost most by learning his trade?

"De te fabula narratur." Who would have thought that the writer of this fine description and eloquent parable, elsewhere in his pages unequalled, would have fallen into the very trap, error, and sin against which he warns his readers! The "father of waters" is "an image of the mighty world;" the trained pilot, the hardened doctor, is the professional humorist, who has lost the power of seeing the beauty of the universe, because he has come to regard it as a mere text-book for his sadly incessant and ultimately wearisome jests. The price we have to pay for always making others laugh is never being able to admire, seldom even to laugh heartily ourselves. Not only Lear's Fool, but his whole kith and kin, have been, if among the wisest, also among the most melancholy of men.

1883

H. R. HAWEIS

MARK TWAIN in about ten years has achieved cosmopolitan renown. Every English-speaking market is flooded with his *Innocents* of all sorts. About the only book I could get at Rome—outside the magic Tauchnitz circle—was *The Jumping Frog*.

Roughing It has consoled me in some of the worst inns on the "Continong"; and whenever, like those celebrated travellers afoot, I have steadily declined to walk, and got into the nearest train, cab, carriage, boat, or railway car sooner than wear out my boots—whenever, I say, I have indulged in these easy "promenades" *en voiture,* I have been forcibly reminded of the *New Pilgrims' Progress* and the *Tramp Abroad.*

Many people regard Twain merely as an extravagant wag with a long bow. It is the fate of all wags. Yet a man may be more than a wag. It matters not. The direct impact power of a joke is so much quicker than that of any other known projectile, that it is sure to hit the public sooner than any other qualities in a man, however superior and forcible. Oliver Wendell Holmes never counselled more wisely than when he said, "Make a reputation first by your more solid acquirements. You can't expect to do anything great with Macbeth, if you first come on flourishing Paul Pry's umbrella!"

Now, Mark Twain came on first with his "Jumping Frog," his horse "Jericho," and the bucking "Mexican Plugs." Had he done no

---

"Mark Twain," from American Humorists *(London: Chatto & Windus, 1883), pp. 165-71.*

more, he would have deserved well of the public; but he has done more, and in all he has done he is oddly sound and quaintly thorough besides.

I believe this is not the general view. He is supposed to lie like truth; but in my opinion he as often speaks truth like lies, and utters many verities in jest—ay, and in earnest too. When serious he is, I believe, generally reliable. You can usually tell when he has got hold of the long bow, and when he is shooting fair; and I must say, that whenever I have taken the trouble to verify his statements of fact and descriptions of scenery, I have found them minutely accurate and photographically true. If I want to know about the shoals of that big American stream called the Mississippi, and the look of its banks, and the set of its craft, and the ways of its voyagers, I would read Mark Twain's *Mississippi Pilot*. Dean Stanley is graphic and elaborate enough on Palestine, and Ernest Renan touches its Past and Present like a poet and philosopher; but any one who wants to understand without going there exactly how it looks now, had better read the *Innocents Abroad*.

The wild mining life of Nevada and California may be coloured, but it is coloured entirely in keeping with reality. There is no difference, except in wit and graphic force, between Mark Twain's sketches of the swashbucklers and bullies like "Slade" and "Arkansas" and the newspaper police reports and cuttings of the period.

The truth about Switzerland is not far to seek. There, at least, Twain knows what he is about, and he either trifles outrageously or not at all. Nothing brief about the glaciers has ever been better put together than his awful narrative of the men who fell into crevices, and were yielded up by the slow-moving mass of ice at the end of fourteen or forty years. "Home, sweet home! there's no place like home!" more than once seemed to me an altogether plausible sentiment as I read these cheerful and precipitous narratives.

Mark Twain's strong points are his facile but minute observation, his power of description, a certain justness and right proportion, and withal a great firmness of touch and peculiar—I had almost said personal—vein of humour. By right proportion I mean putting things substantially in their right light. I might almost say that Twain never makes a mistake here. At times he no doubt indulges openly in a certain rollicking exaggeration and fun, but when he *estimates,* he is always just—just to the wild miner, but no unscrupulous panegyrist or obsequious idolater of him, like Bret Harte; just to the eccentricities of tourists, whether English, French, German, or American; and always just to religion—never, I believe, wantonly irreverent, though occasionally a little free with subjects too sacred in the eyes of many to be so lightly touched. 'Tis, after all, a fault of taste rather than of morals. The value of religion itself is not more tenderly, than is the sham and cant of hypocrisy severely handled.

As a Humorist, of course, Twain deals with the various kinds of mental shock quite inseparable from all wit and humour. The shock of exaggeration, as in the "Jumping Frog," a conceit which to me is the least witty of all his well-known skits; for what, I should like to know, is the fun of saying that a frog who has just been caused to swallow a quantity of shot cannot jump so high as he did before? I should have said, after such a digestive exercise he could not jump at all!

The shock of the impossible, the incongruous, and a general inversion of ideas is common of course to Twain and every other humorist; but he seldom flashes like Artemus. He *distils* his fun drop by drop through a whole page, instead of condensing it into a sentence. With every touch the atmosphere is intensified, and the picture slowly comes together until the page, or even the chapter, stands out a perfect pyramid of fun. This is his gift—the long-drawn-out, elaborately spun witticism; the carefully finished, photographically minute picture. That he *never* flashes I do not say, but his swiftest sallies—done in chalk, with a few strokes—are pictorial; the image is scratched firmly, unmistakably, as when he describes the passage through the Alps and down into Italy, he says, all the way through Mount Cenis and right on, "The train is profusely decorated with tunnels." Or when describing the effect of his own withering sarcasm upon his agent Harris, he remarks, "When the musing spider steps on to the red-hot shovel, he first exhibits a wild surprise, then he shrivels."

Mark Twain's secret is a tolerably open one. He is always wide awake, therefore he keeps you awake. He is full of observation, therefore he is pleasant company. He is not too full, therefore he is not a bore. He jokes habitually, and therefore he makes you laugh. The jokes are generally easy ones, so they do not make you think. This is important, for the slow discovery of a joke is always a wearing process. His descriptions are so vivid that you feel, after reading them, that you know all about those places, so you need not go there. This saves trouble. In this way, Mark Twain himself ascended Mont Blanc. He found he could make the entire ascent for three francs—through the telescope. Harris, the agent, was allowed to go with him for two more. Harris was afraid, and did not want to go, but Twain "heartened him up," and said he would hold his hand all the way. So they started, and in a very few minutes reached the top, and were able to describe the various peaks. "The 'Yodel-horn,' and the 'Dinner-horn' and 'Scrabble-horn,' and the soaring domes of the 'Bottle-horn,' and the 'Saddle-horn,' and the 'Shovel-horn'; and in the 'west-south-west' they beheld the stately range of the Himalayas, which lay dreaming in the purple gloom." This is very pleasant fooling, but it is not difficult, and is evidently *"calqué,"* as the French say, upon the experiences of "little Billee," who, under far more trying circumstances, beheld from the topmast of H.M.S. ———

> "Jerusalem and Madagascar
> And North and South Amerikee."

Then last, but not least, Twain has shown that he can *go on*. He is not the man of one book or one idea. Put him down anywhere, and he will create a situation and spread like that American water-plant which infests the Cam, and has stretched itself over most English rivers. He will soon crowd most waters he can get access to.

What can be more unlike any of his previous works than *The Prince and the Pauper,* Twain's 1881 Christmas book? There the fun lies in the fancy that Edward VI, in a freak just before he ascended the throne, changed clothes with a romantic beggar boy who resembled him closely. The beggar boy is found in the palace, and the courtiers cannot be persuaded that he is not the prince; only the prince, alas! changed—gone mad! Meanwhile, the prince, once in the beggar's clothes, cannot convince any one outside the palace that he is really the king in disguise. So the freak ends in a prolonged struggle on both sides, the prince trying to get back to the palace; the beggar at first trying to get out of the palace, then whimsically resigning himself, up to the moment of coronation, when the *dénouement,* of course, is managed, as intellectual readers will find set down in quaint English in this same showy picture-book.

In freshness and fertility Twain resembles poor Artemus, and rises above Bret Harte, though he is less intense and pathetic than the latter. Artemus, like Twain, rejoiced in variety. He created everywhere; you could not play him out. In California or the great lone silver land, a new pilgrims' progress was ever before him. Most men who can write at all can write one book if they try, but many men can do no more. I confess I do not care much for your dog with one trick, and the public soon get tired of him.

1885

OLIVER WENDELL HOLMES

Ah Clemens, when I saw thee last,—
    We both of us were younger,—
How fondly mumbling o'er the past
    Is Memory's toothless hunger!

So fifty years have fled, they say,
    Since first you took to drinking,—
I mean in Nature's milky way,—
    Of course no ill I'm thinking.

But while on life's uneven road
    Your track you've been pursuing,
What fountains from your wit have flowed—
    What drinks you have been brewing!

I know whence all your magic came,—
    Your secret I've discovered,—
The source that fed your inward flame—
    The dreams that round you hovered:

To Mark Twain on his fiftieth birthday. From The Critic, *VII (November 28, 1885), 253.*

Before you learned to bite or munch
    Still kicking in your cradle,
The Muses mixed a bowl of punch
    And Hebe seized the ladle.

Dear babe, whose fiftieth year to-day
    Your ripe half-century rounded,
Your books the precious draught betray
    The laughing Nine compounded.

So mixed the sweet, the sharp, the strong,
    Each finds its faults amended,
The virtues that to each belong
    In happier union blended.

And what the flavor can surpass
    Of sugar, spirit, lemons?
So while one health fills every glass
    Mark Twain for Baby Clemens!

1891

ANDREW LANG

THE DUTY of self-examination is frequently urged upon us by moralists. No doubt we should self-examine our minds as well as our conduct now and then, especially when we have passed the age in which we are constantly examined by other people. When I attempt to conduct this delicate inquiry I am puzzled and alarmed at finding that I am losing Culture. I am backsliding, I have not final perseverance, unless indeed it is Culture that is backsliding and getting on to the wrong lines. For I ought to be cultured; it is my own fault if I have not got Culture.

I have been educated till I nearly dropped; I have lived with the earliest Apostles of Culture, in the days when Chippendale was first a name to conjure with, and Japanese art came in like a raging lion, and Ronsard was the favorite poet, and Mr. William Morris was a poet too, and blue and green were the only wear, and the name of paradise was Camelot. To be sure, I cannot say that I took all this quite seriously, but "we too have played" at it, and know all about it. Generally speaking, I have kept up with Culture. I can talk (if desired) about Sainte-Beuve, and Mérimée, and Félicien Rops; I could rhyme "Ballades" when they were "in," and knew what a *pantoom* was. I am acquainted with the scholia on the Venetus A. I have a pretty taste in Greek gems. I have got beyond the stage of thinking Mr. Cobden Sanderson a greater binder than Bau-

"The Art of Mark Twain," *from* Illustrated News of the World, *XCVIII (February 14, 1891), 222.*

zonnet. With practice I believe I could do an epigram of Meleager's into a bad imitation of a sonnet by Joachim du Bellay, or a sonnet of Bellay's into a bad imitation of a Greek epigram. I could pass an examination in the works of M. Paul Bourget. And yet I have not Culture. My works are but a tinkling brass, because I have not Culture. For Culture has got into new regions where I cannot enter, and, what is perhaps worse, I find myself delighting in a great many things which are under the ban of Culture.

This is a dreadful position, which makes a man feel like one of those Liberal politicians who are always "sitting on the fence," and who follow their party, if follow it they do, with the reluctant acquiescence of the prophet's donkey. Not that I do follow it. I cannot rave with pleasure over Tolstoi, especially as he admits that "The Kreutzer Sonata" is not "only his fun" but a kind of Manifesto. I have tried Hartmann, and I prefer Plato. I don't like poems by young ladies in which the verses neither scan nor rhyme, and the constructions are all linguistically impossible. I am shaky about Blake, though I am stalwart about Mr. Rudyard Kipling.

This is not the worst of it. Culture has hardly a new idol but I long to hurl things at it. Culture can scarcely burn anything, but I am impelled to sacrifice to that same. I am coming to suspect that the majority of Culture's modern disciples are a mere crowd of very slimly educated people, who have no natural taste or impulse; who do not really know the best things in literature; who have a feverish desire to admire the newest thing, to follow the latest artistic fashion; who prate about "style" without the faintest acquaintance with the ancient examples of style, in Greek, French, or English; who talk about the classics and criticise the classical critics and poets, without being able to read a line of them in the original. Nothing of the natural man is left in these people; their intellectual equipment is made up of ignorant vanity, and eager desire of novelty, and a yearning to be in the fashion.

Take, for example—and we have been a long time in coming to him—Mark Twain. If you praise him among the persons of Culture, they cannot believe that you are serious. They call him a Barbarian. They won't hear of him, they hurry from the subject; they pass by on the other side of the way. Now I do not mean to assert that Mark Twain is "an impeccable artist," but he is just as far from being a mere coarse buffoon. Like other people, he has his limitations. Even Mr. Gladstone, for instance, does not shine as a Biblical critic, nor Mark Twain as a critic of Italian art nor as a guide to the Holy Land. I have abstained from reading his work on an American at the Court of King Arthur, because here Mark Twain is not, and cannot be, at the proper point of view. He has not the knowledge which would enable him to be a sound critic of the ideal of the Middle Ages. An Arthurian Knight in New York or in Washington would find as much to blame, and justly, as a Yankee at Camelot. Let it be admitted that Mark Twain often and often sins against good taste, that some of his waggeries are mechanical, that his books are full of passages which were only good enough for the corner of a newspaper. Even so, the man who does not "let a laugh out of him"—like the Gruagach Gaire —at the story of the Old Ram, or of the Mexican Plug, or of the editing of the country newspaper, or of the Blue Jay, or at the lecture on the German language, can hardly have a laugh in him to let out. Chesterfield very gravely warns his son that it is wrong and vulgar to laugh; but the world has agreed to differ from Chesterfield. To "Homo Ridens" Mark Twain is a benefactor beyond most modern writers, and the Cultured, who do not laugh, are merely to be pitied.

But his art is not only that of a maker of the scarce article— mirth. I have no hesitation in saying that Mark Twain is one among the greatest contemporary makers of fiction. For some reason, which may perhaps be guessed, he has only twice chosen to exercise this art seriously, in *Tom Sawyer* and in *Huckleberry Finn*. The reason, probably, is that old life on the Mississippi is the only form of life in which Mark Twain finds himself so well versed that he can deal with it in seriousness. Again, perhaps his natural and cultivated tendency to extravagance and caricature is only to be checked by working on the profound and candid seriousness of boyhood. These are unlucky limitations, if they really exist, for they have confined him, as a novelist, to a pair of brief works, masterpieces which a fallacious appearance has confounded with boys' books and facetiae. Of the two, by an unheard-of stroke of luck, the second, the sequel, is by far the better. I can never forget nor be ungrateful for the exquisite pleasure with which I read *Huckleberry Finn* for the first time, years ago. I read it again last night, deserting *Kenilworth* for Huck. I never laid it down till I had finished it. I perused several passages more than once, and rose from it with a higher opinion of its merits than ever.

What is it that we want in a novel? We want a vivid and original picture of life; we want character naturally displayed in action, and if we get the excitement of adventure into the bargain, and that adventure possible and plausible, I so far differ from the newest school of criticism as to think that we have additional cause for gratitude. If, moreover, there is an unstrained sense of humor in the narrator, we have a masterpiece, and *Huckleberry Finn* is nothing less. Once more. If the critics are right who think that art should so far imitate nature as to leave things at loose ends, as it were, not pursuing events to their conclusions, even here *Huckleberry Finn* should satisfy them. It is the story of the flight down the Mississippi of a white boy and a runaway slave. The stream takes them through the fringes of life on the riverside; they pass feuds and murders of men, and towns full of homicidal loafers, and are intermingled with the affairs of families, and meet friends whom they would wish to be friends always. But the current carries them on: they leave the murders unavenged, the lovers in full flight; the friends they lose for ever; we do not know, any more than in reality we would know, "what became of them all." They do not return, as in novels, and narrate their later adventures.

As to the truth of the life described, the life in little innocent towns, the religion, the Southern lawlessness, the feuds, the lynchings, only persons who have known this changed world can say if it be truly painted, but it looks like the very truth, like an historical document. Already *Huckleberry Finn* is an historical novel, and more valuable, perhaps, to the historian than *Uncle Tom's Cabin,* for it is written without partisanship, and without "a purpose." The drawing of character seems to be admirable, unsurpassed in its kind. By putting the tale in the mouth of the chief actor, Huck, Mark Twain was enabled to give it a seriousness not common in his work, and to abstain from comment. Nothing can be more true and more humorous than the narrative of this outcast boy, with a heart naturally good, with a conscience torn between the teachings of his world about slavery and the promptings of his nature. In one point Mark Twain is Homeric, probably without knowing it. In the Odyssey, Odysseus frequently tells a false tale about himself, to account for his appearance and position when disguised on his own island. He shows extraordinary fertility and appropriateness of invention, wherein he is equalled by the feigned tales of Huckleberry Finn.

The casual characters met on the way are masterly: the woman who detects Huck in a girl's dress; the fighting families of Shepherdson and Grangerford; the homicidal Colonel Sherburn, who cruelly shoots old Boggs, and superbly quells the mob of would-be lynchers; the various old aunts and uncles; the negro Jim; the two wandering impostors; the hateful father of Huck himself. Then Huck's compliment to Miss Mary Jane, whom he thought of afterwards "a many and a many million times," how excellent it is! "In my opinion she had more sand in her than any girl I ever see; in my opinion she was just full of sand. It sounds like flattery, but it ain't no flattery. And when it comes to beauty—and goodness, too—she lays over them all."

No novel has better touches of natural description: the starlit nights on the great river, the storms, the whole landscape, the sketches of little rotting towns, of the woods, of the cotton-fields, are simple, natural, and visible to the mind's eye. The story, to be sure, ends by lapsing into burlesque, when Tom Sawyer insists on freeing the slave whom he knows to be free already, in a manner accordant with "the best authorities." But even the burlesque is redeemed by Tom's real unconscious heroism. There are defects of taste, or passages that to us seem deficient in taste, but the book remains a nearly flawless gem of romance and of humour. The world appreciates it, no doubt, but "cultured critics" are probably unaware of its singular value. A two-shilling novel by Mark Twain, with an ugly picture on the cover, "has no show," as Huck might say, and the great American novel has escaped the eyes of those who watch to see this new planet swim into their ken. And will Mark Twain never write such another? One is enough for him to live by, and for our gratitude, but not enough for our desire.

1893

FRANK R. STOCKTON

MARK TWAIN'S most notable characteristic is courage. Few other men—even if the other men could think of such things—would dare to say the things that Mark Twain says. To describe the travels of a man on a glacier, with particular reference to the fact that being pressed for time, he rode upon the middle of the glacier, which moves faster than the edges, is one of the bravest things in literature. It required courage to write "She," but She could not possibly exist, and glaciers do move.

Any one with a lively fancy may invent odd and even amusing characters and incidents, but the humorous situation of the highest order cannot be created; it must be evolved from a real situation. To do this requires not only skill but a bold spirit, for the humorist knows that an intelligent reader will probably see both situations, and if he compares unfavorably the evolved condition of affairs with the real one, the battle with that reader is lost. A pure creation of fancy does not presuppose courage; it gives little opportunity for comparative criticism.

Mark Twain is a high jumper, but he always jumps from the solid rock of fact and is not afraid of breaking his neck by falling back upon it. His funniest things are so funny because they are possible. An impossibility is a mill-stone about the neck of a joke. To load a frog with shot so that it cannot engage in a leaping-match is funny; but

"Mark Twain and His Recent Works," from Forum, *XV (August, 1893), 673-79.*

if one were to write of a whale inflated with balloon-gas so that it might shoot out of the water and skim through the air like a flying-fish, it would not be funny, it would be merely fantastic. In his humorous creations Mark Twain seldom plays upon words, he plays upon ideas; and as a pun would have no value were the words played upon treated without reference to their legitimate use, so he never forgets what a character is in the habit of doing when he makes him do something out of the common, and in his comical situations he uses the antithesis as if he were making a pun or an epigram.

It is the disposition of humorists to be prudent; they are careful about the rebounds of their missiles. It would be hard to find one who would not be afraid to ask if Adam were dead. Mark Twain's courage is shown not only in his combinations but in his descriptions. Take this account of the father of Huckleberry Finn—

He was fifty and he looked it. His hair was long and tangled and greasy, and hung down, and you couldn't see his eyes shining through, like he was behind vines. It was all black, no gray; so was his long mixed up whiskers. There warn't no color in his face, where his face showed; it was white; not like another man's white, but a white to make a body sick, a white to make a body's flesh crawl—a tree-toad white, a fish belly white. As for his clothes—just rags, that was all. He had one ankle resting on t'other knee; the boot on that foot was busted, and two of his toes stuck through, and he worked them now and then. His hat was laying on the floor; an old black slouch, with the top caved in like a lid.

Another characteristic of Mark Twain is his use of pure and unadulterated fun. In this regard he differs from the older humorists. A great many of the things they wrote about are not funny in themselves; they are made so by the wonderful manner in which their witty authors have handled them. Mark Twain offers us the crude ore of fun. If he puts his private mark upon it, it will pass current; it does not require the mint stamp of the schools of humor. He is never afraid of not being laughed at. Consider, for instance, the passage in which the Yankee at the Court of King Arthur discovers St. Stylites at the top of his column—

His stand was a pillar sixty feet high, with a broad platform on the top of it. He was now doing what he had been doing every day for twenty years up there—bowing his body ceaselessly and rapidly almost to his feet. It was his way of praying. I timed him with a stop watch, and he made

1244 revolutions in twenty-four minutes and forty-six seconds. It seemed a pity to have all this power going to waste. It was one of the most useful motions in mechanics, the pedal movement; so I made a note in my memorandum book, purposing some day to apply a system of elastic cords to him and run a sewing machine with it. I afterwards carried out that scheme, and got five years' good service out of him; in which time he turned out upwards of eighteen thousand first class tow-linen shirts, which was ten a day.

This is the pure ore of fun, just as it comes from the mine. It has not been coined or even cast into bars.

It must be remembered, however, that Mark Twain does not depend entirely upon the humor of his situations and conditions to make his points. His faculty and range of expression are wonderful, and it is his courage which gives to his expressions, as well as his inventions, their force and unique effect. His glittering phrases are as daring as they are bright, and they sparkle through all his books like stars in the sky. A humiliated person has the aspect of a "bladder that has been stepped on by a cow." A disguised king, practising obeisances, looks about "as humble as the leaning tower of Pisa," and an orator is described "who loved to stand forth before a dazed world and pour forth flame and smoke, and lava, and pumice stone, into the skies, and work his subterranean thunders, and shake himself with earthquakes, and stench himself with sulphur fumes. If he consumed his own fields and vineyards, that was a pity, yes; but he would have his eruptions at any cost." The Yankee at King Arthur's court speaks thus of a damsel of the period—

I was gradually coming to have a mysterious and shuddery reverence for this girl; for nowadays whenever she pulled out from the station and got her train fairly started on one of those horizonless trans-continental sentences of hers, it was borne in upon me, that I was standing in the awful presence of the Mother of the German Language.

Examples of the poignancy of expression with which Mark Twain spurs his readers into a proper appreciation of what he is telling them, are too abundant for further reference, but although he uses them so easily, he does not always find them necessary. Some of the funniest passages of his later works, as well as in those by which he made his reputation, contain not a flash of wit nor any unusual expressions. A combination is presented in the plainest and simplest way, and as the substances are poured together the humor effervesces, not in the author's story, but in the reader's mind.

We have an example of this in an article on ships in his last book. The author asserts that in these days Noah would not be allowed to sail from Bremen in the ark, without first being subjected to an official inspection. After discovering that Noah's ship is six hundred feet long and very large otherwise, the inspector asks him how many passengers he has, to which Noah answers, "Eight."

"Sex?"

"Half male, the other female."

"Ages?"

"From a hundred years up."

"Up to where?"

"Six hundred."

"Crew?"

"The same eight."

"Have any of you ever been to sea?"

"No, sir."

"Where were you reared?"

"On a farm,—all of us."

"Who is Captain?"

"I am."

"You must get a Captain. Also a chambermaid. Also sick nurses for the old people. Who designed this vessel?"

"I did, sir."

"Is it your first attempt?"

"Yes, sir."

"I partly suspected it. Cargo?"

"Animals."

"Wild or tame?"

"Mainly wild."

"Securely caged?"

"No, not caged."

"They must have iron cages. Who feeds and waters the menagerie?"

"We do."

"The old people?"

"Yes, sir."

"It is dangerous—for both. The animals must be cared for by a competent force. How many are there?"

"Big ones, seven thousand; big and little together, ninety-eight thousand."

"You must provide twelve hundred keepers."

"How many pumps have you?"

"None, sir."

"You must provide pumps."

"What is the nature of your steering apparatus?"

"We haven't any."

"Haven't you a rudder?"

"No, sir."

"How do you steer the vessel?"

"We don't."

"You must provide a rudder. How many anchors have you?"

"None."

"Provide twenty-five. Did I understand you to say this was your first attempt at ship-building?"

"My very first. I built this ark without having ever had the slightest training or experience or instruction in marine architecture."

"It is a remarkable work, sir. I consider it contains more features that are new—absolutely new and unhackneyed—than are to be found in any other vessel that swims the sea."

Sometimes a witty point in a remark is omitted in such a way that the effect is a great deal stronger than if it had been left in. In "A Petition to the Queen of England," Mark Twain objects to an income-tax which has been demanded of him as an author, and points out the fact that authors are not mentioned in the official schedule. Mr. Bright, a clerk of the Inland Revenue Office, has said to him, "You are taxed under Schedule D, section 14." Then writes Mark Twain—

I turned to that place, and found these three things; "Trades, Offices, Gas Works." Of course, after a moment's reflection, hope came up again, and then certainty: Mr. Bright was in error and clear off the track; for authorship is not a trade, it is an inspiration; authorship does not keep an office, its habitation is all out under the sky, and everywhere that the winds are blowing and the sun is shining and the creatures of God are free. Now then, since I have no trade and keep no office, I am not taxable under Schedule D, section 14. Your Majesty sees that.

In this deft omission of a reference to gas-works the author draws out the wit of his readers as a magnet draws needles from a cushion.

We who remember Mark Twain when his light first rose above the horizon cannot help thinking of him as a humorist above everything else, for it was as such he rose, and as such his radiance increased. We soon came to know that he was also a philosopher and after a time that he was a story-teller, but for all that and despite our added knowledge of him, we still think first of his brightness, and often forget that his surface may be inhabited or that he has an influence upon our tides.

His philosophy of course, came in with his humor and although the fact was not always noticed, it often formed part of it. Later this philosophic spirit grew and strengthened until it was able to stand alone, and in some of his more recent writings it not only stands up very steadily but it does some bold fighting. As illustrations of the workings of the reasoning powers in his characters, we give two extracts from *Huckleberry Finn*. In the first of these the boy deprecates the upbraiding of his conscience in a case where he was not at all to blame—

But that's always the way; it don't make no difference whether you do right or wrong, a person's conscience ain't got no sense, and just goes for him *anyway*. If I had a yaller dog that didn't know no more than a person's conscience does, I would pisen him. It takes up more room than all the rest of a person's insides and ain't no good, nohow.

In the following, Huckleberry is on a raft with Jim, a negro, who is trying to escape from slavery, and they are approaching Cairo, the nearest point of free soil—

Jim said it made him all over trembly and feverish to be so close to freedom. Well, I can tell you, it made me all over trembly and feverish, too, to hear him, because I begun to get it through my head that he *was* most free—and who was to blame for it? Why *me*. I couldn't get that out of my conscience, no how, nor no way. It got to troubling me so I couldn't rest; I couldn't stay still in one place. It hadn't ever come home to me before, what this thing was that I was doing. But now it did; and it staid with me, and scorched me more and more. I tried to make out to myself that *I* warn't to blame, because *I* didn't run off Jim from his rightful owner; but it warn't no use, conscience up and says, every time, "But you knowed he was running for his freedom, and you could have paddled ashore and told somebody." That was so— I couldn't get around that noway. That was where it pinched. Conscience says to me, "What had poor Miss Watson done to you, that you should see her nigger go off right under your eyes and never say a single word? What did that poor old woman do to you, that you could treat her so mean? Why, she tried to learn you your book, she tried to learn you your manners, she tried to be good to you every way she knowed how. *That's* what she's done."

I got to feeling so mean and miserable I most wished I was dead. I fidgeted up and down the raft, abusing myself to myself, and Jim was fidgeting up and down past me. We neither of us could keep still. Every time he danced around and says "Dah's Cairo!" it went through me like a shot, and I thought if it *was* Cairo I reckoned I would die of miserableness.

Jim talked out loud all the time while I was talking to myself. He was saying how the first thing he would do when he got to a free state he would go to saving up money and never spend a single cent, and when he got enough he would buy his wife, which was owned on a farm close to where Miss Watson lived; and then they would both work to buy the two children, and if their master wouldn't sell them, they'd get an Ab'litionist to go and steal them.

It most froze me to hear such talk. He wouldn't ever dare to talk such talk in his life before. Just see what a difference it made in him the minute he judged he was about free. It was according to the old saying, "Give a nigger an inch and he'll take an ell." Thinks I, this is what comes of my not thinking. Here was a nigger which I had as good as helped to run away, coming right out flat-footed and saying he would steal his children —children that belonged to a man I didn't even know; a man that hadn't done me no harm. I was sorry to hear Jim say that, it was such a lowering of him. My conscience got to stirring me up hotter than ever.

In these passages the humor is merely sprinkled on the rest of the substance. It is like the fun of a circus-clown taking the money at the door; he may be a queer fellow, but he means business.

These extracts lead us insensibly from the consideration of Mark Twain as a funny man and as an expert in logical processes, to Mark Twain as a story-teller. In *The Prince and the Pauper* he took his stand as a writer of fiction with but little reference to his other and then better known qualifications. Of the success of this departure there can be no doubt, and there are critics of high order who consider *The Prince and the Pauper* our author's best work. But it must be remembered that in the average family the boys are as good as the girls; and if some of us marry the one and some of us the other, it is because of our own difference of sex.

It was quite natural that Mark Twain should become a story-teller. The man of broad sympathies, who is able, with interest to himself and others, to evolve the *may be* from the *is,* is sure to end by writing stories, no matter how he begins. He may do it in verse or he may do it in prose, but he will do it. He may set out on his career by describing his own travels, but this field will surely become too small for him, no matter how deep he may dig down into it, or how high he may build above it, and he will leap the wall into regions where he will make people who will travel wherever he chooses to send them, and do and say whatever he chooses to make them do and say. Thus came *Tom Sawyer* and *Huckleberry Finn,* and thus came shorter stories, such as "The £1,000,000 Bank Note." In this we recognize, first of all, that unbounded courage which rises, as we have said, above all other characteristics of Mark Twain; what other author would have dared to put five million dollars into the hands of an intelligent tramp, and to tell him to go forth with it and seek adventures?

It is well known that the actor of comedy often casts longing glances toward the tragic mask, and when he has an opportunity to put it on, he often wears it so well that one cannot say he has no right to it. The same pen-point which will make a man laugh out in church, if gently pricked by it, will not only slay a bride at the altar, but will go entirely through her and kill her father who is giving her away. The figure with the tragic mask stalks through much of Mark Twain's work. In *The Prince and the Pauper* he darkens the page like a semi-weekly eclipse; while in the feud of the Shepherdsons and the Grangerfords in *Huckleberry Finn,* he throws himself with such earnestness into his tragic action that his comic mask drops unnoticed from his hand and might be lost forever, were it not caught on one of the six arms of the picture of the young woman about to jump from the bridge.

Long live that comic mask! With such a forest of points for it to catch upon, there will be no danger of its ever being lost, and while Mark Twain lives he will not cease to be the man of the double stroke —the Bismarck of humorists.

1894

HENRY C. VEDDER

THE IMMEDIATE and permanent popularity of *Innocents Abroad* is not wonderful; it is a book of even greater merit than the public gave it credit for possessing. It was read and enjoyed for its fun, and though nearly twenty-five years have passed, it is still a funny book, whether one reads it now for the first or the forty-first time. But underneath the fun was an earnest purpose that the great mass of readers failed to see at the time, and even yet imperfectly appreciate. This purpose was to tell, not how an American ought to feel on seeing the sights of the Old World, but how he actually does feel if he is honest with himself. From time immemorial, books of travel had been written by Americans purporting to record their experiences, but really telling only what the writers thought they might, could, would, or should have experienced. This is a very familiar type of the genus globe-trotter; specimens of it are seen everywhere in Europe, Murray or Baedeker constantly in hand and carefully conned, lest they dilate with the wrong emotion—or, what is almost as bad, fail to dilate with the proper emotion at the right instant. For sham sentiment, sham love of art, sham adventures, Mark Twain had no tolerance, and he gave these shams no quarter in his book. "Cervantes smiled Spain's chivalry away" is a fine phrase of Byron's which, like most fine phrases, is not true. What Cervantes did was to "smile away" the ridiculous romances of chivalry—chivalry had been long

"Mark Twain," *from* American Writers of To-day *(New York: Silver, Burdett & Co., 1894), pp. 124-40.*

dead in his day—the impossible tales of knightly adventure, outdoing the deeds of the doughty Baron Munchausen, that were produced in shoals by the penny-a-liners of his time. Not since this feat of Cervantes has a wholesome burst of merriment cleared the air more effectually or banished a greater humbug from literature than when *The Innocents Abroad* laughed away the sentimental, the romantic book of travels.

Mark Twain, perhaps, erred somewhat on the other side. His bump of reverence must be admitted to be practically non-existent; and while his jests about the saints may make the unskilful laugh, the judicious grieve. The fact seems to be that he sees so clearly the humbug and pretence and superstition beneath things conventionally held to be sacred that he sometimes fails to see that they are not all sham, and that there is really something sacred there. In truth, Mark Twain has been slow to learn that "quips and cranks and wanton wiles" are not always in good taste. Throughout the book the author was just a little too hard-headed, too realistic, too unimpressionable, too frankly Philistine, for entire truthfulness and good taste; but it may have seemed necessary to exaggerate something on this side in order to furnish an antidote to mawkish sentimentality. His lesson would have been less effective if it had not been now and then a trifle bitter to the taste. Since that time travellers have actually dared to tell the truth; or shall we say that they have been afraid to scribble lies so recklessly? Whichever way one looks at the matter, there is no doubt that American literature, so far as it has dealt with Europe and things European, has been more natural, wholesome, and self-respecting since the tour of this shrewd Innocent.

The same earnestness of purpose underlies much else that Mark Twain has written, especially *The Prince and the Pauper,* and *A Yankee at King Arthur's Court.* The careless reader no doubt sees nothing in the first of these books but a capital tale for boys. He cannot help seeing that, for it is a story of absorbing interest, accurate in its historical setting, and told in remarkably good English. In the latter book he will no doubt discover nothing more than rollicking humor and a burlesque of *Morte d'Arthur.* This is to see only what lies on the surface of these volumes, without comprehending their aim, or sympathizing with the spirit. Not the old prophet of Chelsea himself was a more inveterate hater of sham and cant than Mark

Twain. Much of the glamour of chivalry is as unreal as the tinsel splendors of the stage; to study history is like going behind the scenes of a theatre, a disenchantment as thorough as it is speedy. *Morte d'Arthur* and Tennyson's *Idylls of the King* present to the unsophisticated a very beautiful, but a very shadowy and unsubstantial picture of Britain thirteen centuries ago. Even in these romances a glimpse of the real sordidness and squalor and poverty of the people may now and then be caught amid all the pomp and circumstance of chivalry, and yet nobody has had the pitiless courage heretofore to let the full blaze of the sun into these regions where the lime-light of fancy has had full sway, that we might see what the berouged heroes and heroines actually are.

But Mark Twain has one quality to which Carlyle never attained; joined to his hatred of shams is a hearty and genuine love of liberty. His books could never have been written by one not born in the United States. His love of liberty is characteristic in its manifestation. In a Frenchman it would have found vent in essays on the text of *liberté, fraternité, égalité,* but eloquent writing about abstractions is not the way in which an American finds voice for his sentiments. Mark Twain's love of liberty is shown unostentatiously, incidentally as it were, in his sympathy for, and championship of, the downtrodden and oppressed. He says to us, in effect: "Here you have been admiring the age of chivalry; this is what your King Arthur, your spotless Galahad, your valiant Launcelot made of the common people. Spending their lives in the righting of imaginary wrongs, they were perpetuating with all their energy a system of the most frightful cruelty and oppression. Cease admiring these heroes, and execrate them as they deserve." This, to be sure, is a one-sided view, but it is one that we need to take in endeavoring to comprehend the England of King Arthur. There is no danger that we shall overlook the romantic and picturesque view while Malory and Tennyson are read, but it is wholesome for us sometimes to feel the weight of misery that oppressed all beneath the privileged classes in England's days of chivalry. No books are better fitted to help a student of history "orient himself," as the French phrase it, than these two of Mark Twain's.

Except in the two books that may be called historic romances, Mark Twain has been a consistent realist. He was probably as innocent of intent to belong to the realist school when he began writing as Molière's old gentleman had all his life been of the intent to talk prose. He was realistic because it "came sort o' nateral" to him, as a Yankee would say. His first books were the outcome of his personal experiences. These were many and varied, for few men have knocked about the world more, or viewed life from so many points. Bret Harte has written of life on the Pacific coast with greater appreciation of its romantic and picturesque features, but one suspects with considerably less truthfulness in detail. The shady heroes and heroines of Bret Harte's tales are of a quality that suggests an amalgam of Byron and Smollett; they smack strongly of Bowery melodrama. Mark Twain's *Roughing It* is a wholesome book, and as accurate in its details as a photograph, but there is nothing romantic or thrilling about it.

It is in the Mississippi Valley, however, that our author finds himself most at home, not only because his knowledge of it is more comprehensive and minutely accurate, but because it is a more congenial field. Mark Twain understands California, admires it even, but he loves the great river and the folk who dwell alongside it. He is especially happy in his delineation of the boy of this region. If ever any writer understood boy nature in general, from A to izzard, the name of that writer is Mark Twain. He has explored all its depths and shallows, and in his characters of Tom Sawyer and Huckleberry Finn he has given us such a study of the American boy as will be sought in vain elsewhere. He has done more than this; he has given us a faithful picture, painfully realistic in details, of the *ante bellum* social condition of the Mississippi Valley. This realism redeems the books from what would otherwise seem worthlessness, and gives them a positive value.

One ought also to recognize the great merit of this writer's short stories. Most of these stories are humorous in their fundamental conception, or have a vein of humor running through them, but they are not, for the most part, boisterously funny. They range in style from the avowedly funny tale of "The Jumping Frog of Calaveras" to the surface sobriety of "The £1,000,000 Bank Note." In the composition of the short story, Mark Twain is so evidently perfecting his art as to warrant one in hazarding the prediction that much of his best work in future is likely to be done along this line.

Even our English cousins—as a rule, not too lenient in their judgments of kin across the sea—admit that American humor has a distinct flavor. Not only so, they also admit that this flavor is delightful. To their tastes there is something wild and gamy about American humor, a tang that is both a new sensation and a continuous source of enjoyment. British commendation of American humor, however, is not always as discriminating as it is hearty. We must allow Englishmen the praise of having been prompt to appreciate Artemus Ward the only; but of late years they seem impervious to American humor, except of one type—that which depends for its effect on exaggeration. Exaggeration is, no doubt, one legitimate species of humor. The essence of humor lies in the perception of incongruity, and the effect of incongruity may be produced by exaggeration. This is the more effectively done if the style is dry; the writer must give no sign, until the very end (if even there) that he does not take himself seriously. The narrator must not by a tone of voice or change of facial expression betray any lack of exact veracity in his tale, or the effect is measurably lost. Mark Twain has frequently shown himself to be master of this style of humor. He can invent the most tremendous absurdities, and tell them with such an air of seriousness as must frequently deceive the unwary.

But this is not, as English readers mistakenly imagine, the best type of American humor; it is not even the type in which Mark Twain reaches his highest level. Exaggeration is comparatively cheap humor. Anybody can lie, and the kind of Mark Twain's humor most admired abroad is simply the lie of circumstance minus the intent to deceive. It is morally innocuous, therefore, but it is bad art. No doubt it is frequently successful in provoking laughter, but the quality of humor is not to be gauged by the loudness of the hearers' guffaws. The most delightful fun is that which at most provokes no more than a quiet smile, but is susceptible of repeated enjoyment when the most hilarious joke is received in a grim silence more expressive than words. To borrow a metaphor from science, humor is the electricity of literature, but in its finest manifestation it is not static but dynamic. The permanent charm of humorous writing is generally in inverse ratio to its power to incite boisterous merriment when first read. The joker who at first gives one a pain in the side soon induces "that tired feeling" which is fatal to continued interest. It is Mark Twain's misfortune at present to be appreciated abroad mainly for that which is ephemeral in his writings. His broad humanity, his gift of seeing far below the surface of life, his subtle comprehension of human nature, and his realistic method, are but dimly apprehended by those Britons who go off in convulsions of laughter the moment his name is mentioned. It is probably in vain for us to protest against this misjudgment of American authors by Britons—

> Against stupidity the very gods
> Themselves contend in vain.

A false standard of what is truly "American" has been set up abroad, and only what conforms to that standard wins admiration. For that reason British readers have gone wild over Bret Harte and Joaquin Miller, while they neglected Bryant and Holmes, and for a time even Lowell, on the ground that the latter were "really more English than American, you know." Their own countrymen have a juster notion of the relative standing of American authors. In the case of Mark Twain they do not believe that he is rated too high by foreign critics and readers, but that his true merits are very imperfectly comprehended.

1897

CHARLES MINER THOMPSON

THE HORRID LITTLE TOWN [Hannibal, Mo.], with its poverty of intellectual life, its complete barrenness of all the means for aesthetic cultivation, is hardly the place in which to expect the birth of a refined literary genius. There is a deal of truth in Mr. Barrie's remark that "nothing that happens after we are twelve matters very much." And these early years, impressionable as a photographic plate, were those which supplied him [Mark Twain] with the vivid memories upon which he based his strongest works, *Tom Sawyer* and *Huckleberry Finn*. One piece of singular good fortune was indeed his: by his home flowed the mighty Mississippi. The river was the one thing which he knew in all his early days that could appeal to his imagination and uplift it. Its fascination was upon all the boys in the village. They had passing ambitions, he says—such, for example, as that "if they lived and were good, God would permit them to become pirates;" but the one unchanging desire of their hearts was to be "steamboat men."

Anyone who can remember his boyhood can easily understand how their young thoughts were always of the river, which, huge and sombre, flowed out of the land of mystery, by their commonplace doors, into the land of promise, and how they envied the rivermen to whom both lands were as familiar as the streets of Hannibal. Poor lads, they doubtless found out in after-life that the river touched

"*Mark Twain as an Interpreter of American Character*," *from* Atlantic Monthly, *LXXIX (April, 1897), 443-50.*

neither of these enchanting countries, but simply flowed on, not bored only because it was an insensate thing, past thousands of doors little if any less tedious than their own! But fact is unimportant in the training of a sensitive imagination, and the influence of the river upon that of Mark Twain can hardly be exaggerated. Nor is it difficult to comprehend how it is that through whatever of his books the Mississippi flows, it fills them with a certain portion of its power and beauty. To it is owing all that in his work which is large and fine and eloquent. The river is what makes *Huckleberry Finn* his most vivid story, and *Life on the Mississippi* his most impressive autobiographic narrative.

Unfortunately, there was nothing else in the boy's early surroundings which could help him to become a literary artist, for the river, however it might dominate and uplift his imagination, could not teach him the most delicate and beautiful art of writing well. For that the child must at least have books, good works of the imagination, from which he may unconsciously learn the modest secret of good taste, the value of the apt word, the mysteries of the rise and fall of the rhythm of lovely prose. When one recalls the lack of aesthetic advantages which was so plentiful in his boyhood, in that "loafing, out-at-the-elbows, down-at-the-heels, slaveholding" village, in his wandering, unprosperous youth in cis-Mississippi printing-offices, and in his impecunious journalistic young manhood in the rough and lawless West, one cannot wonder that he is so imperfectly an artist. He has a rude native gift for firm and vigorous narration. He has, too, an inborn eloquence which sometimes rises superior to his faulty periods, and at its best carries the critical reader out of the mood of fastidious objection. But his style—which he has improved steadily—even when correct, is technically without distinction.

He fails no less in the handling of large masses of composition: he is singularly devoid of any aptitude for construction. The narrative in which incidents of about even value succeed each other is the highest variety of literary form in which he has attained good measure of success. Such are *Huckleberry Finn,* and that picturesque failure as an historical novel, *The Personal Recollections of Joan of Arc.* Such, still more frankly, are his earlier successes, *Roughing It, Innocents Abroad,* and *Life on the Mississippi.* And in spite of highly colored incidents thrown in at the end with a delusive air of forming the climax which denotes a plot, *Tom Sawyer,* also, and *The Connecticut Yankee* belong in the same group. *The Gilded Age, The Prince and the Pauper,* and *Pudd'nhead Wilson* are more pretentious; but it is from the passages wherein the author, forgetful of weaving the incidents into a pattern, is content to chronicle them with a broidery of his own shrewd and humorous thought that they have their merit.

No, he is not a great or a skillful writer. The influences of his early years were not such as would make him one. What a disadvantage they were to him may be illustrated by contrasting him, for a moment, with another American writer—like him, a humorist. That other had little, if any, more natural power—perhaps not so much; he had his greatest successes, as Mark Twain had his more popular ones, in the form of the humorous, half-dramatic monologue; but as he had the best training of intellect and taste, he attained a firm place among the semi-great who alone as yet form the most distinguished group of American authors. That writer is Dr. Holmes.

Neither is Mark Twain—bold as the assertion may seem—a great humorist or a great wit. The soul of a jest is immortal. If it defies definition and analysis, experience seems to show that when it leaves its envelope of words standing cold and insignificant, dead upon the page, it usually does so only for the brief space which must elapse before its next incarnation. If the soul of one's grandam may haply inhabit a bird, the soul of the dear lady's jest may more than haply inhabit a sentence—none too sprightly, one may fear—in the corner of the latest comic paper. Rarely indeed is the perfectly crystallized phrase created which can withstand, like a diamond, the wear and tear of time, and eternally imprison the bright sparkle of wit that it contains. In other words, the special incongruities of circumstance change, and the jests change with them: only that humor lives which is expressed in perfect, limpid phrases that take no color from temporary things. Wit lives on from age to age when given form by such a masterly cutter of sentences as La Rochefoucauld; humor survives when embodied in some unchanging type of character such as that to which Cervantes gave the finest time-resisting form. La Rochefoucauld may be considered the type of the great wit, Cervantes the type of the great humorist.

Mark Twain has shaken the sides of the round world with laughter; but after all, has he, in the mass of his writings, uttered any witticism which touches intimately, much less radiantly expresses, some eternal truth of life? Has he ever created any character bearing so plainly a lasting relationship to human nature that it will live on to be hailed brother by future men? Unless indeed some of the clever sayings of Pudd'nhead Wilson have greater depth and reach of meaning than they now seem to have, the answer to the first question is plainly "No." Not many of Mark Twain's witticisms will appear in the Familiar Quotations of the coming century. The answer to the second question is perhaps susceptible of a moment's debate. But probably not more than two characters will rise in the memory of anyone who may wish to answer it otherwise than also by a "No." These will be Tom Sawyer and Huckleberry Finn. And surely Tom Sawyer is only one presentment more of the general idea—boy—added to the thousands which anyone familiar with the commercial industry of writing books for boys can name only too readily. Quite in the line of Mark Twain's variation of the standard type, and its superior as a human portrait, stands the Bad Boy of Mr. Thomas Bailey Aldrich. Huck, however, is not so easily brushed aside. He is at his best, not in the book which wears for title the name of his chief youthful friend, but in the astonishing volume which is named after himself. For he, the best of Mark Twain's creations, has the good fortune—which is not that of the best character of many an author—of being the hero of his originator's best book. In that wild, youthful, impossible Odyssey, the record of his voyage on a frail raft down the strong Mississippi, he assumes in a manner epic proportions.

Still, if a sensitive and candid reader were somewhat carefully to analyze his impressions, perhaps these are the conclusions at which, with a tempered enthusiasm, he would ultimately arrive: that Huck gains in apparent stature by being kept clear of taller rivals in the centre of the stage; that he gains enormously in picturesqueness through his surroundings—the incredibly fantastic scamps who impose themselves upon him, and who, by contrast, make him seem so honest; the childlike negro whom he befriends, and who, by contrast, makes him seem so much more the man; the wild and solemn and beautiful stretches of the huge river, which make him seem, by contrast, so pitiful a waif; that the story is, a few exceptions granted, a tale of what happened to him rather that of what he did, and consequently is not a presentation of character, is not dramatic. What

Huck really is, the sensitive and candid reader would conclude, is simply the usual vagabond boy, with his expected shrewdness and cunning, his rags, his sharp humor, his practical philosophy. The only difference between him and his type would be found in his essential honesty, his strong and struggling moral nature, so notably Anglo-Saxon. The most delightful thing in the portrait, from the point of view of character-drawing, would be seen to be the interminable debate and puzzle in which he is, to reconcile his respect for the law that declares him a criminal for aiding a runaway slave and his instinctive honest perception that his ward is a man, not a chattel. If the literary critic had a field-book, like the botanist—may he some day be so lucky!—in which to trace any unfamiliar specimen, he would find, if engaged in the present search, his finger fall at last upon some such line as this: "Huckleberry Finn: species, *Gavroche.* Locally found in the Mississippi Valley, in the United States, and by some authorities erected"—such is the word of the men of science!—"into a separate variety."

Now, if Mark Twain has neither uttered memorable witticisms nor created any finely humorous character, it will not be as a great humorist that he will survive. Nor is the reason for his failure hard to find. His lack of mastery of form, his constant offense against taste, is, of course, a large part of it, but not all. The humor which finds in him its chief source of expression is that of a shifting and evanescent semi-civilization, the humor of new men in new circumstances in a suddenly developing country, wherein the ups and downs of life, immensely exaggerated both in speed and in span, made a grotesque appeal to the sense of incongruity of a naturally humorous people. The society of the West is not yet settled into its final form, as that of the East may be considered to be; but already it, and we who know it, have traveled far from the possibility of appreciating fully its special humor. A few years more, and most of its fun will seem to all, as it seems to many now, the merest extravagance, as hard to understand as the spirit which prompted the gargoyle on the mediaeval church. A humor based upon the transient conditions of such a life can hardly be more permanent than the life itself.

Not in the technical sense a skillful writer, not a good novelist or story-teller, not a great wit or a great humorist, Mark Twain occupies a strangely conspicuous position in the world of contemporary letters.

He has long been accepted of the people, never of the critics. Although his name is a household word in all places where the English language is spoken, and in many where it is not, he has never been accorded any serious critical notice. There have been, indeed, in various magazines, a few articles—mostly of no critical intention or pretension—about him, but almost the only fact which looks like a recognition of him as a real author, and not as an inconsequential buffoon, is the publication, now going forward, by Messrs. Harper and Brothers, of a uniform edition of his complete works. Yet a general sense of his importance may be found existing even among the critical who neglect him, and some natural, mild wonder why it has never found expression. The critics, with the disdain that comes easily to men, perhaps a bit ostentatiously preoccupied with what is earnest in thought and artistic in form, have let him write and win an unregarded popularity.

The circus clown were as likely to attract the attention of the dramatic critic as Mark Twain that of the serious reviewers. But his enormous vogue should have won the notice of some inquiring mind, and led its possessor to ask if his popularity had not some deeper cause than the love of the crowd for the antics of one who professionally wears the cap and bells. If deeper cause there be, it may well prove something which throws light upon American life and character. Perhaps it were as well to attribute the popularity of Abraham Lincoln to his jokes as to ascribe that of Mark Twain to his extravagant foolery. In the conventional sense, Mark Twain is no more a literary artist than, in the conventional sense, Lincoln was a gentleman. But in spite of lack of polish Lincoln was great: may not Mark Twain, the writer, in spite of his crude literary manners, be great, also? The mere possibility ought to be enough in itself to secure him sympathetic and thoughtful consideration.

Criticism is always concerned with the man behind the book. Veiled as the questioning may be, its object is always to determine if the personality of the author is one which has value, aesthetic or other, for the world. If an author is not able to justify himself on aesthetic grounds, criticism requires him to supply other and good ones. If he is not an artist, he can have no value for any intelligent human being except through his personality.

The remark is too sweeping; he can have value for the student. And Mark Twain has this value abundantly. He has recorded the life of certain southwestern portions of our country, at one fleeting stage of their development, better than it is possible it will ever be done again. From his superficially frivolous pages much can be learned of the causes of the fierce family feuds which prevailed there, of lynching, of the effects of slavery. Under the humorist in Mark Twain lies the keen observer, the serious man, the ardent reformer, and he took note of all that was evil in the life he knew and proclaimed it indignantly to the world. His tenacious memory for detail, his microscopic imagination, and his real interest in the serious side of life make his pictures of the crude society in which he was born both absolutely accurate and surprisingly comprehensive. His writings cannot be neglected by anyone who wishes to know that life, and it is one which is in many respects highly important for us to understand. But it is not for his historical value that an author is popular. To point to that of Mark Twain is not to account for his acceptance by the multitude. That must rest somehow on his character.

Like Dr. Holmes, Mark Twain belongs to the race of literary egotists. The narrations which are his best work are almost entirely autobiographic. *Roughing It* relates his experiences in the West. *Innocents Abroad* sets forth his own peculiarly American view of Europe. *Life on the Mississippi* is very Twain, and naught else. Tom Sawyer is less real than Huckleberry Finn, because—one cannot doubt —he is less the young Clemens than is Huck. Indeed, the rule may be laid down that the interest of Mark Twain's books is in direct proportion to the amount of autobiographic matter in them. What he is gifted to express is plainly himself, his own thoughts, feeling, experiences. That was the gift of Dr. Holmes, also, and where the personality was so engaging, the taste so perfect, the success was easy to understand. But if one were to be told that another writer, born with a smaller gift of invention and with as little trace of constructive imagination, and having only such education as he might be able to pick up in a youth spent among rough surroundings, would take the same literary form and win an even greater popularity, he would scoff at the mere idea. Nevertheless this is what Mr. Clemens has done. The remarkable achievement is strong evidence of the charm of his character.

Perhaps it is possible to discover in what that charm consists. The comparison between Abraham Lincoln and Mark Twain which was suggested a little while ago doubtless appeared fantastical enough. But after all, is not the feeling of kinship which the people had with the statesman the same which they have with the writer? There is certainly no way to a nation's heart more nearly direct than to make it feel that you are of one flesh and blood with it. It loves to see itself literally personified in the executive chair; it likes best that writer who thoroughly expresses its own ideas, gives form to its own moral and mental nature. That is always the secret of success—the one thing in common between popularly successful mediocrities and popularly successful great men.

Such is the conclusion that has been reached by the editors of our most popular periodicals; the working theory by following which they have attained success. Such, again, is the conclusion that those writers who would be popular have arrived at after studying the works of writers who are popular. They have ever discovered the painful if flattering fact that they are not as common men are, and that therefore they cannot effectually appeal to the public taste. If lack of likeness and consequent lack of sympathy are indeed the secret of scant sales, then the average man should be the most popular writer.

An eccentric friend of mine wholly accepts this doleful doctrine. Whatever is widely liked must, he says, appeal to the general public, which is a vulgar body with crude tastes, and, generally speaking, anything which satisfies it is bad. He therefore carefully avoids all greatly popular books—and it must be confessed he escapes in this way the reading of an intolerable deal of writing which, charitably speaking, is not choice. He admits, however, that he misses some excellent authors, and the admission implies that the public does occasionally enjoy good literary work. He explains this by saying that the good book is liked for other than literary reasons. If it is conceivable that the master of a superb literary style should have, for instance, the mental and moral equipment of the late E. P. Roe, my friend avers that the crowd would read him in spite of his style. Mr. Henry James finds it easy to be artistic, The Duchess found it easy to be popular; Mr. Kipling finds it easy to be both. In other words, the great writer is one who to generous artistic and intellectual gifts adds the further good fortune of being the type of a multitude. In the field of politics, the same theory will explain the common success among us of mediocrities, the very great success of some really great men like Lincoln. The same theory explains the vogue of Mark Twain.

If one were to summon his vague recollections of the figure set forth as that of the typical American by such various authorities as the playwright, the caricaturist, the story-teller, and the novelist, there would gradually emerge from the haze a certain quite definite figure of a man. Let us recall, quite at random, a few memories. There is the shrewd, humorous, resourceful, ill-bred Senator as played by Mr. Crane. There is Uncle Sam as he is shown us in the comic press. There is the American in Mr. Kipling's ballad of the "Imperial Rescript," whose ideal is a house of his own, "With gas and water connections, and steam-heat through to the top." There is the ready and scheming Fulkerson in Mr. Howells's *Hazard of New Fortunes,* who thinks of literature as a hardware dealer thinks of nails. There is his counterpart, Pinkerton, in Stevenson's romance, *The Wrecker.* There is the uncouth Lincoln as he appears in Mr. Herndon's *Life.* These figures which chance to come to mind blend easily—do they not?—into a sort of composite personality, a shrewd, ready, practical, irreverent, humorous, uncultivated man, who is apt to jeer at art and the civilization of Europe, but for whom you have, nevertheless, a large affection and a high respect, partly because he has, to a striking degree, such excellent qualities as essential seriousness of character, self-reliance, courage, kindliness, honesty and simplicity of heart, the domestic virtues; and still more, perhaps, because you are a good American yourself, and know him to be the man you would like to be were good manners and cultivation added to him.

This is, after all, the type among the many that we recognize as American which is most generally found throughout the United States. It is a type with which, indeed, the American people are a little too well satisfied. Our public is too apt to be to his virtues very kind, and very blind to his faults—a course of conduct admirable to adopt toward your friend, but not toward yourself if you aim to improve. And is it not this type which Mark Twain is continually drawing? Tom Sawyer and Huckleberry Finn are certainly the typical American in little. Is not the view of Europe expressed in *Innocents Abroad* that of the same humorous, irreverent, uncultivated man? The Connecticut Yankee who went to King Arthur's court would undoubtedly have preferred to any castle in England that house in America "With gas and water connections, and steam-heat through to the top." Pudd'nhead Wilson and the pilots in *Life on the Mississippi* conform perfectly to the type. They are all Americans—raw, if you will, but real, native, typical. Essentially they and the others are one and the same man always. Now, let the reader recall that Mark Twain's work is almost wholly autobiographic, and he will at once perceive the obvious corollary: this man, this typical American, is Mark Twain himself.

His life has been typically American. There is something delightfully national in that "two-story brick with a large tree in front" in which it had its beginnings. To attain fame and fortune is supposed to be the special privilege of the poor, self-educated American boy. American versatility, which has been our doubtful boast, is strikingly exemplified in this man's variety of occupation—printer, pilot, private secretary, miner, reporter, lecturer, inventor (that is especially American!), author, publisher. It all recalls the biographies—not likely, one may guess, to be written in the future as they have been in the past—of the From the Towpath to the White House sort. It is American through and through. Having lived this life, how could Mark Twain fail to go straight to the hearts of his countrymen, attracting them to himself at first through their sense of humor, holding them afterwards through their sense of kinship? If a man can thoroughly express the individuality of a nation, he may fairly be called great. We may lament the artist lost, but we may rejoice in the man. He has drawn the national type, interpreted the national character. For that service we may be grateful. And he has taught unobtrusively, but none the less powerfully, the virtues of common sense and honest manliness. If it comes to a choice, these are better than refinement.

1901

WILLIAM DEAN HOWELLS

TWO RECENT EVENTS have concurred to offer criticism a fresh excuse, if not a fresh occasion, for examining the literary work of Mr. Samuel L. Clemens, better known to the human family by his pseudonym of Mark Twain. One of these events is the publication of his writings in a uniform edition, which it is to be hoped will remain indefinitely incomplete; the other is his return to his own country after an absence so long [ten years] as to form a psychological perspective in which his characteristics make a new appeal. . . .

. . . .

So far as I know, Mr. Clemens is the first writer to use in extended writing the fashion we all use in thinking, and to set down the thing that comes into his mind without fear or favor of the thing that went before or the thing that may be about to follow. I, for instance, in putting this paper together, am anxious to observe some sort of logical order, to discipline such impressions and notions as I have of the subject into a coherent body which shall march columnwise to a conclusion obvious if not inevitable from the start. But Mr. Clemens, if he were writing it, would not be anxious to do any such thing. He would take whatever offered itself to his hand out of that mystical chaos, that divine ragbag, which we call the mind, and leave the reader to look after relevancies and sequences for himself.

"Mark Twain: An Inquiry," from North American Review, *CLXXII (February, 1901), 306-21.*

These there might be, but not of that hard-and-fast sort which I am eager to lay hold of, and the result would at least be satisfactory to the author, who would have shifted the whole responsibility to the reader, with whom it belongs, at least as much as with the author. In other words, Mr. Clemens uses in work on the larger scale the method of the elder essayists, and you know no more where you are going to bring up in *The Innocents Abroad* or *Following the Equator* than in an essay of Montaigne. The end you arrive at is the end of the book, and you reach it amused but edified, and sorry for nothing but to be there. You have noted the author's thoughts, but not his order of thinking; he has not attempted to trace the threads of association between the things that have followed one another; his reason, not his logic, has convinced you, or, rather, it has persuaded you, for you have not been brought under conviction.

It is not certain that this method is of design with Mr. Clemens; that might spoil it; and possibly he will be as much surprised as anyone to know that it is his method. It is imaginable that he pursues it from no wish but to have pleasure of his work, and not to fatigue either himself or his reader; and his method may be the secret of his vast popularity, but it cannot be the whole secret of it. Anyone may compose a scrapbook and offer it to the public with nothing of Mark Twain's good fortune. Everything seems to depend upon the nature of the scraps, after all; his scraps might have been consecutively arranged, in a studied order, and still have immensely pleased; but there is no doubt that people like things that have at least the appearance of not having been drilled into line. Life itself has that sort of appearance as it goes on; it is an essay with moments of drama in it rather than a drama; it is a lesson, with the precepts appearing haphazard, and not precept upon precept; it is a school, but not always a school-room; it is a temple, but the priests are not always in their sacerdotal robes; sometimes they are eating the sacrifice behind the altar and pouring the libations for the god through the channels of their dusty old throats. An instinct of something chaotic, ironic, empiric in the order of experience seems to have been the inspiration of our humorist's art, and what finally remains with the reader, after all the joking and laughing, is not merely the feeling of having had a mighty good time, but the conviction that he has got the worth of his money. He has not gone through the six hundred pages of *The Innocents Abroad,* or *Following the Equator,* without having learned more of the world as the writer saw it than any but the rarest traveller is able to show for his travel; and possibly, with his average practical American public, which was his first tribunal, and must always be his court of final appeal, Mark Twain justifies himself for being so delightful by being so instructive. If this bold notion is admissible, it seems the moment to say that no writer ever imparted information more inoffensively.

But his great charm is his absolute freedom in a region where most of us are fettered and shackled by immemorial convention. He saunters out into the trim world of letters, and lounges across its neatly kept paths, and walks about on the grass at will, in spite of all the signs that have been put up from the beginning of literature, warning people of dangers and penalties for the slightest trespass.

One of the characteristics I observe in him is his single-minded use of words, which he employs as Grant did to express the plain, straight meaning their common acceptance has given them with no regard to their structural significance or their philological implications. He writes English as if it were a primitive and not a derivative language, without Gothic or Latin or Greek behind it, or German and French beside it. The result is the English in which the most vital works of English literature are cast, rather than the English of Milton and Thackeray and Mr. Henry James. I do not say that the English of the authors last named is less than vital, but only that it it not the most vital. It is scholarly and conscious; it knows who its grandfather was; it has the refinement and subtlety of an old patriciate. You will not have with it the widest suggestion, the largest human feeling, or perhaps the loftiest reach of imagination, but you will have the keen joy that exquisite artistry in words can alone impart, and that you will not have in Mark Twain. What you will have in him is a style which is as personal, as biographical as the style of anyone who has written, and expresses a civilization whose courage of the chances, the preferences, the duties, is not the measure of its essential modesty. It has a thing to say, and it says it in the word that may be the first or second or third choice, but will not be the instrument of the most fastidious ear, the most delicate and exacting sense, though it will be the word that surely and strongly conveys intention from the author's mind to the reader's. It is the

Abraham Lincolnian word, not the Charles Summerian; it is American, Western.

Now that Mark Twain has become a fame so world-wide, we should be in some danger of forgetting, but for his help, how entirely American he is, and we have already forgotten, perhaps, how truly Western he is, though his work, from first to last, is always reminding us of the fact. But here I should like to distinguish. It is not alone in its generous humor, with more honest laughter in it than humor ever had in the world till now, that his work is so Western. Anyone who has really known the West (and really to know it one must have lived it) is aware of the profoundly serious, the almost tragical strain which is the fundamental tone in the movement of such music as it has. Up to a certain point, in the presence of the mystery which we call life, it trusts and hopes and laughs; beyound that it doubts and fears, but it does not cry. It is more likely to laugh again, and in the work of Mark Twain there is little of the pathos which is supposed to be the ally of humor, little suffusion of apt tears from the smiling eyes. It is too sincere for that sort of play; and if after the doubting and the fearing it laughs again, it is with a suggestion of resentment which youth feels when the disillusion from its trust and hope comes, and which is the grim second-mind of the West in the presence of the mystery.

It is not so much the race-effect as the region-effect; it is not the Anglo-American finding expression, it is the Westerner, who is not more thoroughly the creature of circumstances, of conditions, but far more dramatically their creature than any prior man. He found himself placed in them and under them, so near to a world in which the natural and primitive was obsolete, that while he could not escape them, neither could he help challenging them. The inventions, the appliances, the improvements of the modern world invaded the hoary eld of his rivers and forests and prairies, and, while he was still a pioneer, a hunter, a trapper, he found himself confronted with the financier, the scholar, the gentleman. They seemed to him, with the world they represented, at first very droll, and he laughed. Then they set him thinking, and, as he never was afraid of anything, he thought over the whole field and demanded explanations of all his prepossessions—of equality, of humanity, of representative government and revealed religion. When they had not their answers ready, without accepting the conventions of the modern world as solutions or in any manner final, he laughed again, not mockingly, but patiently, compassionately. Such, or somewhat like this, was the genesis and evolution of Mark Twain.

Missouri was Western, but it was also Southern, not only in the institution of slavery, to the custom and acceptance of which Mark Twain was born and bred without any applied doubt of its divinity, but in the peculiar social civilization of the older South from which his native State was settled. It would be reaching too far out to claim that American humor, of the now prevailing Western type, is of Southern origin, but without staying to attempt it I will say that I think the fact could be established; and I think one of the most notably Southern traits of Mark Twain's humor is its power of seeing the fun of Southern seriousness, but this vision did not come to him till after his liberation from neighborhood in the vaster Far West. He was the first, if not the only, man of his section to betray a consciousness of the grotesque absurdities in the Southern inversion of the civilized ideals in behalf of slavery, which must have them upside down in order to walk over them safely.

No American of Northern birth or breeding could have imagined the spiritual struggle of Huck Finn in deciding to help the negro Jim to his freedom, even though he should be forever despised as a negro thief in his native town, and perhaps eternally lost through the blackness of his sin. No Northerner could have come so close to the heart of a Kentucky feud, and revealed it so perfectly, with the whimsicality playing through its carnage, or could have so brought us into the presence of the sardonic comi-tragedy of the squalid little river town where the store-keeping magnate shoots down his drunken tormentor in the arms of the drunkard's daughter, and then cows with bitter mockery the mob that comes to lynch him.

The strict religiosity compatible in the Southwest with savage precepts of conduct is something that could make itself known in its amusing contrast only to the native Southwesterner, and the revolt against it is as constant in Mark Twain as the enmity to New England orthodoxy is in Doctor Holmes. But he does not take it with such serious resentment as Doctor Holmes is apt to take his inherited Puritanism, and it may be therefore that he is able to do it more perfect justice, and impart it more absolutely. At any rate, there are no more vital passages in his fiction than those which embody character as it is affected for good as well as evil by the severity of the local Sunday-schooling and church-going.

I find myself, in spite of the discipline I intend for this paper, speaking first of the fiction, which by no means came first in Mark Twain's literary development. It is true that his beginnings were in short sketches, more or less inventive, and studies of life in which he let his imagination play freely; but it was not till he had written *Tom Sawyer* that he could be called a novelist. Even now I think he should rather be called a romancer, though such a book as *Huckleberry Finn* takes itself out of the order of romance and places itself with the great things in picaresque fiction. Still, it is more poetic than picaresque, and of a deeper psychology. The probable and credible soul that the author divines in the son of the town drunkard is one which we might each own brother, and the art which portrays this nature at first hand in the person and language of the hero, without pose or affectation, is fine art. In the boy's history the author's fancy works realistically to an end as high as it has reached elsewhere, if not higher; and I who like *The Connecticut Yankee in King Arthur's Court* so much have half a mind to give my whole heart to *Huckleberry Finn*.

Both *Huckleberry Finn* and *Tom Sawyer* wander in episodes loosely related to the main story, but they are of a closer and more logical advance from the beginning to the end than the fiction which preceded them, and which I had almost forgotten to name before them. We owe to *The Gilded Age* a type in Colonel Mulberry Sellers which is as likely to endure as any fictitious character of our time. It embodies the sort of Americanism which survived through the Civil War, and characterized in its boundlessly credulous, fearlessly adventurous, unconsciously burlesque excess the period of political and economic expansion which followed the war. Colonel Sellers was, in some rough sort, the American of that day, which already seems so remote, and is best imaginable through him. Yet the story itself was of the fortuitous structure of what may be called the autobiographical books, such as *The Innocents Abroad* and *Roughing It*. Its desultory and accidental character was heightened by the coöperation of Mr. Clemens's fellow-humorist, Charles Dudley Warner, and such coherence as it had was weakened by the diverse qualities of their minds and their irreconcilable ideals in literature. These never combined to a sole effect or to any variety of effects that left the reader very clear what the story was all about; and yet from the cloudy solution was precipitated at least one character which, as I have said, seems of as lasting substance and lasting significance as any which the American imagination has evolved from the American environment.

If Colonel Sellers is Mr. Clemens's supreme invention, as it seems to me, I think that his *Connecticut Yankee* is his highest achievement in the way of a greatly imagined and symmetrically developed romance. Of all the fanciful schemes in fiction, it pleases me most, and I give myself with absolute delight to its notion of a keen East Hartford Yankee finding himself, by a retroactionary spell, at the court of King Arthur of Britain, and becoming part of the sixth century with all the customs and ideas of the nineteenth in him and about him. The field for humanizing satire which this scheme opens is illimitable; but the ultimate achievement, the last poignant touch, the most exquisite triumph of the book, is the return of the Yankee to his own century, with his look across the gulf of the ages at a period of which he had been a part and his vision of the sixth-century woman he had loved holding their child in her arms.

It is a great fancy, transcending in aesthetic beauty the invention in *The Prince and the Pauper,* with all the delightful and affecting implications of that charming fable, and excelling the heartrending story in which Joan of Arc lives and prophesies and triumphs and suffers. She is, indeed, realized to the modern sense as few figures of the past have been realized in fiction; and is none the less of her time and of all time because her supposititious historian is so recurrently of ours. After Sellers, and Huck Finn, and Tom Sawyer, and the Connecticut Yankee, she is the author's finest creation; and if he had succeeded in portraying no other woman-nature, he would have approved himself its fit interpreter in her. I do not think he succeeds so often with that nature as with the boy-nature or the man-nature, apparently because it does not interest him so much. He will not trouble himself to make women talk like women at all times; oftentimes they talk too much like him, though the simple, homely sort express themselves after their kind; and Mark Twain does not always write men's dialogue so well as he might. He is apt to burlesque the lighter colloquiality, and it is only in the more serious and most tragical junctures that his people utter themselves with veracious simplicity and dignity. That great, burly fancy of his is always tempting him to the exaggeration which is the condition of so much of his personal humor, but which when it invades the drama spoils the illusion. The illusion renews itself in the great moments, but I wish it could be kept intact in the small, and I blame him that he does not rule his fancy better.

His imagination is always dramatic in its conceptions, but not always in its expressions; the talk of his people is often inadequate caricature in the ordinary exigencies, and his art contents itself with makeshift in the minor action. Even in *Huck Finn,* so admirably proportioned and honestly studied, you find a piece of lawless extravagance hurled in, like the episode of the two strolling actors in the flatboat; their broad burlesque is redeemed by their final tragedy— a prodigiously real and moving passage— but the friend of the book cannot help wishing the burlesque was not there. One laughs, and then despises one's self for laughing, and this is not what Mark Twain often makes you do. There are things in him that shock, and more things that we think shocking, but this may not be so much because of their nature as because of our want of naturalness; they wound our conventions rather than our convictions.

As most women are more the subjects of convention than men, his humor is not for most women; but I have a theory that, when women like it, they like it far beyond men. Its very excess must satisfy that demand of their insatiate nerves for something that there is enough of; but I offer this conjecture with instant readiness to withdraw it under correction. What I feel rather surer of is that there is something finally feminine in the inconsequence of his ratiocination, and his beautiful confidence that we shall be able to follow him to his conclusion in all those turnings and twistings and leaps and bounds by which his mind carries itself to any point but that he seems aiming at. Men, in fact, are born of women, and possibly Mark Twain owes his literary method to the colloquial style of some far ancestress who was more concerned in getting there, and amusing herself on the way, than in ordering her steps.

Possibly, also, it is to this ancestress that he owes the instinct of right and wrong which keeps him clear as to the conditions that formed him, and their injustice. Slavery in a small Missouri River town could not have been the dignified and patriarchal institution which Southerners of the older South are fond of remembering or imagining. In the second generation from Virginia ancestry of this sort, Mark Twain was born to the common necessity of looking out for himself, and, while making himself practically of another order of things, he felt whatever was fine in the old and could regard whatever was ugly and absurd more tolerantly, more humorously than those who bequeathed him their enmity to it. Fortunately for him, and for us who were to enjoy his humor, he came to his intellectual consciousness in a world so large and free and safe that he could be fair to any wrong while seeing the right so unfailingly; and nothing is finer in him than his gentleness with the error which is simply passive and negative. He gets fun out of it, of course, but he deals almost tenderly with it, and hoards his violence for the superstitions and traditions which are arrogant and active. His pictures of that old river-town, Southwestern life, with its faded and tattered aristocratic ideals and its squalid democratic realities, are pathetic, while they are so unsparingly true and so inapologetically and unaffectedly faithful.

The West, when it began to put itself into literature, could do so without the sense, or the apparent sense, of any older or politer world outside of it; whereas the East was always looking fearfully over its shoulder at Europe, and anxious to account for itself as well as represent itself. No such anxiety as this entered Mark Twain's mind, and it is not claiming too much for the Western influence upon American literature to say that the final liberation of the East from this anxiety is due to the West, and to its ignorant courage or its indifference to its difference from the rest of the world. It would not claim to be superior, as the South did, but it could claim to be humanly equal, or, rather, it would make no claim at all, but would simply be, and what it was, show itself without holding itself responsible for not being something else.

The Western boy of forty or fifty years ago grew up so close to the primeval woods or fields that their inarticulate poetry became part of his being, and he was apt to deal simply and uncritically with literature when he turned to it, as he dealt with nature. He took what he wanted, and left what he did not like; he used it for the playground, not the workshop of his spirit. Something like this I find true of Mark Twain in peculiar and uncommon measure. I do not see any proof in his books that he wished at any time to produce literature, or that he wished to reproduce life. When filled up with an experience that deeply interested him, or when provoked by some injustice or absurdity that intensely moved him, he burst forth, and the outbreak might be altogether humorous, but it was more likely to be humorous with a groundswell of seriousness carrying it profoundly forward.

In all there is something curiously, not very definably, elemental, which again seems to me Western. He behaves himself as if he were the first man who was ever up against the proposition in hand. He deals as newly, for instance, with the relations of Shelley to his wife, and with as personal and direct an indignation, as if they had never attracted critical attention before; and this is the mind or the mood which he brings to all literature. Life is another affair with him; it is not a discovery, not a surprise; everyone else knows how it is; but here is a new world, and he explores it with a ramping joy, and shouts for the reader to come on and see how, in spite of all the lies about it, it is the same old world of men and women, with really nothing in it but their passions and prejudices and hypocrisies.

At heart he was always deeply and essentially romantic, and once must have expected life itself to be a fairy dream. When it did not turn out so he found it tremendously amusing still, and his expectation not the least amusing thing in it, but without rancor, without grudge or bitterness in his disillusion, so that his latest word is as sweet as his first. He is deeply and essentially romantic in his literary conceptions, but when it comes to working them out he is helplessly literal and real; he is the impassioned lover, the helpless slave of the concrete. For this reason, for his wish, his necessity, first to ascertain his facts, his logic is as irresistible as his laugh.

All life seems, when he began to find it out, to have the look of a vast joke, whether the joke was on him or on his fellow-beings, or if it may be expressed without irreverence, on their common creator. But it was never wholly a joke, and it was not long before his literature began to own its pathos. The sense of this is not very apparent in *The Innocents Abroad,* but in *Roughing It* we began to be distinctly aware of it, and in the successive books it is constantly imminent, not as a clutch at the heartstrings, but as a demand of common justice, common sense, the feeling of proportion. It is not sympathy with the under dog merely as under dog that moves Mark Twain; for the under dog is sometimes rightfully under. But the probability is that it is wrongfully under, and has a claim to your inquiry into the case which you cannot ignore without atrocity.

Mark Twain never ignores it; I know nothing finer in him than his perception that in this curiously contrived mechanism men suffer for their sorrows rather oftener than they suffer for their sins; and when they suffer for their sorrows they have a right not only to our pity but to our help. He always gives his help, even when he seems to leave the pity to others, and it may be safely said that no writer has dealt with so many phases of life with more unfailing justice. There is no real telling how anyone comes to be what he is; all speculation concerning the fact is more or less impudent or futile conjecture; but it is conceivable that Mark Twain took from his early environment the custom of clairvoyance in things in which most humorists are purblind, and that being always in the presence of the under dog, he came to feel for him as under with him. If the knowledge and vision of slavery did not tinge all life with potential tragedy, perhaps it was this which lighted in the future humorist the indignation at injustice which glows in his page. His indignation relieves itself as often as not in a laugh; injustice is the most ridiculous thing in the world, after all, and indignation with it feels its own absurdity.

It is supposable, if not more than supposable, that the ludicrous incongruity of a slaveholding democracy nurtured upon the Declaration of Independence, and the comical spectacle of white labor owning black labor, had something to do in quickening the sense of contrast which is the fountain of humor, or is said to be so. But not to drive too hard a conjecture which must remain conjecture, we may reasonably hope to find in the untrammelled, the almost unconditional life of the later and farther West, with its individualism limited by nothing but individualism, the outside causes of the first overflow of the spring. We are so fond of classification, which we think is somehow interpretation, that one cannot resist the temptation it holds out in the case of the most unclassifiable things; and I must yield so far as to note that the earliest form of Mark Twain's work is characteristic of the greater part of it. The method used in *The Innocents Abroad* and in *Roughing It* is the method used in *Life on the Mis-*

sissippi, in *A Tramp Abroad,* and in *Following the Equator,* which constitute in bulk a good half of all his writings, as they express his dominant aesthetics.

If he had written the fictions alone, we should have had to recognize a rare inventive talent, a great imagination and dramatic force; but I think it must be allowed that the personal books named overshadow the fictions. They have the qualities that give character to the fictions, and they have advantages that the fictions have not and that no fiction can have. In them, under cover of his pseudonym, we come directly into the presence of the author, which is what the reader is always longing and seeking to do; but unless the novelist is a conscienceless and tasteless recreant to the terms of his art, he cannot admit the reader to his intimacy. The personal books of Mark Twain have not only the charm of the essay's inconsequent and desultory method, in which invention, fact, reflection, and philosophy wander after one another in any following that happens, but they are of an immediate and most informal hospitality which admits you at once to the author's confidence, and makes you frankly welcome not only to his thoughts but to his way of thinking. He takes no trouble in the matter, and he asks you to take none. All that he requires is that you will have common sense, and be able to tell a joke when you see it. Otherwise the whole furnishing of his mental mansion is at your service, to make such use as you can of it, but he will not be always directing your course, or requiring you to enjoy yourself in this or that order.

In the case of the fictions, he conceives that his first affair is to tell a story, and a story when you are once launched upon it does not admit of deviation without some hurt to itself. In Mark Twain's novels, whether they are for boys or for men, the episodes are only those that illustrate the main narrative or relate to it, though he might have allowed himself somewhat larger latitude in the old-fashioned tradition which he has oftenest observed in them. When it comes to the critical writings, which again are personal, and which, whether they are criticisms of literature or of life, are always so striking, he is quite relentlessly logical and coherent. Here there is no lounging or sauntering, with entertaining or edifying digressions. The object is in view from the first, and the reasoning is straightforwardly to it throughout. This is as notable in the admirable paper on the Jews, or on the Austrian situation, as in that on Harriet Shelley, or that on Cooper's novels. The facts are first ascertained with a conscience uncommon in critical writing of any kind, and then they are handled with vigor and precision till the polemic is over. It does not so much matter whether you agree with the critic or not; what you have to own is that here is a man of strong convictions, clear ideas, and ardent sentiments, based mainly upon common sense of extraordinary depth and breadth.

In fact, what finally appeals to you in Mark Twain, and what may hereafter be his peril with his readers, is his common sense. . . . The danger which he now runs with us is neither heightened nor lessened by the spread of his fame, but is an effect from intrinsic causes. Possibly it might not have been so great if he had come back comparatively forgotten; it is certain only that in coming back more remembered than ever, he confronts a generation which began to know him not merely by his personal books and his fiction, but by those criticisms of life and literature which have more recently attested his interest in the graver and weightier things.

Graver and weightier, people call them, but whether they are really more important than the lighter things, I am by no means sure. What I am amused with, independently of the final truth, is the possibility that his newer audience will exact this serious mood of Mr. Clemens, whereas we of his older world only suffered it, and were of a high conceit with our liberality in allowing a humorist sometimes to be a philosopher. Some of us indeed, not to be invidiously specific as to whom, were always aware of potentialities in him, which he seemed to hold in check, or to trust doubtfully to his reader as if he thought they might be thought part of the joke.

Looking back over his work now, the later reader would probably be able to point out to earlier readers the evidence of a constant growth in the direction of something like recognized authority in matters of public import, especially those that were subject to the action of the public conscience as well as the public interest, until now hardly any man writing upon such matters is heard so willingly by all sorts of men. All of us, for instance, have read somewhat of the conditions in South Africa which have eventuated in the present effort of certain British politicians to destroy two free republics in the interest of certain British speculators; but I doubt if we have found the case anywhere so well stated as in the closing chapters of Mark Twain's *Following the Equator*. His estimate of the military character of the belligerents on either side is of the prophetic cast which can come only from the thorough assimilation of accomplished facts; and in those passages the student of the actual war can spell its anticipative history. It is by such handling of such questions, unpremeditated and almost casual as it seems, that Mark Twain has won his claim to be heard on any public matter, and achieved the odd sort of primacy which he now enjoys.

But it would be rather awful if the general recognition of his prophetic function should implicate the renunciation of the humor that has endeared him to mankind. It would be well for his younger following to beware of reversing the error of the elder, and taking everything in earnest, as these once took nothing in earnest from him. To reverse that error would not be always to find his true meaning, and perhaps we shall best arrive at this by shunning one another's mistakes. In the light of the more modern appreciation, we elders may be able to see some things seriously that we once thought pure drolling, and from our experience his younger admirers may learn to receive as drolling some things that they might otherwise accept as preaching.

What we all should wish to do is to keep Mark Twain what he has always been: a comic force unique in the power of charming us out of our cares and troubles, united with as potent an ethic sense of the duties, public and private, which no man denies in himself without being false to other men. I think we may hope for the best he can do to help us deserve our self-respect, without forming Mark Twain societies to read philanthropic meanings into his jokes, or studying the Jumping Frog as the allegory of an imperializing republic. I trust the time may be far distant when the Meditation at the Tomb of Adam shall be memorized and declaimed by ingenuous youth as a mystical appeal for human solidarity.

1907

WILLIAM LYON PHELPS

DURING the last twenty years, a profound change has taken place in the attitude of the reading public toward Mark Twain. I can remember very well when he was regarded merely as a humorist, and one opened his books with an anticipatory grin. Very few supposed that he belonged to literature; and a complete, uniform edition of his *Works* would perhaps have been received with something of the mockery that greeted Ben Jonson's folio in 1616. Professor Richardson's *American Literature,* which is still a standard work, appeared originally in 1886. My copy, which bears the date 1892, contains only two references in the index to Mark Twain, while Mr. Cable, for example, receives ten; and the whole volume fills exactly 990 pages. Looking up one of the two references, we find the following opinion:

> But there is a class of writers, authors ranking below Irving or Lowell, and lacking the higher artistic or moral purpose of the greater humorists, who amuse a generation and then pass from sight. Every period demands a new manner of jest, after the current fashion.... The reigning favorites of the day are Frank R. Stockton, Joel Chandler Harris, the various newspaper jokers, and "Mark Twain." But the creators of *Pomona* and *Rudder Grange,* of *Uncle Remus and His Folk-lore Stories* and *Innocents Abroad,* clever as they are, must make hay while the sun shines. Twenty years hence, unless they chance to enshrine their wit in some higher literary achievement, their unknown successors will be the privileged comedians of the republic. Humor alone never gives its masters a place in literature;

"*Mark Twain," from* North American Review, *CLXXXV (July 5, 1907), 540-48.*

it must co-exist with literary qualities, and must usually be joined with such pathos as one finds in Lamb, Hood, Irving or Holmes.

It is interesting to remember that before this pronouncement was published, *Tom Sawyer* and *Huckleberry Finn* had been read by thousands. Professor Richardson continued: "Two or three divisions of American humor deserve somewhat more respectful treatment," and he proceeds to give a full page to Petroleum V. Nasby, another page to Artemus Ward and two and one-half pages to Josh Billings, while Mark Twain had received less than four lines. After stating that, in the case of authors like Mark Twain, "temporary amusement, not literary product, is the thing sought and given," Professor Richardson announces that the department of fiction will be considered later. In this "department," Mark Twain is not mentioned at all, although Julian Hawthorne receives over three pages!

I have quoted Professor Richardson at length, because he represents an attitude toward Mark Twain that was common all during the eighties. Another college professor, who is today one of the best living American critics, says in his *Initial Studies in American Letters* (1895), "Though it would be ridiculous to maintain that either of these writers [Artemus Ward and Mark Twain] takes rank with Lowell and Holmes, . . . still it will not do to ignore them as mere buffoons, or even predict that their humors will soon be forgotten." There is no allusion in his book to *Tom Sawyer* or *Huckleberry Finn,* nor does the critic seem to regard their creator as in any sense a novelist. Still another writer, in a passing allusion to Mark Twain, says, "Only a very small portion of his writing has any place as literature."

Literary opinions change as time progresses; and no one could have observed the remarkable demonstration at the seventieth birthday of our great national humorist without feeling that most of his contemporaries regarded him, not as their peer, but as their Chief. Without wishing to make any invidious comparisons, I cannot refrain from commenting on the statement that it would be "ridiculous" to maintain that Mark Twain takes rank with Oliver Wendell Holmes. It is, of course, absolutely impossible to predict the future; the only real test of the value of a book is Time. Who now reads Cowley? Time has laughed at so many contemporary judgments that it would be foolhardy to make positive assertions about literary stock quotations one hundred years from now. Still, guesses are not prohibited: and I think it not unlikely that the name of Mark Twain will outlast the name of Holmes. American Literature would surely be the poorer if the great Boston Brahmin had not enlivened it with his rich humor, his lambent wit and his sincere pathos; but the whole content of his work seems slighter than the big American prose epics of the man of our day.

Indeed, it seems to me that Mark Twain is our foremost living American writer. He has not the subtlety of Henry James or the wonderful charm of Mr. Howells; he could not have written *Daisy Miller,* or *A Modern Instance,* or *Indian Summer,* or *The Kentons*— books of which every American should be proud, for they exhibit literary quality of an exceedingly high order. I have read these books over and over again, with constantly increasing profit and delight. I wish that Mr. Howells might live forever, and give to every generation the pure intellectual joy that he has given to ours. But the natural endowment of Mark Twain is still greater. Mr. Howells has made the most of himself; God has done it all for Mark Twain. If there be a living American writer touched with true genius, whose books glow with the divine fire, it is he. He has always been a conscientious artist; but no amount of industry could ever have produced a *Huckleberry Finn.*

When I was a child at the West Middle Grammar School of Hartford, on one memorable April day, Mark Twain addressed the graduating class. I was thirteen years old, but I have found it impossible to forget what he said. The subject of his "remarks" was Methuselah. He informed us that Methuselah lived to the ripe old age of nine hundred and sixty-nine. But he might as well have lived to be several thousand—nothing happened. The speaker told us that we should all live longer than Methuselah. Fifty years of Europe are better than a cycle of Cathay, and twenty years of modern American life are longer and richer in content than the old patriarch's thousand. Ours will be the true age in which to live, when more will happen in a day than in a year of the flat existence of our ancestors. I cannot remember his words; but what a fine thing it is to hear a speech, and carry away an idea!

I have since observed that this idea runs through much of his literary work. His philosophy of life underlies his broadest burlesque

—for *A Connecticut Yankee in King Arthur's Court* is simply an exposure of the "good old times." Mark Twain believes in the Present, in human progress. Too often do we apprehend the Middle Ages through the glowing pages of Spenser and Walter Scott; we see only glittering processions of "ladies dead and lovely knights." Mark Twain shows us the wretched condition of the common people, their utter ignorance and degradation, the coarseness and immorality of technical chivalry, the cruel and unscrupulous ecclesiastical tyranny and the capricious insolence of the barons. One may regret that he has reversed the dynamics in so glorious a book as Malory's *Morte d'Arthur,* but, through all the buffoonery and roaring mirth with which the knights in armor are buried, the artistic and moral purpose of the satirist is clear. If I understand him rightly, he would have us believe that *our* age, not theirs, is the "good time;" nay, ours is the age of magic and wonder. We need not regret in melancholy sentimentality the picturesqueness of bygone days, for we ourselves live, not in a material and commonplace generation, but in the very midst of miracles and romance. Merlin and the Fay Morgana would have given all their petty skill to have been able to use a telephone or a phonograph, or to see a moving picture. The sleeping princess and her castle were awakened by a kiss; but in the twentieth century a man in Washington touches a button, and hundreds of miles away tons of machinery begin to move, fountains begin to play and the air resounds with the whir of wheels. In comparison with today, the age of chivalry seems dull and poor. Even in chivalry itself our author is more knightly than Lancelot; for was there ever a more truly chivalrous performance than Mark Twain's essay on Harriet Shelley, or his literary monument to Joan of Arc? In these earnest pages, our national humorist appears as the true knight.

Mark Twain's humor is purely American. It is not the humor of Washington Irving, which resembles that of Addison and Thackeray; it is not delicate and indirect. It is genial, sometimes outrageous, mirth—laughter holding both his sides. I have found it difficult to read him in a library or on a street-car, for explosions of pent-up mirth or a distorted face are apt to attract unpleasant attention in such public places. Mark Twain's humor is boisterous, uproarious, colossal, overwhelming. As has often been remarked, the Americans are not naturally a gay people, like the French; nor are we light-hearted and careless, like the Irish and the Negro. At heart, we are intensely serious, nervous, melancholy. For humor, therefore, we naturally turn to buffoonery and burlesque, as a reaction against the strain and tension of life. Our attitude is something like that of the lonely author of the *Anatomy of Melancholy,* who used to lean over the parapet of Magdalen Bridge, and shake with mirth at the horrible jokes of the bargemen. We like Mark Twain's humor, not because we are frivolous, but because we are just the reverse. I have never known a frivolous person who really enjoyed or appreciated Mark Twain.

The essence of Mark Twain's humor is Incongruity. The jumping frog is named Daniel Webster; and, indeed, the intense gravity of a frog's face, with the droop at the corners of the mouth, might well be envied by many an American Senator. When the shotted frog vainly attempted to leave the earth, he shrugged his shoulders "like a Frenchman." Bilgewater and the Dolphin on the raft are grotesquely incongruous figures. The rescuing of Jim from his prison cell is full of the most incongruous ideas, his common-sense attitude toward the whole transaction contrasting strangely with that of the romantic Tom. Along with the constant incongruity goes the element of surprise—which Professor Beers has well pointed out. When one begins a sentence, in an apparently serious discussion, one never knows how it will end. In discussing the peace that accompanies religious faith, Mark Twain says that he has often been impressed with the calm confidence of a Christian with four aces. Exaggeration —deliberate, enormous hyperbole—is another feature. Rudyard Kipling, who has been profoundly influenced by Mark Twain, and has learned much from him, often employs the same device, as in "Brugglesmith."

Irreverence is also a noteworthy quality. In his travel-books, we are given the attitude of the typical American Philistine toward the wonders and sacred relics of the Old World, the whole thing being a gigantic burlesque on the sentimental guide-books which were so much in vogue before the era of Baedeker. With so much continuous fun and mirth, satire and burlesque, it is no wonder that Mark Twain should not always be at his best. He is doubtless sometimes flat, sometimes coarse, as all humorists since Rabelais have been. The wonder is that his level has been so high. I remember, just before the appearance of *Following the Equator,* I had been told that Mark Twain's inspiration was finally gone, and that he could not be funny if he tried. To test this, I opened the new book, and this is what I found on the first page:

> We sailed for America, and there made certain preparations. This took but little time. Two members of my family elected to go with me. Also a carbuncle. The dictionary says a carbuncle is a kind of jewel. Humor is out of place in a dictionary.

Although Mark Twain has the great qualities of the true humorist —common sense, human sympathy and an accurate eye for proportion—he is much more than a humorist. His work shows very high literary quality, the quality that appears in first-rate novels. He has shown himself to be a genuine artist. He has done something which many popular novelists have signally failed to accomplish—he has created real characters. His two wonderful boys, Tom Sawyer and Huckleberry Finn, are wonderful in quite different ways. The creator of Tom exhibited remarkable observation; the creator of Huck showed the divine touch of imagination. Tom is the American boy —he is "smart." In having his fence whitewashed, in controlling a pool of Sabbath-school tickets at the precise psychological moment, he displays abundant promise of future success in business. Huck, on the other hand, is the child of nature, harmless, sincere and crudely imaginative. His reasonings with Jim about nature and God belong to the same department of natural theology as that illustrated in Browning's *Caliban.* The night on the raft with Jim, when these two creatures look aloft at the stars, and Jim reckons the moon laid them, is a case in point.

> We had the sky up there, all speckled with stars, and we used to lay on our backs and look up at them, and discuss about whether they was made or only just happened. Jim he allowed they was made, but I allowed they happened; I judged it would have took too long to *make* so many Jim said the moon could 'a' *laid* them; well, that looked kind of reasonable, so I didn't say nothing against it, because I've seen a frog lay most as many, so of course it could be done. We used to watch the stars that fell, too, and see them streak down. Jim allowed they'd got spoiled and was hove out of the nest.

Again, Mark Twain has so much dramatic power that, were his literary career beginning instead of closing, he might write for us the great American play that we are still awaiting. The story of the feud between the Grangerfords and the Shepherdsons is thrillingly dramatic, and the tragic climax grips one by the heart. The shooting of the drunken Boggs, the gathering of the mob and its control by one masterful personality, belong essentially to true drama, and are written with power and insight. The pathos of these scenes is never false, never mawkish or overdone; it is the pathos of life itself. Mark Twain's extraordinary skill in descriptive passages shows, not merely keen observation, but the instinct for the specific word—the one word that is always better than any of its synonyms, for it makes the picture real—it creates the illusion, which is the essence of all literary art. The storm, for example:

It was my watch below till twelve, but I wouldn't 'a' turned in anyway if I'd had a bed, because a body don't see such a storm as that every day in the week, not by a long sight. My souls, how the wind did scream along! And every second or two there'd come a glare that lit up the white-caps for a half a mile around, and you'd see the islands looking dusty through the rain, and the trees thrashing around in the wind; then comes a *h-whack!*—bum! bum! bumble-umble-um-bum-bum-bum-bum—and the thunder would go rumbling and grumbling away, and quit—and then *rip* comes another flash and another sockdolager. The waves most washed me off the raft sometimes, but I hadn't any clothes on, and didn't mind. We didn't have no trouble about snags; the lightning was glaring and flittering around so constant that we could see them plenty soon enough to throw her head this way or that and miss them.

Tom Sawyer and *Huckleberry Finn* are prose epics of American life. The former is one of those books—of which *The Pilgrim's Progress, Gulliver's Travels* and *Robinson Crusoe* are supreme examples —that are read at different periods of one's life from very different points of view; so that it is not easy to say when one enjoys them the most—before one understands their real significance or after. Nearly all healthy boys enjoy reading *Tom Sawyer,* because the intrinsic interest of the story is so great, and the various adventures of the hero are portrayed with such gusto. Yet it is impossible to outgrow the book. The eternal Boy is there, and one cannot appreciate the nature of boyhood properly until one has ceased to be a boy. The other masterpiece, *Huckleberry Finn,* is really not a child's book at all.

Children devour it, but they do not digest it. It is a permanent picture of a certain period of American history, and this picture is made complete, not so much by the striking portraits of individuals placed on the huge canvas, as by the vital unity of the whole composition. If one wishes to know what life on the Mississippi really was, to know and understand the peculiar social conditions of that highly exciting time, one has merely to read through this powerful narrative, and a definite, coherent, vivid impression remains.

By those who have lived there, and whose minds are comparatively free from prejudice, Mark Twain's pictures of life in the South before the war are regarded as, on the whole, nearer the truth than those supplied by any other artist. One reason for this is the aim of the author; he was not trying to support or defend any particular theory—no, his aim was purely and wholly artistic. In *Uncle Tom's Cabin,* a book by no means devoid of literary art, the red-hot indignation of the author largely nullified her evident desire to tell the truth. If one succeeds in telling the truth about anything whatever, one must have something more than the *desire* to tell the truth; one must know how to do it. False impressions do not always, probably do not commonly, come from deliberate liars. Mrs. Stowe's astonishing work is not really the history of slavery; it is the history of abolition sentiment. On the other hand, writers so graceful, talented and clever as Mr. Page and Mr. Hopkinson Smith do not always give us pictures that correctly represent, except locally, the actual situation before the war; for these gentlemen seem to have *Uncle Tom's Cabin* in mind.

Mark Twain gives us both points of view; he shows us the beautiful side of slavery—for it had a wonderfully beautiful, patriarchal side—and he also shows us the horror of it. The living dread of the negro that he would be sold down the river, has never been more vividly represented than when the poor woman in *Pudd'nhead Wilson* sees the water swirling against the snag, and realizes that she is bound the wrong way. That one scene makes an indelible impression on the reader's mind, and counteracts tons of polemics. The peculiar harmlessness of Jim is beautiful to contemplate. Although he and Huck really own the raft, and have taken all the risk, they obey implicitly the orders of the two tramps who call themselves Duke and King. Had that been a raft on the Connecticut River, and had

Huck and Jim been Yankees, they would have said to the intruders, "Whose raft is this, anyway?"

Mark Twain may be trusted to tell the truth; for the eye of the born caricature artist always sees the salient point. Caricatures often give us a better idea of their object than a photograph; for the things that are exaggerated, be it a large nose, or a long neck, are, after all, the things that differentiate this particular individual from the mass. Everybody remembers how Tweed was caught by one of Nast's cartoons.

Mark Twain is through and through American. If foreigners really wish to know the American spirit, let them read Mark Twain. He is far more American than their favorite specimen, Walt Whitman. The essentially American qualities of common sense, energy, enterprise, good humor and Philistinism fairly shriek from his pages. He reveals us in our limitations, in our lack of appreciation of certain beautiful things, fully as well as he pictures us in coarser but more triumphant aspects. It is, of course, preposterous to say that Americans are totally different from other humans; we have no monopoly of common sense and good humor, nor are we all hide-bound Philistines. But there is something pronounced in the American character, and the books of Mark Twain reveal it. He has also more than once been a valuable and efficient champion. Without being an offensive and blatant Jingo, I think he is well satisfied to be an American.

Mark Twain is our great Democrat. Democracy is his political, social and moral creed. His hatred of snobbery, affectation and assumed superiority is total. His democracy has no limits; it is bottomless and far-reaching. Nothing seems really sacred to him except the sacred right of every individual to do exactly as he pleases; which means, of course, that no one can interfere with another's right, for then democracy would be the privilege of a few, and would stultify itself. Not only does the spirit of democracy breathe out from all his greater books, but it is shown in specific instances, such as "Travelling with a Reformer;" and Mark Twain has more than once given testimony for his creed, without recourse to the pen.

At the head of all American novelists, living and dead, stands Nathaniel Hawthorne, unapproached, possibly unapproachable. His fine and subtle art is an altogether different thing from the art of our mighty, democratic, national humorist. But Literature is wonderfully diverse in its content; and the historian of American Letters, in the far future, will probably find it impossible to omit the name of Mark Twain, whose books have warmed human hearts all over the world.

1907

[CHARLES WHIBLEY]

FOR THE LAST MONTH London has suffered from a violent attack of hilarity. Painfully she has held her poor sides. So fiercely has she rocked with noisy laughter that her public monuments have been in danger of destruction. For Mark Twain has been in her midst, and has transmitted, through the voices of obsequious journalists, his messages of mirth. Mark Twain is a humourist, a simple truth which nobody is permitted to forget. He is a humourist who cannot open his mouth without provoking the wonder of the world, and, thanks to the industry of energetic reports, we have not lost one single pearl of his speech.

It is not Mark's fault—Mark they call him, to prove their familiarity,—nor the fault of the reporters, if a word spoken by the humourist has escaped us. All the world knows that the sublime heights of fun were climbed when Mark Twain referred happily to his own funeral. The compositors who set up this brilliant sally were so keenly conscious of their privilege that they fitted the master's incongruity with a bold series of misprints. Mark Twain designing his own funeral! Isn't it funny? Lives there a curmudgeon who will refrain from laughter when he hears of it? Still gayer was the phantasy which accused Mark Twain of stealing the Ascot Gold Cup. There's imagination for you! There's a pretty invention! Fleet Street accepted the joke as one man and it will be surprising if the great man's luggage

"The Sin of Exaggeration," from Blackwood's Edinburgh Magazine, *CLXXXII (August, 1907), 279-86. Authorship revealed in letter from Wm. Blackwood & Sons, Ltd., October 12, 1953.*

is not ransacked for the lost treasure by the Customs officers of his free and independent fatherland.

At last the humourist has left these shores. The echo of his last joke has died away, though the throats of his admirers are still husky with appreciative laughter. And so well did London play her part that if he rang his bell or asked for a lucifer match, the neighborhood of Dover Street palpitated with excitement. Unhappily, upon this enthusiasm, as upon most others, time has and will have a chastening effect. Our exhausted capital is beginning to understand that it can have too much of a good joke, and that nothing stales so rapidly as the thing called "humour."

Humour as a solid quality and a lucrative trade is of modern invention. The ancients knew well that its effect was an effect of light and shade. They were humorous in flashes, and their humour was infinitely enhanced, because it was set against a background of gravity. To be funny at all hours and in all places is as vile a sin against taste as it would be to dissolve in floods of tears before strangers. The great men who dared to laugh in an earlier age than ours laughed in moderation and with a wise purpose. Aristophanes and Lucian, Chaucer and Rabelais, Shakespeare and Fielding, are the true humourists of the world. They did not jest and jibe out of season. They held up folly to ridicule, not to amuse the groundlings, but to reveal, in a sudden blaze of light, the eternal truths of wisdom and justice. Their humour is precious on account of its parsimony. They do not at every turn slap their reader on the back and assure him that there is nothing congruous in the visible world. Of the irreverence that turns whatever is beautiful or noble into a stupid jest they knew nothing. They kept their humour in its proper place; they used it for a wise purpose; they did not degrade it to catch an easy round of applause; and, fortunately for them, they are today refused the august title of humourist, which sits so appositely upon the shoulders of Mark Twain.

The essence of humour is that it should be unexpected. The modern humourist is never unexpected. He beats the drum from the moment at which he appears upon the stage. He does not cease to beat it until he quits the stage for the last time. His mouth is always awry, as though he fed upon sour apples, and he demands that his auditors also should twist their lips. From morning till night he grins through a horse-collar, and is surprised if all the world does not applaud his grimaces. To the rash fellow who confesses that he does not understand his fun, the professional humourist has a ready answer. He tells the wretch, with a shrug of pity, that he has no sense of humour, and has no right to criticise wholesome ribaldry. The boot, of course, is on the other leg. The professional humourist is the one person to whom the proper exercise of humour is forbidden, and he does but add insult to injury when he dares to criticise his victim's understanding.

Yet the professional humourist today inherits the earth. He is the most popular of God's creatures. He has his own "organs," in which he makes a desperate attempt to look at all things from a ridiculous point of view. He assures you, with a sentimental leer, that his fun is always amiable, as though amiability were a sufficient atonement for an imbecile lack of taste. He is prepared to tickle you with his jokes from early morn to nightfall, and he has been so grossly flattered that he believes there is a positive virtue in his antics. He is perfectly convinced that he is doing good, and he needs very little persuasion to believe that he is the only regenerator of mankind. Gradually, too, he is encroaching upon all the professions which are not legitimately his own. The pulpit knows him and the senate. Worse still, he has invaded the Courts of Law, and sits grinning upon the bench at his own ineptitude, which appears to the obsequious barristers who hope some day to wear his cap and bells, to sparkle with the brilliance of true Attic wit.

The secret of modern humour is revealed to all. Its basis is an obvious incongruity. Not the subtle [counter-expectation] of the ancients, not a whimsical turn of phrase or twist of idea, which surprises us in the masters, but a coarse, crass confusion of past with present or of grave with gay. Its inventors, we regret to remind our readers, were Englishmen, aided and abetted by such Frenchmen as Motteux and D'Urfey, who were driven to these shores before or at the revocation of the Edict of Nantes, and whose native gaiety was not wholly extinguished by the persecutions endured by their fathers. Tom Brown the Facetious and the Inimitable Ned Ward were characteristic innovators. Inspired by joyousness and brandy, they laughed to scorn life and all its works. They were as cheerful a pair of ruffians as ever beat the pavement of a populous city since the infamous creatures of Petronius went splendidly upon the pad. They knew London as they knew their pockets, and they haunted the taverns with a zeal and an understanding worthy of their high purpose and higher spirits. They recall the beggar-students of an earlier age, or the poets who, in Elizabeth's time, brought their plays to the Bankside. Ned Ward, inn-keeper though he was, had still a regard for letters, and Tom Brown was a real scholar. His style was flippant; his muse was ever down at heel, and wore a dressing-gown; his prose was alive with the slang of the gutter and the quip of the street corner. But when he took up his pen his mind went back to Lucian and to Horace; he kept always in the great tradition; and though he was determined to laugh at all things, he had too quick a sense of his art to be a humourist and nothing more.

Nevertheless, he sowed the seeds of the easy incongruity which has debauched the humour of today. He delighted in such mock-heroic exercises as an "Oration in praise of Drunkenness," and he taught the world to believe that nothing was beyond the reach of jocularity. One of the earliest of our comic reporters, he wore the cap and bells with a light indifference, and, Ned Ward aiding him, he understood that the journal and pamphlet were a useful substitute for the generosity of patrons. Had they lived under the Tudors or early Stuarts, Brown and Ward would have been jesters at court or in a country house. They would have worn the livery of king or duke, and repaid the munificence of their masters with a licensed effrontery. The liberal age of Anne threw them upon the people, and they forced their note to suit the foolish rufflers who bought their wares. Thus they showed the way, and their descendants in the world of humour have been only too ready to follow them.

Humour, in this baser sense, is a foolish travesty of life; and before Brown split the sides of Grub Street, Charles Cotton, fisherman and Cockney, had already converted travesty into a form of literature. If the poor humourists of today descend in one line from Tom Brown, in another they may trace their pedigrees back to the admirable Cotton. Now Cotton, as became a gentleman of his education and pursuits, founded his humour upon the classics. He treated Virgil and Lucian precisely as the modern Yankee treats the older civilisation of Europe. He translated them into his own lingo, and asked you to laugh with him at them. He delighted to trick out the heroes of antiquity in his own poor fustian, and as his knowledge of slang was as great as his daring, the result is often ludicrous. A passage or two in illustration will make the purpose of the old travesties as clear as daylight. Here is Dido's address of farewell to Aeneas in Cotton's version:

> "But I'll waste on thee no more Breath,
> For whom the Wind, that fumes beneath,
> Is far too sweet: Avaunt, thou Slave!
> Thou lying coney-catching Knave,
> Be moving, do as thou hast told me!
> Nobody here intends to hold thee!
> Go: seek thy Farm, I hope 'twill be
> I' th' very bottom of the Sea:
> But shd'st thou 'scape, and not in Dike lie
> Drown'd like a Puppy, as 'tis likely,
> Since in the Proverb old 'tis found,
> Who's born to hang, will ne'er be drowned;
> Yet shd'st thou not be much the nigher
> I'll haunt thee like a going Fire,
> As soon as I can turn to a Ghost,
> Which will be in a week at most."

That is a fair specimen of Cotton's familiar style, and Cotton had many imitators. His contempt for grandeur, which is characteristic of the Cockney spirit, was emulated by many ingenious writers. The example which he set was followed for a century and more, and the best of his pupils handled the style with an even greater effrontery than his. Perhaps none of them, in ease of manner or bold anachronism, exceeded Bridges, whose burlesque translation of Homer is still ranked among "curiosities" in the catalogues. It is thus that in Bridges' version Agamemnon rates the angry Achilles:

> "The general gave him tit for tat,
> And answer'd, cocking first his hat,
> Go, and be hang'd, you blust'ring whelp,
> Pray, who the murrain wants your help?
> When you are gone, I know there are
> Col'nels sufficient for the war,
> Militia bucks that know no fears,
> Brave fishmongers and auctioneers;
> Besides, great Jove will fight for us,
> What need we then this mighty fuss?
> Thou lov'st to quarrel, fratch, and jangle,
> To scold and swear, and fight and wrangle.

Great strength thou hast, and pray what then?
Art thou so stupid, canst not ken,
The gods that ev'ry thing can see
Give strength to bears as well as thee?"

There in its origin and in its purpose is the whole of modern humour. The same flippant impertinence which distresses us in the works of popular Americans is already alive and alert. The same confusion of ancient and modern is already designed to evoke a hasty chuckle. We do not mean that the imitation is conscious; we do not suppose that Mark Twain or his predecessors ever heard the name of Charles Cotton; but when once the spirit of contempt for grave and reverend things was evoked, the worst enormities of contemporary humour were obvious and natural.

The end and aim of Mark Twain, then, are the end and aim of Cotton and Bridges. For him the art of Europe and the chivalry of King Arthur serve the purpose of Virgil and Homer. He travesties them with a kind of malignant joy. He brings whatever time has honoured down to the level of a Yankee drummer. In *The Innocents Abroad* he sets a slur of commonness upon beauty and splendour. With the vanity of a crude civilisation he finds every custom ridiculous that does not conform with the standard of the United States. The restraints of honour are food for his mirth. He holds his sides when he thinks of the old masters. They are not brought down to this our date. Nor does he understand that there are certain institutions, certain manifestations of genius, which should be sacred even for the jester. Newness is not the only virtue known to the world, and he who laughs at what is old, merely because it is old, proves a lack of intelligence which no whimsicality can excuse.

In other words, Mark Twain the humourist is a bull in the chinashop of ideas. He attempts to destroy what he could never build up, and assumes that his experiment is eminently meritorious. When, as in *A Yankee at the Court of King Arthur,* he gave full rein to his fancy, he achieved such a masterpiece of vulgarity as the world has never seen. His book gives you the same sort of impression which you might receive from a beautiful picture over which a poisonous slug had crawled. The hint of magnificence is there, pitilessly deformed and defaced. That Mark Twain is in perfect sympathy with his creature is perfectly evident. He frankly prefers Hartford, Conn., to

Camelot. He believes that in all respects his native land is superior to the wisest and noblest society that the eye of Arthur saw or any other eye has seen. He is sure that refinement and "gentility" were unknown before his own time. The Knights of the Round Table, he declares, used words which would have made a Comanche blush. "Indelicacy is too mild a term to convey the idea." In our own nineteenth century, he informs us, "the earliest samples of the real lady and real gentleman discoverable in English history—or in European history, for that matter—may be said to have made their appearance." That is what it is to be a humourist. But even if we permit the humour we must still question the historical accuracy of the statement, and regret that Mark Twain ever thought it necessary to comment upon the ancients, against whom he cherishes a fierce antipathy.

His verbal humour, if less reckless than his history, is far more dismally deplorable. Here is his comment upon Merlin: "He is always blethering around in my way, everywhere I go; he makes me tired. He don't amount to shucks as a magician." Who can resist this amazing humour? And again, who, save a churl, would refuse the tribute of a laugh to the following exquisite criticism of the same wonder-worker? "Merlin's stock was flat," writes Mark Twain, "the King wanted to stop his wages: he even wanted to banish him; but I interfered. I said he would be useful to work the weather, and attend to small matters like that, and I would give him a lift now and then when his poor little parlour-magic soured on him." Isn't there a snigger in every word of it? And before this brilliancy must we not confess that humour, like delicacy and all the other virtues, made its first appearance in the nineteenth century and in America?

This monstrous incongruity demands two qualities for its indulgence: a perfect self-esteem, and an exaggerated common-sense. No one who is not confident that he engrosses the graces can affect to find pleasure in thus insulting the past. No one whose sense is not common in all respects can apply all the resources of a vulgar logic to the creations of fancy and emotion. That Mark Twain is fully equipped for his purpose is only too clear. His humour and his talk alike proclaim it. And it is the more pitiful, because he has a talent which stands in need of no folly for its embellishment. Had he never cut a joke, had he refrained always from grinning at grave and beautiful things, how brilliant a fame would have been his!

When you are tired of his irreverence, when you have deplored his noisy jibes, when his funeral and his theft of the cup alike pall upon your spirit, take down his *Life on the Mississippi,* and see what perfect sincerity and a fine sympathy can accomplish. Mark Twain writes of the noble river as one who knows its every change and chance. Yet he writes of it with an austere restraint and without any desire to humanise it out of its proper character. And there is humour, too, in his descriptions,—not the tortured humour of a later day, but humour sufficient to play, like light upon shade, in the grave places of his history. As he says himself, he loved the pilot's profession far better than any he has followed since, and his love and understanding shine in every page of his masterpiece. As the river kept no secrets from him, so his quick memory enabled him to recover the impressions of his youth. To cite his own expressive words, "The face of the water, in time, became a wonderful book— a book which was a dead language to the uneducated passenger, but which told its mind to me without reserve, delivering its most cherished secrets as clearly as if it uttered them with a voice. And it was not a book to be read once and thrown aside, for it had a new story to tell every day. . . . There was never so wonderful a book written by man." In this passage Mark Twain strikes the real note of his life and experience. With equal truth he tells us at what cost he acquired this deep knowledge of the river and its moods.

Now, when I had mastered the language of this water, and had come to know every trifling feature that bordered the great river as familiarly as I knew the letters of the alphabet, I had made a valuable acquisition. But I had lost something, too. I had lost something which could never be restored to me while I lived. All the grace, the beauty, the poetry had gone out of the majestic river. I still keep in mind a certain wonderful sunset which I witnessed when steam-boating was new to me. . . . But, as I have said, a day came when I began to cease from noting the glories and the charms which the moon and the sun and the twilight wrought upon the river's face: another day came, when I ceased altogether to note them.

Yet the very fact that Mark Twain recognized the change which had come over his vision is the best proof that he submitted willingly to the marvelous spell of the river. His mental process was the reverse of Wordsworth's. Wordsworth learned

> To look on nature, not as in the hour
> Of thoughtless youth; but hearing oftentimes
> The still, sad music of humanity,
> Not harsh nor grating, though of ample power
> To chasten and subdue.

Mark Twain, on the other hand, heard "the still, sad music of humanity" when he but half knew the river. A profounder knowledge silenced the music, and persuaded him to own, with sincerity, that he gazed upon the sunset scene without rapture, but with the understanding of an intimate.

The author of *Life on the Mississippi* was also the creator of Tom Sawyer and Huck Finn, two boys who will survive to cast shame upon all the humour of America. And it is for the sake of a genuine talent that we deplore Mark Twain's studied antics. It should not have been for him to light the thorns which crackle under the pot. It should not have been for him to encourage the gross stupidity of his fellows. The moderation of one who has known men and rivers should have been revealed to all the world. But Mark Twain, in submitting to the common demand, shares the general love of exaggeration. "Govern a great country as you would cook a small fish," said the Chinese philosopher; "that is, do not overdo it." The tendency of today is to overdo all things. Humour, which should be a relief, and nothing more, is now an end in itself. . . . Some day there will be a reaction, and then it will be recognised that pleasure counts in life as much as success, and that solid blocks of humour are as blatant an outrage upon good sense as a daily pageant, or as games played with no other aim than by hook or by crook to snatch a victory.

1909

ARCHIBALD HENDERSON

I've a theory that every author while living has a projection of himself, a sort of eidolon, that goes about in near and distant places and makes friends and enemies for him out of folk who never knew him in the flesh. When the author dies this phantom fades away, not caring to continue business at the old stand. Then the dead writer lives only in the impression made by his literature; this impression may grow sharper or fainter, according to the fashions and new conditions of the time.—*Letter of Thomas Bailey Aldrich to William Dean Howells, December 23. 1901.*

DESPITE THE AVERAGE American's complacent and chuckling satisfaction in his country's possession of that superman of humor, Mark Twain, there is room for serious doubt whether a realization of the unique and incomparable position of Mark Twain in the republic of letters has fully dawned upon the American consciousness. On reflection, the number of living writers to whom can justly be attributed what a Frenchman would call *mondial éclat* is startlingly few. It was not so many years ago that Rudyard Kipling, with vigorous, imperialistic note, won for himself the unquestioned title as militant spokesman for the Anglo-Saxon race. Today, Bernard Shaw has a fame more world-wide than that of any other literary figure in the British Isles, and his dramas are played from Madrid to Helsingfors, from Budapest to Stockholm, from Vienna to St. Petersburg, from Paris to Berlin. Since Ibsen's death, Tolstoi exerts unchallenged the profoundest influence upon the thought and consciousness of the world—not

"*Mark Twain*," *from* Harper's Monthly, *CXVIII (May, 1909)*, [948]-55.

so much by his intellect as by the passionate integrity of his moral aspiration. But, in a sense not easily misunderstood, Mark Twain has a place in the minds and hearts of the great mass of humanity throughout the civilized world which, if measured in terms of affection, sympathy, and spontaneous enjoyment, is without a parallel.

The robust nationalism of Kipling challenges the defiant opposition of foreigners; while his reportorial realism offends many an inviolable canon of European taste. With all his incandescent wit and radiant comic irony, Bernard Shaw makes his most vivid impression upon the upper strata of society; while his legendary character is perpetually standing in the light of the serious reformer. Tolstoi's works are Russia's greatest literary contribution to posterity; yet his extravagant ideals, his unrealizable hopes, in their almost maniacal mysticism, continue to detract from his fame. If Mark Twain makes a more generally popular appeal, it is because the instrument of his appeal is the universal solvent of humor. That *eidolon* of which Aldrich speaks—a compact of good humor, robust sanity, and large-minded humanity—has diligently "gone about in near and distant places," everywhere making warm and lifelong friends of folk of all nationalities who have never known Mark Twain in the flesh. The stevedore on the dock, the motorman on the street-car, the newsboy on the street, the riverman on the Mississippi—all speak with exuberant affection of this quaint figure in his white suit, ever wreathed in clouds of tobacco smoke. In one day an emperor and a *concierge* vie with each other in tributes of admiration and esteem for the man and his works. It is Mark Twain's imperishable glory, not simply that his name is more widely known than that of any other living man, but that it is remembered with infinite and irrepressible zest.

Not without wide significance in its bearing upon the general outlines of contemporary literature is the circumstance that Mark Twain served his apprenticeship to letters in the high school of journalism. Rudyard Kipling awoke the world with a start by the crude, almost barbaric cry of his journalese; and Bernard Shaw acquired that trenchant and forthright style, which imparts such an air of heightened verisimilitude to his plays, in the ranks of the new journalism. "The writer who aims at producing the platitudes which are 'not for an age, but for all time,' " says Bernard Shaw, "has his reward in being unreadable in all ages; while Plato and Aristophanes trying to knock some sense into the Athens of their day, Shakespeare peopling that same Athens with Elizabethan mechanics and Warwickshire hunts, Ibsen photographing the local doctors and vestrymen of a Norwegian parish, Carpaccio painting the life of St. Ursula exactly as if she were a lady living in the next street to him, are still alive and at home everywhere among the dust and ashes of many thousands of academic, punctilious, most archaeologically correct men of letters and art who spent their lives haughtily avoiding the journalist's vulgar obsession with the ephemeral." Mark Twain began by studying the people and period he knew, in relation to his own life; and in writing of his time *à propos* of himself, succeeded in telling the truth about humanity in general and for any time. If it be true that the intellectual life of America for the most part takes its cue from the day, while Europe derives hers from history, then Mark Twain is a typical product of American literature as defined by Johannes V. Jensen: "journalism under exceptionally favorable conditions." Whatever modicum of truth may lurk in this definition, certain it is that Mark Twain is the greatest genius evolved by natural selection out of the ranks of American journalism. Crude, rudimentary, and often coarse as much of his writing was, it bore upon it the fresh stamp of contemporary actuality.

While Mark Twain has solemnly averred that humor is a "subject which has never had much interest" for him, it is nothing more than a commonplace to say that it is as a humorist and as a humorist only that the world persists in regarding him. The philosophy of his early life was what George Meredith has aptly termed the "philosophy of the Broad Grin"; and Mark Twain has had a great struggle to "live down his past." Mr. Gilbert Chesterton once said that "American humor, neither unfathomably absurd like the Irish, nor transfiguringly lucid and appropriate like the French, nor sharp and sensible and full of the realities of life like the Scotch, is simply the humor of imagination. It consists in piling towers on towers and mountains on mountains; of heaping a joke up to the stars and extending it to the end of the world." This partial and somewhat conventional foreign conception of American humor is admirably descriptive of the cumulative and sky-breaking humor of the early Mark Twain. Then no exaggeration was too absurd for him, no phantasm too unreal, no climax too extreme. After a while he learned on the platform that the unpardonable sin is to "sell" an audience, and in the study that "comic copy" will never win real fame.

In spite of these wholesome lessons learned through actual experience, Mark Twain has had to pay in full the penalty of comic greatness. The world is loath to accept a popular character at any rating other than its own. Whosoever sets to himself the task of amusing the world must realize the almost insuperable difficulty of inducing the world to regard him as a serious thinker. *"C'est une étrange entreprise que celle de faire rire les honnêtes gens,"* says Molière; and the strangeness of the undertaking is no less pronounced than the rigor of its obligations. Mark Twain began his career as a professional humorist and fun-maker; and the man in the street is not easily persuaded that the basis of the comic is not uncommon nonsense, but glorified common sense. The French have a fine-flavored distinction in *ce qui remue* from *ce qui émeut;* and if *remuage* was the defining characteristic of *A Tramp Abroad, Roughing It,* and *Innocents Abroad,* there was much of deep and genuine emotion in *Life on the Mississippi, Tom Sawyer, Huckleberry Finn,* and *Pudd'nhead Wilson.* Think of that admirable passage in which he portrays the marvellous spell laid upon him by that mistress of his youth, the great river:

The face of the water in time became a wonderful book—a book which was a dead language to the uneducated passenger, but which told its mind to me without reserve, delivering its most cherished secrets as if it uttered them with a voice. And it was not a book to be read over and thrown aside, for it had a new story to tell every day. . . . There was never so wonderful a book written by man. . . . When I had mastered the language of this water, and had come to know every trifling feature that bordered the great river as familiarly as I knew the letters of the alphabet, I had made a valuable acquisition. But I had lost something, too. I had lost something which could never be restored to me while I lived. All the grace, the beauty, the poetry, had gone out of the majestic river. . . . A day came when I began to cease from noting the glories and the charms which the moon and the sun and the twilight wrought upon the river's face: another day came when I ceased altogether to note them.

Even today, though long since dissociated in fact from the category of Artemus Ward, John Phoenix, Josh Billings, and Petroleum V. Nasby, Mark Twain can never be sure that his most solemn utterance may not be drowned in roars of thoughtless laughter. "It has been a very serious and a very difficult matter," Mr. Clemens lately remarked to me, "to doff the mask of humor with which the public has always seen me adorned. It is the incorrigible practice of the public, in this or in any country to see only humor in a humorist, however serious his vein. Not long ago I wrote a poem, which I never dreamed of giving to the public, on account of its seriousness; but on being invited to address the women students of a certain great university, I was persuaded by a near friend to read this poem. At the close of my lecture I said: 'Now, ladies, I am going to read you a poem of mine'—which was greeted with bursts of uproarious laughter. 'But this is a truly *serious* poem,' I asseverated—only to be greeted with renewed and, this time, more uproarious laughter. Nettled by this misunderstanding, I put the poem in my pocket, saying, 'Well, young ladies, since you do not believe me serious, I shall not read the poem,' at which the audience almost went into convulsions of merriment."

Humor, it must be remembered, is a function of nationality. The same joke, as related by an American, a Scotsman, an Irishman, a Frenchman, carries with it a distinctive racial flavor and individuality of approach. Indeed, it is open to question whether most humor is not essentially local in its nature, requiring some specialized knowledge of some particular locality. After reading George Ade's *Fables in Slang,* Mr. Andrew Lang was driven to the desperate conclusion that humor varies with the parallels of latitude, a joke in Chicago being a riddle in London! If one would lay his finger upon the secret of Mark Twain's world-wide popularity as a humorist, he must find that secret primarily in the universality and humanity of his humor. Mark Twain is a master in the art of broad contrast; incongruity lurks on the surface of his humor; and there is about it a staggering and cyclopean surprise. But these are mere surface qualities, more or less common, though at lower power, to all forms of humor. Nor is Mark Twain's international reputation as a humorist to be attributed to any tricks of style, to any breadth of knowledge, or even to any depth of intellectuality. His hold upon the world is due to qualities not of the head, but of the heart. I once heard Mr. Clemens say that humor is the key to the hearts of men, for it springs from the heart; and worthy of record is his dictum that there is far more of feeling than of thought in genuine humor.

Mark Twain has a remarkable feeling for words and their uses; and the merit of his style is its admirable adaptation to the theme.

And though Mr. Henry James may have said that one must be a very rudimentary person to enjoy Mark Twain, there is unimpeachable virtue in a rudimentary style in treatment of rudimentary—or, as I should prefer to phrase it, fundamental—things. Mark Twain has always written with utter individuality, untrammelled by the limitations of any particular sect of art. Style bears translation ill; in fact, translation is not infrequently impossible. But as Mr. Clemens once pointed out to me, *humor has nothing to do with style.* Mark Twain's humor has international range, since, constructed out of a deep comprehension of human nature and a profound sympathy for human relationships and human failings, it successfully surmounts the difficulties of translation into alien tongues.

Mark Twain is a great figure, not because he is an American, paradoxical and even unpatriotic as this may sound, but because he is America's greatest cosmopolitan. He is a true cosmopolitan in the Higginsonian sense in that, unlike Mr. Henry James, he is "at home even in his own country." Above all, he has sympathized with and admired the citizens of every nation, seeking beneath the surface veneer the universal traits of that nation's humanity. It is a matter, not of argument, but of fact, that he has made far more damaging admissions concerning America than concerning any other nation. He disclaims any "attitude" toward the world, for the very simple reason that his relation toward all peoples has been one of effort at comprehension and identification with them in feeling. Lafcadio Hearn best succeeded in interpreting poetry to his Japanese students by freeing it from all artificial and local restraints, and using as examples the simplest lyrics which go straight to the heart and soul of man. And his remarkable lecture on *Naked Poetry* is the most signal illustration of his profoundly suggestive mode of interpretation. In the same way Mark Twain as humorist has sought the highest common factor of all nations. "My secret, if there is any secret," Mr. Clemens said to me, "is to create humor independent of local conditions. Though studying humanity as exhibited in the people and localities I best knew and understood, I have sought to winnow out the encumbrance of the local. *Humor, like morality, has its eternal verities.* Most American humorists have not been widely famous because they have failed to create humor independent of local conditions not found or realized elsewhere."

It must be conceded that the history of literature furnishes forth no great international figures whose fame rests solely upon the basis of humor, however human, however sympathetic, however universal that humor may be. Behind that humor must lurk some deeper and more serious implication which gives breadth and solidity to the art-product. Genuine humor, as Landor has pointed out, requires a "sound and capacious mind, which is always a grave one." There is always a breadth of philosophy, a depth of sadness, or a profundity of pathos in the very greatest humorists. Both Rabelais and La Fontaine were reflective dreamers; Cervantes fought for the progressive and the real in pricking the bubble of Spanish chivalry; and Molière declared that, for a man in his position he could do no better than attack the vices of his time with ridiculous likenesses. Though exhibiting little of the melancholy of Lincoln, Mark Twain has much of the Yankee shrewdness and bed-rock common sense of Franklin; and commingled with all his boyish and exuberant fun is a note of pathos subdued but unmistakable. That "disposition for hard hitting with a moral purpose to sanction it," which George Meredith pronounces the national disposition of British humor, is Mark Twain's racial hereditament; and it is, perhaps, because he relates us to our origins, as Mr. Brander Matthews has suggested, that Mark Twain is the foremost of American humorists. It is impossible to think of him in his maturer development as other than a moralist. His impassioned and chivalric defence of Harriet Shelley, his eloquent tribute to the Maid of Orleans, his philippic against King Leopold and the atrocities in the Congo, are all, in essence, vindications of the moral principle. "Was it Heaven or Hell?" in its simple pathos, and "The Man that Corrupted Hadleyburg," in its shrieking irony, present that same transvaluation of current moral values which marks the age of Nietzsche, of Ibsen, of Tolstoi, of Zola, and of Shaw. In her unfinished biography of him, Mark Twain's little daughter Susy credited him with being "as much of a pholosopher [sic] as anything"; and insists that "he is more interested in earnest books and earnest subjects to talk upon than in humorous ones." Mr. Clemens' first essay on a philosophical subject—doubting the existence of free will and declaring that every man was under the immitigable compulsion of his temperament, his training, and his environment—was too heretical for the Hartford Club of orthodox religionists to which he belonged; and so was never read. But in the last thirty years he has amplified his original conception into a philosophical and ethical system; and to-day his injunction for right living is best concretized in these words: "Diligently train your ideals upward and still upward toward a summit where you will find your chiefest pleasure in conduct which, while contenting you, will be sure to confer benefits upon your neighbors and the community." As Lassalle once said, "History forgives mistakes and failures, but not want of conviction." In Mark Twain posterity will never be called upon to forgive any want of conviction.

Mark Twain is a great humorist—more genial than grim, more good-humored than ironic, more given to imaginative exaggeration than to intellectual sophistication, more inclined to pathos than to melancholy. He is a great story-teller; and he has enriched the literature of the world with a gallery of portraits so human in their veracious likeness as to rank them with the great figures of classic comedy. He is a remarkable observer and faithful reporter, never allowing himself, in Ibsen's phrase, to be "frightened by the venerableness of the institution;" and his sublimated journalism reveals a mastery of the naively comic thoroughly human and democratic. He is the most eminent product of our American democracy; and, in profoundly shocking Great Britain by preferring Connecticut to Camelot, he exhibited that robustness of outlook, that buoyancy of spirit, and that faith in the contemporary which stamps America in perennial and inexhaustible youth. Throughout his long life he has been a factor of high ethical influence in our civilization; and the philosopher and the humanitarian look out from the twinkling eyes of the humorist.

But, after all, Mark Twain's supremest title to distinction as a great writer inheres in his mastery in that highest sphere of thought, embracing religion, philosophy, morality, and even humor, which we call sociology. Mr. Bernard Shaw once remarked to me that he regarded Poe and Mark Twain as America's greatest achievements in literature; and that he thought of Mark Twain primarily, not as humorist, but as sociologist. "Of course," he added, "Mark Twain is in much the same position as myself: he has to put matters in such a way as to make people who would otherwise hang him believe he is joking!" And Mark Twain once said that whenever he had diverged from custom and principle to utter a truth, the rule has been that the hearer hadn't strength of mind enough to believe it. There is a "sort of contemporaneous posterity" which has registered its verdict that Mark Twain is the world's greatest living humorist; but there is yet to come that greater posterity of the future which will, I dare say, class Mark Twain as America's greatest sociologist in letters. He is the historian in art of a varied and unique phase of civilization on this continent that has passed forever. And it is inconceivable that any future investigator into the sociological phase of that civilization can fail to find priceless and unparalleled documents in the wild yet genial, rudimentary yet sane, boisterous yet universally human writings of Mark Twain.

It is a far cry from the steamboat on the Mississippi to the Italianate villa, from the overalls of the river pilot to the gray and scarlet of the Oxford gown. And in recalling the various vicissitudes of his varied life the mind irresistibly reverts to that day when Mark Twain, at the age of sixty, accompanied by his wife, set forth to retrieve his fallen fortunes. When the publishing-house in which he was interested, against his advice and through no fault of his own, continued a policy which led to ruin, Mr. and Mrs. Clemens discovered that even if they sacrificed all their effects they could pay the creditors only about forty cents on the dollar. But Mrs. Clemens' passion for morals manifested itself, and they agreed together that at any cost they must pay nothing less than dollar for dollar. With her courageous company, Mr. Clemens began his career a second time, setting off on a tramp abroad which has ended in "Stormfield" and autumn peace. With obligations satisfied, business integrity magnificently maintained, and fortune made, Mr. Clemens has earned that dignified and honorable leisure for congenial work and humanitarian service it was the tragic fate of Sir Walter Scott never to realize. Nothing can disturb the even tenor of his care-free existence—not even that direst of all terrors to the man of letters, the expiration of copyright. For he has incorporated the very name of *Mark Twain!*

1910

G. K. CHESTERTON

WE ARE ALWAYS TOLD that there is something specially sinister in the death of a great jester. I am not so sure about the point myself, seeing that so many thousand human beings, diplomatists, financiers, kings, bankers, and founders of philosophies, are engaged in functions far more ultimately fruitless and frivolous than really making the smallest schoolboy laugh. If the death of a clown makes pantomimes for a moment tragic, it is also true that the death of a statesman makes statesmanship for a moment highly comic; the irony cuts both ways. But in the case of the great man whom Englishmen and Americans must now join in lamenting (not because they are all Anglo-Saxons, but because they can all admire good literature written in English) — in the case of Mark Twain there is a particular cause which at once emphasises and complicates this contrast between the comic and the serious. The point I mean is this: that while Mark Twain's literary merits were very much of the uproarious and topsy-turvy kind, his personal merits were very much of the stoical or even puritanical kind. While irresponsibility was the energy in his writings, an almost excessive responsibility was the energy in his character. The artistic European might feel that he was, perhaps, too comic when he was comic; but such a European would also feel that he was too serious when he was serious.

"Mark Twain," from T. P.'s Weekly *(April 29, 1910), pp. 535-36.*

His wit.

The wit of Mark Twain was avowedly and utterly of the extravagant order. It had that quality of mad logic carried further and further into the void, a quality in which many strange civilisations are at one. It is a system of extremes, and all extremes meet in it; thus houses piled one on top of the other is the idea of a flat in New York and of a pagoda in Pekin. Mark Twain was a master of this mad lucidity. He was a wit rather than a humorist; but I do not mean by this (as so many modern people will certainly fancy) that he was something less than a humorist. Possibly, I think, he was something more than a humorist. Humour, a subtle relish for the small incongruities of society, is a thing that exists in many somewhat low society types, in many snobs and in some sneaks. Like the sense of music, it is exquisite and ethereal; but, like the sense of music, it can exist (somehow or other) in utter blackguards or even in utter blockheads; just as one often meets a fool who can really play the fiddle, so one often meets a fool who can really play the fool. But wit is a more manly exercise than fiddling or fooling; wit requires an intellectual athleticism, because it is akin to logic. A wit must have something of the same running, working, and staying power as a mathematician or a metaphysician. Moreover, wit is a fighting thing and a working thing. A man may enjoy humour all by himself; he may see a joke when no one else sees it; he may see the point and avoid it. But wit is a sword; it is meant to make people feel the point as well as see it. All honest people saw the point of Mark Twain's wit. Not a few dishonest people felt it.

Great art.

But though it was wit it was wild wit, as wild as the pagoda in China or the other pagodas in New York. It was progressive, and the joke went forward by arithmetical progression. In all those excruciating tales of his, which in our youth made us animally ill with laughing, the idea always consisted in carrying some small fact or notion to more and more frantic lengths of deduction. If a man's hat was as high as a house Mark Twain would think of some way of calling it twenty times higher than a house. If his hat was smashed as flat as a pancake Mark Twain would invent some startling and happy metaphor to prove that it was smashed twenty times flatter than a pancake. His splendid explosive little stories, such as that which describes how he edited an agricultural paper, or that which explains how he tried to decipher a letter from Horace Greeley, have one tremendous essential of great art. I mean that the excitement mounts up perpetually; they grow more and more comic, as a tragedy should grow more and more tragic. The rack, tragic or comic, goes round until something breaks inside a man. In tragedy it is his heart, or, perhaps, his stiff neck. In farce I do not quite know what it is — perhaps his funny-bone is dislocated; perhaps his skull is slightly cracked.

Niagara the vulgar.

Anyhow, the humour or wit of Mark Twain was of this ascending and exaggerative order. As such it was truly mountainous, and almost apocalyptic. No writer of modern English, perhaps, has had such a genius for making the cow jump over the moon; that is, for lifting the heaviest and most solemn absurdity high up into the most starry adventures. He was never at a loss for a simile or a parable, and they were never, strictly speaking, nonsense. They were rather a kind of incredible sense. They were not suddenly inconsequent, like Lewis Carroll; rather they were unbearably consequent, and seemed capable of producing new consequences for ever. Even that fantastic irreverence and fantastic ignorance which sometimes marked his dealings with elements he insufficiently understood were never abrupt departures, but only elaborate deductions from his idea. It was quite logical that when told that a saint's heart had burst his ribs he should ask what the saint had had for dinner. It was quite logical that his delightful musician, when asked to play music appropriate to the Prodigal Son, would play, "We all get blind drunk when Johnny comes marching home." These are things of real wit, like that of Voltaire; though they are not uttered with the old French restraint, but with a new American extravagance. Voltaire is to them as the Rhone is to Niagara; not inferior in quality, but merely in quantity, for Niagara is not only one of the violences, but almost one of the vulgarities of Nature. The laughter of Mark Twain was literally like Niagara.

Samuel Clemens.

Such was Mark Twain; such was not Samuel Clemens. His lonely figure stands up in strange solitude and severity against the confusion and extravagance of the background of his works. The virtues which we have all now to regret in their return to God were specially virtues rather of the restrained than of the riotous or sympathetic order. We know, indeed, that he rose from the ranks, in the sense that he was poor and pugnacious in a rich and pugnacious society; that he came of Southern folk, served with the heroic Southern armies, but that the greater part of his life was such a scramble of incalculable successes and unavoidable failures as Stevenson has well described in the once convincing picture of a Good American, Jim Pinkerton, in "The Wrecker." The words Stevenson used of Pinkerton might quite truly be used of Clemens: "He was stuffed full of manly virtues. Thrift and courage glowed in him." When his hair was white and his soul heavy with years an accident led him into liabilities which the law would have discharged by the ordinary arrangements of bankruptcy. The old man refused to accept the ordinary arrangements which the law allowed him. He set to work strenuously, writing and lecturing as if he were at the beginning of his life rather than at the end of it. He repaid his unrecognised and unlegal debt, and a little later he died. Thus the primary paradox is emphasised almost in the article of death; the man whom ten million people had adored as a tom-fool was too serious even for the expectation of his own creditors.

Republican virtue.

The credit of such glowing thrift and courage (to quote an admirable phrase again) must be ascribed to something or somebody; I will no longer disguise the dreadful fact that I ascribe it exactly where Mark Twain would have ascribed it. I ascribe it to the Republican virtue of America. Of course, if Mark Twain had said that in so many words, everybody in England would have thought he was making one of his best jokes; whereas, in truth, he would have been indulging in one of his worst pieces of seriousness. Somebody in an advanced Socialist paper that I saw the other day said that Mark Twain was a cynic. I suppose there never was a person so far removed from cynicism as Mark Twain. A cynic must at least mean a man who is flippant about serious things; about things that he thinks serious. Mark Twain was always serious to the verge of madness. He was not serious about St. Francis; he did not think St. Francis serious. He honestly supposed the marvels of St. Francis to be some ecclesiastical trick of Popes and Cardinals. He did not happen to know that the Franciscan movement was something much more certainly popular than the Revolution that rent America from England. He derided King Arthur's Court as something barbaric. He did not happen to know that the only reason why that dim and highly-dubious Court has made a half-entry into history is that it stood, if it ever stood at all, for the remnant of high civilisation against the base advance of barbarism. He did not happen to know that, in his time, St. Francis stood for the ballot-box. He did not happen to know that, in his time, King Arthur stood for the telephone. He could never quite get rid of the American idea that good sense and good government had begun quite a little while ago; and that the heavier a monumental stone was to lift the more lightly it might be thrown away. But all these limitations of his only re-emphasise the ultimate fact: he never laughed at a thing unless he thought it laughable. He was an American; that is, an unfathomable solemn man. Now all this is due to a definite thing, an historical thing, called Republican virtue. It *was* worth while to issue the Declaration of Independence if only that Mark Twain might declare his independence also.

Austere love.

In this the great humorist not only represents his country, but a big mistake about his country. The apparent clamour and complexity of America is very superficial; America is not really advanced or aggressively civilised. New York, Philadelphia, Chicago are jokes; just such tall jokes as Mark Twain would have made. American commerce is all one tall story; American commerce is a vast American lie. But the American lie is a very serious, separate, and authoritative institution, which could only exist among a singularly truthful people. Behind these extravagances, whether in words or wealth, whether in books or bricks, there remains a grave simplicity which is truly American. The genuine value of the Yankee is not his forwardness.

Rather it is his backwardness that is the real beauty of the Yankee. There is in the depths of him the rural stillness of an intellectual backwater: he is a great rustic. The log-hut, and not the sky-scraper, is the American home. Therefore, despite the revolting vices of wealth and all the vulgarities of unhistorical individualism, there does remain in the Americans a certain average of virile virtues, equality, hard work, patriotism, and a plain ideality. Corrupt fatigue is uncommon; unclean despair is almost unknown. You could not have made Mark Twain even understand either of these things. He was radiant with a rectitude none the less noble for being slightly naïve; he carried everywhere those powerful platitudes that are like clubs of stone. With these he hammered Calvinism in his youth and Christian Science in his old age. But he was not an "advanced" thinker, not a mind in revolt; rather he was a conservative and rustic grandfather older than all such follies. But this strength in him and his country truly came from a great spirit which England resisted and has forgotten; the spirit which, when all is said, made it no nonsense to compare Washington to Cincinnatus; the austere love of liberty and of the ploughshare and the sword.

1910

STUART P. SHERMAN

NO AMERICAN WRITER has ever enjoyed a more purely democratic reputation than Mark Twain. From village celebrity to international renown, he has been advanced stage after stage by popular suffrage. The plain, unbookish burgess holding both his sides at a public lecture has helped roar him into eminence. The freckled, brown-legged pirate who finds Tom Sawyer nearer to his business and his bosom than Robinson Crusoe has played no negligible part in the campaign. The vote of the retired merchant reading *A Tramp Abroad* in preparation for a European holiday told decisively in his favor before the tardy voice of the professional critic assented. When an overwhelming majority of his fellow countrymen had established his position, the universities recognized the fact, so that one day not long ago, he strolled into the Sheldonian Theatre, clad in scarlet, and, after a "very satisfactory hurrah" from the audience, was created doctor of letters by the University of Oxford.

During the last few years of his life, he attained a still higher honor. It is to be hoped that no one will attempt to distinguish the customary "three periods" of his development, because, contrary to custom he was essentially the same in all parts of his career. One may distinguish, however, three aspects of his reputation. Like a political orator making his maiden speech or invading hostile territory, he broke through the reserve of his audience with a string of irresistible stories. Handicapped by uproarious laughter, he produced two or

---

"Mark Twain," from the Nation, *XC (May 12, 1910), 477-80.*

three pieces of fiction which demanded serious attention; but his leonine head had grown gray before he lived down his record as a "platform humorist." At his seventieth birthday, he obtained a reconsideration of his case, and the highest tribunals decided that he indubitably belonged in the history of literature, if, indeed, he was not the "foremost American man of letters." After that, national feeling about him crystallized rapidly. He appeared in white flannels in midwinter, declaring that white was the only wear for a man with seventy clean years behind him; we were significantly pleased. After our newspapers had made one of their little breaks, he sent word to us that the reports of his death were "greatly exaggerated." It was a phrase that we all envied, from the President down; we saw that he was no mere literary man—he was a public man. When he died, we abandoned the last reservation. We said with one voice: He was an American.

To the foreign critic this ultimate tribute may seem perplexingly cheap and anticlimactic. That is, of course, due to the mistaken notion that we number some four score millions of Americans. As a matter of fact, we number our Americans on our ten fingers; the rest of us are merely citizens of the United States. Anyone who will take a little pains with the alphabet may become a citizen; to become an American demands other talents. We are more than doubtful about Washington. Lowell said that Lincoln was the first American, but he forgot Franklin. There have been one or two since Lincoln's time. From certain indications, it looks as if Mr. Roosevelt might turn out to be an American. Only the other day, he sent us a message to this effect: "I know that the American people will agree that I could have acted in no other way than I did act." The American is a man of destiny. His word and deed flow inevitably out of the American character. On the one hand, he does a thing because it is right; on the other hand, the thing is right because he does it. Revising the thought of Henry V, we may say, Nice customs curtsy to great Americans.

The point is strikingly illustrated by a story which Mark Twain tells on himself in one of the chapters of his autobiography. It was in 1877, before a company including all the leading geniuses of New England, banqueting in honor of Whittier's birthday. When Mark Twain's turn came, he rose and entered upon a fictitious "reminiscence." Out in southern California he had knocked at a miner's cabin, and announced himself as a literary man. The miner replied with marked ill-humor that he had just got rid of three of them, "Mr. Longfellow, Mr. Emerson, Mr. Oliver Wendell Holmes—consound the lot. . . . Mr. Emerson was a seedy little bit of a chap, red headed; Mr. Holmes as fat as a balloon; he weighed as much as three hundred, and had double chins all the way down to his stomach. Mr. Longfellow was built like a prizefighter. . . . They had been drinking, I could see that." And so on.

At the words "consound the lot," Twain had expected a peal of laughter, but to his amazement "the expression of interest in the faces turned to a sort of black frost." The whole story was a dismal failure; it was years before the author recovered from the shame of it. Speaking as a mere reader of Lamb, Jane Austen, Thackeray, O. W. Holmes, I am not in the least surprised at the New England frost. I know very well that Congreve or Addison or George Meredith would have agreed with the New England geniuses that Mark Twain's reminiscence was a piece of crude, heavy, intellectual horse-play—an impudent affront offered to Puritan aristocracy by a rough-handed plebeian jester from Missouri. But hear Mark Twain thirty years later:

> I have read it twice, and unless I am an idiot, it hasn't a single defect in it from the first word to the last. It is just as good as can be. It is smart; it is saturated with humor. There isn't a suggestion of coarseness or vulgarity in it anywhere. What could have been the matter with that house? . . . If I had those beloved and revered old literary immortals back here . . . I would melt them till they'd run all over that stage!

In his mellow Indian summer Mark Twain himself grew conscious that he had become an American. He knew, therefore, that the speech was right, *because he had made it*. I confess to a doubt whether those "old literary immortals" would laugh at it even now; if they would not, as a countryman of Lincoln I should be ashamed of them. The man who cannot laugh with Twain must be either better or worse than the "overwhelming majority" of his fellow-citizens. To accept him is almost equivalent to accepting the American flag. When once you have sworn allegiance, you may find fault with both for the rest of your life without impeachment of your patriotism. "I paint myriads of heads," cried Walt Whitman, "but I paint no head without its nimbus of gold-colored light." He was prophesying the golden mean, which he called the "divine average," and which he knew was actually rarer than either extreme. He was prophesying Mark Twain. "Who are you, indeed," he exclaims, "who would talk or sing in America?" The antiphonal voice replies:

I swear I will have each quality of my race in myself,
Talk as you like, he only suits These States whose manners favor the audacity and sublime turbulence of The States.

Humor, it is agreed, consists in contrasts and incongruities, and the essence of Mark Twain's most characteristic humor consists in contrasting this typical, nimbused American compacted of golden mediocrities, against the world—consists in showing the incongruity of the rest of the world with this nimbused American. It necessarily follows that the heights and depths of humor are beyond the reaches of Mark Twain's soul. It necessarily follows that his laughter is burly, not fine; broad, not profound; national, not universal. When he that sitteth in the heavens laughs, he is not contrasting the year 1910 with the year 1300, nor the President of the United States with Louis XVI, nor the uncrowned sovereigns of Missouri with the serfs of Russia, Germany, or England. The comparison is intolerable—let us mark a lowlier difference. When Puck in the *Midsummer Night's Dream,* looking out upon the bewildered lovers exclaims, "Lord, what fools these mortals be"; when Titania, waking from magical sleep, murmurs drowsily, "Methought I was enamoured of an ass"— the mirth of these subtle creatures is kindled by the contrast between sentimental and bottom humanity, respectively, and the exquisite manners and passions of elfland. If Twain had written the play, he would have put Puck into overalls and Titania into a hoop-skirt. For he ignored the ethereal hunger which troubled the creator of Falstaff, and never entered into the secret laughter of the idealist. Let us descend once more. It is said that the last book Mark Twain read was Carlyle's *French Revolution.* I suppose he loved it incidentally for its picturesque and savage energy, but mainly because it proclaims that a man's a man for all that. He shows traces both of its style and of its central thought in his own work. But so far as I know, he never shows a trace of its heart-searching irony, of that universal world-humor which arises when the upstart, red-blooded pageant of time's latest hour is confronted with the grim, dim phantasms of eternity—

Charlemagne sleeps at Salzburg, with truncheon grounded, only fable expecting that he will waken. Charles the Hammer, Pepin Bow-legged, where now is their eye of menace, their voice of command? Rollo and his shaggy northmen cover not the Seine with ships, but have sailed off on a longer voyage. The hair of Tow-head (Tête d'étoupes) now needs no combing; Iron-cutter (Taillefer) cannot cut a cobweb; shrill Fredegonda, shrill Brunhilda, have had out their hot life-scold, and lie silent, their hot life-frenzy cooled. . . . They are all gone; sunk—down, down with the tumult they made; and the rolling and trampling of ever new generations passes over them; and they hear it not any more forever.

Carlyle makes ducks and drakes of Charlemagne and shrill Fredegonda, but he laughs with a by-gone eternity. When Whitman asks that stupendous question, "Whom have you slaughtered lately, European headsman?" millions of strange shadows tend on him. He, too, is a humorist, and a grave one. He makes ducks and drakes of the "old literary immortals," for he laughs with an eternity to come. Mark Twain cannot be persuaded that we are such stuff as dreams are made of; looking neither before nor after, he laughs with the present hour; and he cannot stand the comparison.

Not by his subtlety, then, nor his depth, nor his elevation, but by his understanding and his unflinching assertion of the ordinary self of the ordinary American did Mark Twain become our "foremost man of letters."

He was geographically an American; he knew his land and its idioms at first hand—Missouri, the Mississippi River and its banks, Nevada, California, New England, New York, the great cities. It is insufficiently recognized that to love one's country intelligently one must know its body, as well as its mind. He had the good fortune to be born in the West; so that, of course, he had to go East—otherwise he might, instead of becoming an American, have remained a mere Bostonian or New Yorker all his life, and never have learned to love Chicago and San Francisco at all. At various times and places, he was pilot, printer, editor, reporter, miner, lecturer, author, and publisher. But during the first half of his life, he went most freely with "powerful uneducated persons, and with the young, and with the mothers of families." The books in which he embodies his early experiences—*Tom Sawyer, Roughing It, Huckleberry Finn*—are almost entirely delightful. They breathe the spirit of eternal boyhood, they are richly provincial, they spring out of the fresh earth. There is a touch of melodrama in the first and more than a touch of farce in the last, but in the main, they are as native as the bluff to the Mississippi or a pine tree to a red spur of the Rockies. It is when an American carries his virtues abroad that the lines of his character become salient. Mark Twain was a self-made man, of small Latin and less Greek, indifferent to abstractions, deficient in historical sympathy and imagination, insensitive to delicate social differences, content and at home in modern workaday realities. I confess with great apprehension that I do not much care for his books of foreign travel. Like the story told on Whittier's birthday, they are "smart and saturated with humor"; but for some almost indefinable reason my emotions fail to enter into the spirit of the occasion. An uneasy doubt about the point of view binds my mirth as with a "black frost." I find myself concerned for my fellow-citizen, the author behind the books; beneath the surface gayety the whole affair seems to be of appalling seriousness for us both. Ostensibly light-hearted burlesques of the poetical and sentimental volumes of travel, these books are in reality an amazingly faithful record of the way Europe and the Orient strike the "divine average"—the typical American—the man for whom the world was created in 1776. Wandering through exhumed Pompeii, he peoples its solemn ruins with the American proletariat, and fancies that he sees upon the walls of its theatre the placard, "Positively No Free List, Except Members of the Press." He digresses from an account of the ascent of Vesuvius to compare the prices of gloves, linen shirts, and dress suits in Paris and in Italy. At length arrived at the summit of the mountain, he describes its crater as a "circular ditch"; some of the party light their cigars in the fissures; he descends, observing that the volcano is a poor affair when compared with Kilauea, in the Sandwich Islands. He visits the Parthenon in the night; obviously, the memorable feature of the expedition was robbing the vineyards on the way back to the ship. The most famous picture galleries of Europe are hung with "celebrated rubbish"; the immemorial Mosque of St. Sophia is the "mustiest barn in heathendom"; the Sea of Galilee is nothing to Lake Tahoe.

The Mississippi pilot, homely, naive, arrogantly candid, refuses to sink his identity in the object contemplated—that, as Corporal Nym would have said, is the humor of it. He is the kind of travelling companion that makes you wonder why you went abroad. He turns the Old World into a laughing-stock by shearing it of its storied humanity— simply because there is nothing in him to respond to the glory that was Greece, to the grandeur that was Rome—simply because nothing is holier to him than a joke. He does not [merely] throw the comic light upon counterfeit enthusiasm; he laughs at art, history, and antiquity from the point of view of one who is ignorant of them and mightily well satisfied with his ignorance. And, unless I am very much mistaken, the "overwhelming majority" of his fellow-citizens —those who made the success of *Innocents Abroad* and *A Tramp Abroad*—have laughed with him, not at him. So, too, unquestionably, in the nearly parallel case of the bludgeoning burlesque, *A Connecticut Yankee at King Arthur's Court.*

What endears a public man to us is what he has in common with us—not his occasional supereminences. It does not damage Franklin to say that he was not so graceful as Lord Chesterfield; nor Lincoln to say that he was not so handsome as Count D'Orsay; nor Mr. Roosevelt to say that one misses in his literary style I know not what that one finds in the style of Walter Savage Landor. Writing from Khartum, the hunter tells us that, in consequence of hard service in camp, his pigskin books were "stained with blood, sweat, gun oil, dust, and ashes." We have a mystical feeling that this is very appropriate and beautiful—that a good American's books ought to be stained with gun oil and ashes. "Fear grace—fear delicatesse," cries the author of "Chants Democratic." It does not damage Mark Twain to say that there was not a drop of the aristocrat in his veins.

In politics he was an intelligent but unspeculative democrat, committed to the principles of the preamble to the Constitution, preserving a tang of Tom Paine's contempt for kings, and not without a suggestion of the republican insolence caricatured by Dickens in *Martin Chuzzlewit*. I do not think that he gave a "square deal" either to Europe or to the Arthurian realm; but within his own territory he had a very genuine sense of the brotherhood of man. He was not, like some more exquisite men of letters, a democrat in his study and a snob in his drawing-room; he was of the people and for the people at all times. His tender regard for the social contract permeated his humor. It will be remembered that Pudd'nhead Wilson earned his nickname and ruined his chances as a lawyer for twenty years by an incomprehensible remark about a howling dog. "I wish I owned half of that dog," said Wilson. "Why?" somebody asked. "Because I would kill my half." No one understood him—the sensitive, symbolic democracy of the expression was too compact for their intelligence, and they fell into a delicious discussion of how one-half could be killed without injury to the other half. That, to be sure, is also one of the problems of democracy; but Wilson's implications were, I believe, both simpler and deeper than that. In not molesting another man's dog he showed the American reverence for property. The American desire to be moderately well-to-do (Mr. Roosevelt's "neither rich nor poor") he indicated by desiring to own only half the dog. In saying that he would kill his half he expressed his sacred and inalienable right to dispose of his own property as he chose, while at the same time he recognized his neighbor's sacred and inalienable right to let his half of the property howl. Indeed, I am not sure that he did not recognize that the dog itself had a certain property right in the howling.

With almost every qualification for a successful political career, Mark Twain could never have aspired to the Presidency, for he was not a regular attendant at church—a shortcoming, by the way, which interfered seriously with Mr. Taft's campaign till his former pastor testified in the public prints that the candidate had once at a church social taken the part of a fairy. In religion, Twain appeared to be a mugwump, or, more classically speaking, an agnostic over whom had fallen the shadow of Robert Ingersoll of pious memory. The irreligion of that generation is touched with a raw, philistine rationalism, but is thoroughly honest. Like all Americans, the author of *Tom Sawyer* received his religious culture in the Sunday-school, but stumbled over the book of Genesis and kindred difficulties, and was "emancipated." The loss of faith which, in proper conditions, is a terrible bereavement, was to him a blessed relief; when the God of the Sunday-school and the camp meeting ceases to terrify, he ordinarily becomes a deadly bore. Having never known the magnificent poetry of faith, he never felt the magnificent melancholy of unbelief. His experience was typical, however, and his very unspirituality was social. In his examination of Christian Science, he admitted that every man is entitled to his own favorite brand of insanity, and insisted that he himself was as insane as anybody. That was enough to assure most of us that he was sound on "all essentials."

"Be good and you will be lonesome" is, I suppose, one of Mark Twain's most widely quoted utterances on moral topics. At first thought, one may wonder why this apparently Bohemian apothegm should have taken such hold upon the heart of a nation which above all things else adores virtue. But the difficulty disappears the instant one reflects that these seven words express as in a nutshell precisely the kind and temper of virtue that the nation adores. Like Wilson's observation on the dog, the saying is cryptic and requires explication. Twain tells us in his autobiography that when he was a boy his mother always allowed about thirty per cent on what he said for "embroidery" and so "struck his average." The saying means, as I take it, first of all, Don't lose your sense of humor as those do who become infatuated with their own particular hobbies in goodness. Calculate to keep about in the middle of the road, but make allowance for all reasonable shades of difference in taste and opinion. Don't be too good or you will find yourself in a barren and uninfluential minority of one. In America, whatever is not social is not virtue. When he put his shoulder under the debts of his bankrupt publishing house, the author of the apothegm himself explained its meaning. Natively fond of strong language, careless of peccadilloes, tolerant of all human frailties though he was—kin-making touches of nature—his feet were "mortised and tenoned" in domestic rectitude and common morality.

"We cannot live always on the cold heights of the sublime—the thin air stifles"—I have forgotten who said it. We cannot flush always with the high ardor of the signers of the Declaration, nor remain at the level of the address at Gettysburg, nor cry continually, "O Beautiful! My country!" Yet, in the long dull interspaces between these sacred moments we need someone to remind us that we are a nation. For in the dead vast and middle of the years insidious foes are stirring—anaemic refinements, cosmopolitan decadencies, the egotistic and usurping pride of great cities, the cold sickening of the heart at the reiterated exposures of giant fraud and corruption. When our countrymen migrate because we have no kings or castles, we are thankful to anyone who will tell us what we can count on. When they complain that our soil lacks the humanity essential to great literature, we are grateful even for the firing of a national joke heard round the world. And when Mark Twain, robust, big-hearted, gifted with the divine power to use words, makes us all laugh together, builds true romances with prairie fire and Western clay, and shows us that we are at one on all the main points, we feel that he has been appointed by Providence to see to it that the precious ordinary self of the Republic shall suffer no harm.

1910

HENRY VAN DYKE

We know you well, dear Yorick of the West,
The very soul of large and friendly jest,
That loved and mocked the broad grotesque of things
In this new world where all the folk are kings.

Your breezy humor cleared the air, with sport
Of shame that haunts the democratic court;
For even where the sovereign people rule,
A human monarch needs a royal fool.

Your native drawl lent flavor to your wit;
Your arrows lingered, but they always hit;
Homeric mirth around the circle ran,
But left no wound upon the heart of man.

We knew you kind in trouble, brave in pain,
We saw your honor kept without a stain.
We read this lesson of our Yorick's years:
True wisdom comes with laughter and with tears.

"Mark Twain," from The American Academy and the National Institute of Arts and Letters, Public Meeting, Held at Carnegie Hall, New York, November 30, 1910, in Memory of Samuel Langhorne Clemens *(New York, 1922), pp. 102-3.*

1913

JOHN MACY

GULLIVER'S TRAVELS is to be found in two editions, one for adult minds, the other for adventurous immaturity. The texts differ but little, if at all; differences are mainly differences in the reader. For one audience *Gulliver's Travels* is a story book like *Robinson Crusoe* and *Treasure Island*. For the other audience it is a tremendous satire on human nature, a vast portrait of man, the nakedly simple narrative uttering profundities before which the sentimental quail and hypocrites wear an unhappy smile. The boy who follows the strange fortunes of Doctor Gulliver does not know that Swift is talking over his head to the parents who gave the boy the wonder book. All satire is dual in its nature. It speaks in parable, saying one thing and meaning a deeper parallelism. It is a preacher in cap and bells.

To the holiday mood of the world and the wholesomely childish popular mind Mark Twain's books, like *Gulliver's Travels,* appeal instantly. For forty years he has been a favorite comedian, a beloved jester, picturesque, histrionic in all his public attitudes. His books have been sold by hundreds of thousands. Of *Joan of Arc,* one of his least popular books ("I wrote it for love," he says, "and never expected it to sell"), sixteen thousand copies were sold in the years from 1904 to 1908. Mark Twain was the most successful man of letters of his time; in the duration and variety of his powers, in the

"*Mark Twain*," *from* The Spirit of American Literature *(New York: Boni & Liveright, 1913), pp. 248-77.* ©*by author's estate, Arthur Macy.*

number and enthusiasm of his audience he has no rival in English literature after Dickens.

To say in the face of that towering popularity that he is greater than his reputation may seem praise beyond reason, and it may be presumptuous to suggest that the millions who admire him do not all know how great a man they admire or what in him is most admirable. Nevertheless it is true that this incorrigible and prolific joker has kept the world chuckling so continuously that it has not sobered down to comprehend what a powerful, original thinker he is. If you mention his name, someone says, "Oh, yes! do you remember what he said when it was reported that he was dead?" You smile appreciatively and insist, "Yes, but have you read *Joan of Arc?* Have you really read, since you grew up, the greatest piece of American fiction, *Huckleberry Finn?*" The response is apt to be more willing than intelligent. Some men of letters, like Mr. Bernard Shaw, and some critics, such as Professor W. L. Phelps and Professor Brander Matthews, have measured his significance. Mr. Howells, after warning us not to forget the joker in the gravity of our admiration, said it all in a few words, "Clemens, the sole and incomparable, the Lincoln of our literature." Other critics remain truer to the critic type by condescending to contemporary greatness and reserving highest praise for Mark Twain's equals who lived long ago, Swift, Molière, Cervantes, Fielding. As an example of the timid ineptitude of critics in the presence of living greatness, I quote from a handbook of American literature published five or six years ago. In it *A Connecticut Yankee in King Arthur's Court* is called a "cruel parody of Malory's *Morte d'Arthur*." It is not cruel and it is not a parody; in other respects the criticism is profoundly true. "It is unfortunate"— says the same handbook—"it is unfortunate for Mr. Clemens that he is a humorist; no one can ever take such a man seriously." It is unfortunate; just as it is a burning shame that Lamb was not an epic poet and that Swift was not a church historian.

To take humorists seriously is superficially incongruous. We should approach all satirists from Aristophanes to George Meredith in a spirit of gay delight. If we talk too solemnly about them, their spirits will wink us out of countenance. However, it is a well-established custom to discuss masters of humor, who have been dead a long time, as if they were really important in the history of human thought; and, without a too ponderous solemnity, one may seriously praise and expound the wisdom of the great laugh-maker who died two years ago.

Mark Twain began as a newspaper reporter, a "funny-column" man. He was a natural story-teller; his delightful, flexible voice was a melancholy vehicle for outrageous absurdities, and the mask of a grieved and puzzled countenance was a gift of the gods to a platform humorist. His natural talents of mind and manner made him success-ful on the Pacific Coast before he thought of himself as a professional man of letters. As he grew older, he cultivated the gifts which he had discovered by accident, came in time to a perfect and conscious com-mand of his art, and by much reading and writing and experience made himself a very great master of prose.

His first book of sketches, printed in 1867, is of no better quality than the work of hundreds of newspaper men who put a little fun into their day's scribbling and so get a little fun out of it. The sketches had given Clemens a local reputation before they were printed as a book, and prompted the proprietors of the *Alta California* to send him on the famous voyage of the steamer *Quaker City.* The report of that voyage is *Innocents Abroad,* a first-rate book of travel, which revealed at once an accomplished writer of sincere, vigorous English. As if the spirit of incongruities had conspired to make fun doubly funny, *Innocents Abroad* has been regarded, by those who read with any part of their organism except their intellect, as an expression of American irreverence grinning at the august beauties of Europe. So far as it is disrespectful, its satire is aimed at the dishonest American tourist, at the gaping pretender who feigns to see beauty where it is not, or where he does not see it, and misses beauty where it is. Upon the "pilgrims" with their fraudulent enthusiasms, their vandal thefts of "souvenirs" from places that they call sacred, the clerk of the party pours his scornful ridicule. To swindlers who exploit art and antiquity for the sake of the tourist's dollar he gives no quarter. Romances that thoughtless people accept as lovely but which are essentially base, like the story of Abelard, he tears to shreds. The unshakable realist here begins to deal those blows to sentimentality and pretension which ring through all his work to the last.

.   .   .   .

In *Innocents Abroad* the self-deceptions and pious buncome of the pilgrims, the mendacious guides, the "tall" traditional stories told for money to tourists by vergers and ciceroni (stories beside which "American exaggeration" is shrinking understatement)—all these impositions move the recording Innocent to cut capers, to play the vacant idiot, and then to pour out one of his level streams of deadly accurate and demolishing irony. It is a pleasure to read him in his abusive moods, and it was a greater pleasure to hear him in one of his coolly passionate tirades, speaking sentences amazingly finished and constructed as if a prose style were as natural to him as breathing, in a voice even, deliberate, modulated and sweet with rage.

Besides much excellent fooling and vigorous destruction of what is revered but not reverend, there is in *Innocents Abroad* a good deal of fine, clear description of things seen. Indeed the book is on the whole a serious report of sights and events. The characterization of the pilgrims reveals the gift that was later to draw shrewd portraits of human beings, real and fictitious. Mark Twain shows in this book, as in much of his writing, the deep enthusiasm for natural beauty which is impossible to people who can harbour dishonest admirations. The description of Vesuvius is powerful, graphic, as fresh as if no other man had seen and described it.

.   .   .   .

The first strong voice of realism in the western part of America is Mark Twain, and *Roughing It* is its first expression—a statement that some Americans would probably meet by pointing out that Mark Twain changes the names of Nevada people and invents things that really did not happen! Imagination is wasted on a people who hug Mark Twain's jokes as a child hugs a jumping-jack and do not know that *Roughing It* is an important social study, reconstructing in its own unmethodical fashion a phase of American history, a section of the national life. Under the touch of a great instinctive humorist, whose vision is sharp and undeluded, whose lively caricature plays over a cold sense of fact, the silver boom-town, its comedy and tragedy, takes permanent and accurate shape for the benefit of an inquisitive posterity that will wish to study our social history.

In *The Gilded Age* Mark Twain and Charles Dudley Warner worked together two claims, only one of which shows real metal. The story is of two sets of characters brought together in a forced and unconvincing unity. The young people from the east with their commonplace love affairs figure in one plot, which crosses the fortunes and misfortunes of Colonel Sellers and his family. Everything in the book except Colonel Sellers may be sacrificed without great loss to literature. Sellers is a colossal comic creation, the embodied spirit of western mushroom hopes and bubble enterprise. The type is so true to human nature, and especially to American human nature in a land of rapid haphazard exploitation, sudden wealth and disastrous "progress," that the authors were besieged with claimants for the honour of having sat as model. There was a real person, a kinsman of Clemens, who suggested the character, but there was no model except perennial humanity. The book as a whole is amateurish and lacking in cohesion. One suspects that Colonel Sellers kept the two humorists gayly interested in the work, and that they made up the rest of the book in a perfunctory way at a low pitch of creative enthusiasm. Some years later in *The American Claimant* Mark Twain brought Colonel Sellers on the stage again. In this book, as in *The Gilded Age,* the story is nothing (unless it is a "cruel parody" of *Little Lord Fauntleroy).* But Sellers is himself, generous and pathetically lovable, for all his sham wisdom and magniloquent inflation. He is, like Don Quixote and some of Dickens's characters, drawn taller than life-size, but he is true to the outlines of humanity, a pantographic enlargement of man.

The delight with which the public received Colonel Sellers encouraged Clemens to try another work of fiction. He wrote one of the best of boys' books, *Tom Sawyer.* The adventure in the cave and the finding of gold are the good old-fashioned stuff of dime novels. Mark Twain, like that other wise man with the heart of a boy, Stevenson, has taken the traditional boy romance and made it literature. Except for its one affluent adventure in treasure-trove, the book is all actual boy life, a masterly biography of the universal youngster. The adult novel in America is not yet adult, but four men of letters, Aldrich, Warner, Mr. Howells and Mark Twain, have limned us immortally as we all were in the golden age. It may be that *Tom Sawyer* and *Huckleberry Finn,* Aldrich's *Story of a Bad Boy,* Howells's *Flight of Pony Baker,* and Warner's *Being a Boy* are the reaction of humor and naturalism against the era of St. Rollo. Like all true books about boys, *Tom Sawyer* gives glimpses of the social conditions and habits of the older generation. There are wider glimpses in *Huckleberry Finn.* Indeed this is more than a boy's book or a book about boys. It is a study of many kinds of society seen through eyes at once innocent and prematurely sage. Those who are fond of classifying books may see in *Huckleberry Finn* a new specimen of the picaresque novel of adventure; some classifiers, going back further for analogies, have called it the "Odyssey of the Mississippi," which is strikingly inept. It is a piece of modern realism, original, deep and broad, and it is in American literature deplorably solitary. It is one of the unaccountable triumphs of creative power that seem to happen now and again, as *Robinson Crusoe* happened, and the surrounding intellectual territory has not its comrade.

Huck's dialect is a marvel of artistry. As Clemens says in a significant preface, the shadings in the dialects reported by Huck "have not been done in a haphazard fashion, or by guesswork; but painstakingly, and with the trustworthy guidance and support of personal familiarity with these several forms of speech." To maintain Huck's idiom and through it to describe a storm on the Mississippi with intense vividness; through the same dialect to narrate the tragic feud between the Grangerfords and the Shepherdsons; to hint profound social facts through the mouth of a boy and not violate his point of view—this is the work of a very great imagination. Huck's reflection on Tom Sawyer's proposal to "steal a nigger out of slavery" is a more dramatic revelation of the slaveholder's state of mind than *Uncle Tom's Cabin,* and expresses more powerfully than a thousand treatises the fact that "morality" is based on economic and social conditions.

Well, one thing was dead sure, and that was that Tom Sawyer was in earnest, and was actually going to help steal that nigger out of slavery. That was the thing that was too many for me. Here was a boy that was respectable and well brung up; and had a character to lose; and folks at home that had characters; and he was bright and not leather-headed; and knowing and not ignorant; and not mean, but kind; and yet here he was,

without any more pride, or rightness, or feeling, than to stoop to this
business, and make himself a shame, before everybody.

. . . .

The Prince and the Pauper, which like *Huckleberry Finn,* is read
with delight by children, is a parable in democracy. Lazarus and
Dives, in the figures of two pretty boys, change places, and for once
the mighty learn by experience how the other half lives. The same
idea is dramatized in *A Connecticut Yankee in King Arthur's Court,*
where the king, incognito, goes out among the people. Mark Twain
hated the lords of the earth. In *The Czar's Soliloquy* his hatred is
at a white heat. In the course of one of those enchanting monologues
with which he entertained his guests he said that every Russian child
should drink in with his mother's milk the resolution to kill a czar,
"until every Romanoff would rather sit on a stool in his back yard than
on a throne of crime." He laughed also at the hypocrisy of false
republicanism and proved that every democrat loves a lord and why.
Humanity, ridiculous, pathetic and pretentious, is all divided into
castes, each caste merciless and snobbish. Its portrait is drawn in this
passage from *A Connecticut Yankee:* "Toward the shaven monk who
trudged along with his cowl tilted back and the sweat washing his
fat jowls, the coal-burner was deeply reverent; to the gentleman he
was abject; with the small farmer and the free mechanic he was
cordial and gossipy; and when a slave passed by with a countenance
respectfully lowered, this chap's nose was in the air—he couldn't even
see him. Well, there are times when one would like to hang the
whole human race and finish the farce." That is written not about a
mythical England of the dark ages, but about *us.* The book is a satire
on society. Two conditions of uncivilization are thrown into grotesque
contrast primarily for the fun of it all, and also for the sake of
flaying priesthood and kingship. The book is not a "parody" of
Morte d'Arthur, and it is not cruel. Mark Twain would not have
been so witless as to parody a harmless old book; he is not interested
in Malory, but in man, and especially in the conflict between man's
intelligence and his superstitions.

It is, however, worth noting that like all wise men who chance to
give their opinions about books Mark Twain is a good critic. He
touches unerringly on Malory's weaknesses, his lack of humour and

his inability to characterize. In Malory Sir Dinadan is represented as having delivered a convulsing ballad, but Malory cannot give the ballad, or furnish his humourist with anything to say. Mark Twain seizes this chance to make Sir Dinadan the court bore. Sandy tells the Yankee a story which is taken from Malory, and the Yankee makes a comment which is a just and compact criticism of that inchoate bundle of legends. "When you come to figure up results, you can't tell one fight from another, nor who whipped; and as a picture of living, raging, roaring battle, sho! why, it's pale and noiseless—just ghosts scuffling in a fog. Dear me, what would this barren vocabulary get out of the mightiest spectacle?—the burning of Rome in Nero's time, for instance? Why, it would merely say 'Town burned down; no insurance; boy brast a window; fireman brake his neck!' Why, that ain't a picture!"

Clemens was a shrewd critic of books because he was a shrewd critic of men. He was not hypnotized by what other people thought of the good and the great; he thought for himself. The essays on Cooper and Shelley and Mr. Howells are better than most of the work of professional critics. Some of his casual remarks about books and authors are memorable. He disliked *The Vicar of Wakefield,* because the misadventure of Moses at the fair is represented as funny, whereas it is a pathetic and touching thing when a boy is deceived. Clemens had no admiration for Jane Austen and used to argue with Mr. Howells, who adores her. Most people will agree with Mr. Howells, but nobody can forget, once he has heard it, Mark Twain's way of putting his disapproval: "A very good library can be started by leaving Jane Austen out."

.   .   .   .

A Connecticut Yankee is a humourist's jest, not at any true ancient manner of thought or at any class of fairy tale, but at the falsification of history and at idiotic moonshine held up to admiration as serious story and clothed in the grave beauty of poetry. Not that Mark Twain was a conscious critic of nineteenth-century imitation romance, but like all realists he was filled with the spirit of his time, and quite without intention of making romantic poets and other sentimentalists uncomfortable, he sends the world of terrific and really interesting facts crashing into the stage world of false moonlight and tin armour. The knights of legend, as their modern poetic champions portray them, are garrulous boobies and bullies. Their chivalric attitude toward women is a fraud that disgusts a truly chivalrous man. The sentimentalist who admires Arthur as "perfectly lovely" and who thinks it philistine to laugh at him, will never understand, of course, that Tennyson's Idyls are commonplace and the laureate himself a tedious philistine; nor will they ever understand the great realists, Molière, Fielding, Cervantes, Mark Twain. True chivalry is possible only in those who detest false chivalry. Mark Twain was a supremely chivalrous man, a man of exquisite courtesy and of beautiful loyalty to all ancient and contemporary idealisms. I have read somewhere the opinion that he was vulgar, but the unique cannot be vulgar; moreover, as Pudd'nhead Wilson says, "There are no people who are quite so vulgar as the over-refined." Clemens has also been called irreverent. He *was* disrespectful of all superstitions, including his own. Says Pudd'nhead Wilson, "Let me make the superstitions of a nation, and I care not who makes its laws or its songs either."

Mark Twain was a globe-trotter; he knew all grades and conditions of man, and he was a reader of history and biography; he was early cured of the grossest of superstitions, abject patriotism, with which all peoples are drenched and with which Americans, especially, seem to be afflicted.

"You see my kind of loyalty," says the Yankee, "was loyalty to one's country, not to its institutions or its office-holders."

The country is the real thing, the substantial thing, the eternal thing; it is the thing to watch over, and care for, and be loyal to; institutions are extraneous, they are its mere clothing, and clothing can wear out, become ragged, cease to be comfortable, cease to protect the body from winter, disease, and death. To be loyal to rags, to shout for rags, to worship rags, to die for rags—that is a loyalty of unreason, it is pure animal; it belongs to monarchy, was invented by monarchy; let monarchy keep it. I was from Connecticut, whose Constitution declares "that all political power is inherent in the people, and all free governments are founded on their authority and instituted for their benefit; and that they have *at all times* an undeniable and indefeasible right to *alter their form of government* in such a manner as they may think expedient."

Under that gospel, the citizen who thinks he sees that the commonwealth's political clothes are worn out, and yet holds his peace and does not agitate for a new suit, is disloyal; he is a traitor. That he may be the only one who thinks he sees this decay, does not excuse him; it is his duty to agitate anyway, and it is the duty of the others to vote him down if they do not see the matter as he does.

That is the Mark Twain who "jokingly" said that the only distinct native criminal class in America is congressmen, the Mark Twain who despairingly predicted that America, having proved that it was not capable of being truly democratic, would probably set up a monarchy in the course of another century, and who uttered as blasting an arraignment of American plutocracy as ever fell from a man's lips. Americans, complaisant and sentimental, do not yet know the power of Mark Twain's Swiftian attacks on our flimsy-minded patriotism and religiosity. After his death he was slandered by nice critics who purvey optimism and water to the multitude; they spoke of his "kindly wit and humour which never hurt anyone." From such libel may he be defended! Some missionaries, politicians, soldiers, and priests of several churches from Rome to Huntington Avenue, Boston, will, if they have read his works, tell a different story.

Only a man whose heart is purged of counterfeit idealism can be the lofty idealist that Mark Twain was. He worshipped truth and worthy individuals dead and living. His *Personal Recollections of Joan of Arc* is a tribute to a heroine whose nobility is authentic, whose good head and good heart are proved by documents. It is an eloquent book, instinct with such reverence and passion for beauty as are possible in a soul that is not moved by hazy pieties or tricked by too easy credulity. The tone of the book is sustainedly perfect, the style excellently managed by the same imagination that holds unbrokenly true the character and diction of Huckleberry Finn. After he acknowledged the book everybody saw that he must have written it, and pointed to the obvious Mark-Twainisms, but when the story was first published anonymously, many wise critics failed to guess the authorship. In one character Mark Twain is enjoying himself in his everyday manner—in the Paladin, the comic foil, the picturesque liar whom Mark Twain likes to introduce into all human company. The episode in the Fifteenth Chapter of the Second Book, laughter in the lap of tragedy, is one of those wrenching contrasts of human feelings such as only the Shakespeares can draw unfalteringly.

In the work of no modern prose writer is there wider range than in the work of Mark Twain—from *Huckleberry Finn* to *Joan of Arc*. He had wonderful breadth of knowledge and interest; whatever he encountered he pondered. And he seems to have turned almost every experience into a written page. When, at the end of his life, he came to write what was to be "the best and truest autobiography ever written," he confessed in whimsical desperation that he could not tell the truth and never had told the truth, that as Pudd'nhead Wilson says, the very ink with which history is written is prejudice. He must also have found that he had already written in his other books as much of his autobiography as it was possible for him to write. His books are a record of his career from his memories of boyhood to his last travels round the world.

1919

WALDO FRANK

BUT THE LAND of the pioneer has had a more heroic victim [than Jack London]. Jack London was a man of talent: Mark Twain was a man of genius. The mind of Jack London was brilliant: the soul of Mark Twain was great.

Out of the bitter wreckage of his long life, one great work emerges by whose contrasting fire we can observe the darkness. This work is *Huckleberry Finn*. It must go down in history, not as the expression of a rich national culture like the books of Chaucer, Rabelais, Cervantes, but as the voice of American chaos, the voice of a pre-cultural epoch. Mark Twain kept this book long at his side. Ostensibly, it was the sequel to *The Adventures of Tom Sawyer* which appeared in 1875. *Huck* came nine years later. In it for once, the soul of Mark Twain burst its bonds of false instruction and false ideal, and found voice. Mark Twain lived twenty-six years longer. That voice never spoke again.

Huckleberry Finn is the simple story of a young white lad, born on the banks of the Mississippi, who, with an escaped slave named Jim, builds a raft and floats down the mighty current. Mark Twain originally had meant it to be nothing else: had meant it for the mere sequel of another tale. But his theme was too apt a symbol. Into it he poured his soul.

"The Land of the Pioneer," from Our America *(New York: Boni & Liveright, 1919), pp. 37-44. Copyright Waldo Frank, 1947, and reprinted by permission of Liveright Publishing Corp.*

Huck is a candid ignorant courageous child. He is full of the cunning and virtue of the resilient savage. He wears the habiliments of the civilization from which he comes, loosely, like trinkets about the neck. He and his companion build a raft and float. At night they veer their craft into the shallows or sleep on land. They have many adventures. The adventures that Huck has are the material of pioneering life. He always *happens* upon them. At times, he is a mere spectator: at times enforced accessory. Always, he is passive before a vaster fact. Huck is America. And Huck *floats* down the current of a mighty Stream.

Huckleberry Finn is the American epic hero. Greece had Ulysses. America must be content with an illiterate lad. He expresses our germinal past. He expresses the movement of the American soul through all the sultry climaxes of the Nineteenth Century.

The Mississippi with its countless squalid towns and its palatial steamboats was a ferment of commingled and insoluble life. All the elements of the American East and all the elements of Europe seethed here, in the hunt for wealth. A delirium of dreams and schemes and passions, out of which shaped our genius for invention and exploitation. The whole gamut of American beginnings ran with the river. And Huck along. One rises from the book, lost in the beat of a great rhythmic flow: the unceasing elemental march of a vast life, cutting a continent, feeding its soil. And upon the heaving surface of this Flood, a human child: ignorant, joyous and courageous. The American soul like a midge upon the tide of a world.

Mark Twain was fifty when this work appeared. The balance of his literary life, before and after, went mostly to the wastage of half-baked, half-believed, half-clownish labor. And underneath the gibes and antics of the professional jester, brooded the hatred and resentment of a tortured child. Mark Twain, in his conscious mind, shared his people's attitude of contempt for "art and spiritual matters"—shared their standards of success. Mark Twain strove to make money and to please! This great soul came to New York and felt ashamed before the little dancing-masters of the magazines; felt humble before Richard Watson Gilder and William Dean Howells! Shared their conviction that he was only a crude, funny writer from Missouri; changed the texts of his books to suit their fancy. Mark Twain did not believe in his soul, and his soul suffered. Mark Twain believed, with his fellows, that the great sin was to be unpopular and poor, and his soul died. His one great work was the result of a burst of spirit over the dikes of social inhibition and intellectual fear. *Leaves of Grass* came in consequence of a similar bursting of the floodgates. American expression has ever had to break through the bars of pioneer conviction. But in the case of Whitman, the spirit remained free.

I recall vividly the one time I ever saw Mark Twain. There was a Benefit Performance for some Association for the Blind, in the ballroom of a New York hotel. My father took me. The platform was filled with blind men and women; silent faces that had somehow won serenity from their deprivation above the turmoil of those who saw. Joseph H. Choate was the chairman. My father told me that he was our Ambassador to England, and that he was the leader of the American Bar. I remember my vague and unresolved discomfort, looking at Mr. Choate. He had a bland and empty face. The face of a gigantic child. His well-groomed body curved with gracious gestures. It also was childlike, sweet, untrammeled. No passion seemed to have ruffled this great man: no harsh experience stamped him. He seemed to me the symbol of respectable vapidity. I did not realize that he was rather more the symbol of a world which barred experience— the true Ambassador of the pioneer.

Mr. Choate arose and spoke solemn, touching words. Speaking, his face wrinkled with complacence. A blind man was led to the piano: he played. A blind woman sang. And then, a tall spare person, natively graceful, naïvely timid, swung forward from his place among the blind. A vast shock of white hair fell from the clear forehead. Mark Twain! He opened his mouth. He hesitated. The long, nasal twang of the lower Middle-West came with his words. Mark Twain— the humorist—America's funny man! His words were diffident and sad. But everybody laughed. Mark Twain drew back. Turning half about, he seemed to take some heartening he needed from the unseeing eyes, from the wan smiles behind him. He began again. Mark Twain's Western twang. The ballroom laughed once more. For five minutes, the sad soul struggled with this reality about him—this reality that would laugh. His face was strained: his body seemed loose and nervous: his transparent voice withdrew gradually from the obtuse glee of his hearers. And then, Mark Twain gave up. He relaxed. He launched into an anecdote. The audience settled back, wreathed in smiles that somehow suggested to me the folds of an obese body. And Mark Twain rambled on. His jokes came slow and listless. He stood there almost still, with his back to the rows of them who could not see, and dropped the ungainly humor from his mouth. And the audience before him snouted it, guzzled it, roared with delight. At last, Mark Twain stopped. He fell back from the high applause to his seat and was out of sight among the sightless.

I remember how at that time I hated this noble-looking fool. It seemed to me that all the shallowpates I knew called Mark Twain their favorite author, bored me with quotations from his books. I hated Mark Twain because of them who seemed to love him. Now, I love him, because I faintly understand what a cross such love must have bound upon his back.

Mark Twain went through life, lost in a bitter blindness that is far more terrible than the hate of men like Schopenhauer or Jonathan Swift. The mighty pessimists were fertile: they plowed great fields with their wrath and sowed them with their love. Mark Twain's was the misery of a love too feeble to create. In his later days, he wrote a book entitled *What Is Man?* It is the confession of his despondency, and its elucidation. It is the profane utterance of a defeated soul bent upon degrading the world to the low level where it was forced to live, whence came its ruin. An Old Man, in wooden dialogue, proves to a Young Man the folly of all human aspiration: proves to him that man is a machine:

YOUNG MAN: Do you believe in the doctrine that man is equipped with an intuitive perception of good and evil?
OLD MAN: Adam hadn't it.
YOUNG MAN: But has man acquired it since?
OLD MAN: No: I think he has no intuition of any kind. He gets all his ideas, all his impressions from the outside.

The *reductio ad absurdum* of extraversion. And in the mouth of a man who by every inner circumstance and gift was an intuitive giant, belonged to the number of great artists! But Mark Twain knew that this was not the sort of book that his American readers wanted. So out of deference to their taste, or lack of confidence in his own, he hid it among his papers, where it was discovered at his death. Until the end, he held forward to the public gaze the painted and powdered visage of a clown.

The clown tragedy of Mark Twain is prelude to the American drama. The generic Clemens was a tender and dreaming and avid spirit, in love with beauty, in love with love. But he was born in the ranks of a hurling and sweating army. He forced himself to move with it at its own pace. He forced himself to take on its measures of success: to take on that distrust of life and love which so well defended the principal business of its march. For this betrayal of his soul, his soul brought him bitterness, and the mass of his works are failures.

Mark Twain was a giant. Or a giant he would have grown to be, had he been nurtured at his nation's breast. But the centrifugal force was overwhelming. Mark Twain was slung away in outer darkness: where he did not belong, and where only lesser men adapt themselves to live. If we look for Miracle upon these Western plains, we must seek elsewhere.

1920

VAN WYCK BROOKS

WE CANNOT PROPERLY GRASP the significance of Mark Twain's marriage unless we realize that he had been manoeuvered into the rôle of a candidate for gentility. But here, in order to go forward, we shall have to go back. What had been Mark Twain's original, unconscious motive in surrendering his creative life? To fulfill the oath he had taken so solemnly at his dead father's side; he had sworn to "make good" in order to please his mother. In short, when the artist in him had abdicated, the family man, in whom personal and domestic interests and relations and loyalties take precedence of all others, had come to the front. His home had ever been the hub of Mark Twain's universe; "deep down," says Mr. Paine, of the days of his first triumphs in Nevada, "he was lonely and homesick; he was always so away from his own kindred." And at thirty-two, able to go back to his mother "without shame," having at last retrieved his failure as a miner, he had renewed the peculiar filial bond which had remained precisely that of his infancy. Jane Clemens was sixty-four at this time, we are told, "but as keen and vigorous as ever—proud (even if somewhat critical) of this handsome, brilliant man of new name and fame who had been her mischievous, wayward boy. She petted him, joked with him, scolded him, and inquired searchingly into his morals and habits. In turn, he petted, comforted and teased her. She decided that he was the same Sam, and always would be—a true prophecy."

"The Candidate for Gentility," from The Ordeal of Mark Twain, ©*1920 by E. P. Dutton & Co., Inc. Renewal 1948 by Van Wyck Brooks. Reprinted by permission of the publishers.*

It was indeed so true that Mark Twain, who required authority as much as he required affection, could not fail now to seek in the other sex someone who would take his mother's place. All his life, as we know, he had to be mothered by somebody, and he transferred this filial relation to at least one other person before it found its bourn first in his wife and afterwards in his daughters. This was "Mother" Fairbanks of the *Quaker City* party, who had, we are told, so large an influence on the tone and character of those travel letters which established his fame. "She sewed my buttons on," he wrote—he was thirty-two at the time—"kept my clothing in presentable form, fed me on Egyptian jam (when I behaved), lectured me awfully . . . and cured me of several bad habits." It was only natural, therefore, that he should have accepted the rule of his wife "implicitly," that he should have "gloried," as Mr. Howells says, in his subjection to her. "After my marriage," he told Professor Henderson, "she edited everything I wrote. And what is more—she not only edited my works—she edited me!"

What, indeed, were Mark Twain's works in the totality of that relationship? What, for that matter, was Olivia Clemens? . . . For Mark Twain had not married an awakened soul; he had married a young girl without experience, without imagination, who had never questioned anything, understood anything, desired anything, who had never been conscious of any will apart from that of her parents, her relatives, her friends. To win her approval and her pride, therefore—and love compelled him to do that—he had to win the approval and the pride of Elmira itself, he had to win the *imprimatur* of all that vast and intricate system of privilege and convention of which Elmira was the symbol. They had all said of Olivia Langdon, who was the "family idol," that "no one was good enough for her—certainly not this adventurous soldier of letters from the West." Charles Langdon, her brother and Mark Twain's old comrade, was so mortified at having brought this ignominy upon his own household, that he set off on a voyage round the world in order to escape the wedding. Furthermore, Mark Twain's friends in California replied unanimously to Mr. Langdon's enquiries about his character, that, while he was certainly a good fellow, he would make the "worst husband on record." Would not all these things have put any lover on his mettle?

Mark Twain was on probation, and his provisional acceptability in this new situation was due not to his genius but to the fact that he was able to make money by it. What made the Langdons relent and consider his candidacy was quite plainly, as we can see from Mr. Paine's record, the vast success Mark Twain was having as a humourous journalist and lecturer. With the publication of *The Innocents Abroad,* as we know, "he had become suddenly a person of substance —an associate of men of consequence:" even in New York people pointed him out in the street. He was a lion, a conquering hero, and Elmira could not help yielding to that: "it would be difficult," as Mr. Paine says, "for any family to refuse relationship with one whose star was so clearly ascending." . . .

Jervis Langdon gave the young couple a house in a fashionable street in Buffalo, a house newly and fully fitted up, with a carriage and a coachman and all the other appointments of a prosperous *ménage.* It was a surprise, one of the unforeseen delights of Mark Twain's wedding day!—he woke up, so to speak, and found himself, with the confused and intoxicating sensations of a bridegroom, absolutely committed to a scale of living such as no mere literary man at the outset of his career could ever have lived up to. He had been fairly shanghaied into the business man's paradise! But Jervis Langdon had foreseen everything. Mark Twain's ambition at this time, we are told, "lay in the direction of retirement in some prosperous newspaper enterprise, with the comforts and companionship of a home." That was the ambition, already evoked, which his new situation confirmed, the ambition which had now fully become his because the Langdons encouraged it. And as he had no money actually on hand, his father-in-law bound himself to the extent of $25,000 and advanced half of it in cash so that Mark Twain could acquire a third interest in the Buffalo *Express.* Thus, almost without realizing it, he had actually become a business man, with love and honor obliging him to remain one.

The full consequences of this moral surrender—shall we call it? —can only appear as we go on with our story. Meanwhile, we may note that, precisely because of his divided soul, Mark Twain could not consistently and deliberately pursue the main chance. Had he been able to do so he might, in a few years, have bought his liberty; but he lost interest in his journalistic enterprise just as he was to lose interest in so many other lucrative enterprises in the future. And every time he was driven back to make a fresh attempt. "I have a perfect *horror* and heart-sickness over it," Mrs. Clemens wrote to her sister after the bankruptcy of the publishing house of Charles L. Webster and Co. "I cannot get away from the feeling that business failure means disgrace. I suppose it always will mean that to me. Sue, if you were to see me you would see that I have grown old very fast during this last year: I have wrinkled. Most of the time I want to lie down and cry. Everything seems to me so impossible."

Naturally, inevitably; but imagine an author, who was also a devoted lover, having to respond to a stimulus like that! His bankruptcy was, to Mark Twain, like a sudden dawn of joyous freedom. "Farewell—a long farewell—to business!" he exclaimed during those weeks of what might have seemed an impending doom. "I will *never* touch it again! I will live in literature, I will wallow in it, revel in it; I will swim in ink!" But when his release finally comes he writes as follows to his wife, whom he has left in France:

Now and then a good and dear Joe Twichell or Susy Warner condoles with me and says, "Cheer up—don't be downhearted" . . . and none of them suspect what a burden has been lifted from me and how blithe I am inside. *Except* when I think of you, dear heart—then I am not blithe; for I seem to see you grieving and ashamed, and dreading to look people in the face. . . . You only seem to see rout, retreat, and dishonored colors dragging in the dirt—whereas none of these things exist. There is temporary defeat, but no dishonor—and we will march again. Charley Warner said today, "Sho, Livy isn't worrying. So long as she's got you and the children she doesn't care what happens. She knows it isn't her affair." Which didn't convince *me!*

No, Mrs. Clemens, who was so far from being the votary of genius, was not quite the votary of love either; she was, before all, the unquestioning daughter of that "wealthy coal-dealer" of Elmira, who had "held about a quarter of a million in her own right"; her husband might lag and lapse as a literary man, but when he fell behind in the race of pecuniary emulation she could not help applying the spur. She had even invested her own patrimony in her husband's ventures, and all that the Paige Typesetting Machine had spared went up the chimney in the failure of Charles L. Webster and Co. Of course Mark Twain had to retrieve that! And so it went: as the years passed, owing to the very ineptitude that ought to have kept him out of business altogether, he was involved more and more deeply in it.

As we can see now, the condition of Mark Twain's survival, on probation as he was and morally pledged to make a large income, was that he should adopt the whole code of his new environment. It was for love's sake that he had put his head, so to say, into the noose; in his case the matrimonial vow had been almost literally reversed and it was he who had promised not only to love and honor but also to obey. His loyalty was laid under further obligations by certain family disasters that followed his marriage and by the weakness of his wife. A neurotic, hysterical type—at sixteen, through a fall upon the ice, she had become a complete invalid, confined to her bed for two years in a darkened room, unable to sit, even when supported, unable to lie in any position except upon her back till a wizard came one day and told her, with miraculous results, to arise and walk—Mrs. Clemens was of an almost unearthly fragility, and she seems to have remained so during the greater part of her life. "I am still nursing Livy night and day. I am nearly worn out," Mark Twain writes, shortly after his marriage; and the death of their first child, not long after, naturally intensified his almost abnormal absorption in domestic interests, his already excessive devotion to his wife. We recall that passionate promise he had made to his brother: "I am in for it. I must go on chasing [phantoms] until I marry, *then* I am done with literature and all other bosh—that is, literature wherewith to please the general public. I shall write to please myself then." What chance did he have now, preoccupied at home, driven to support the pretentious establishment his father-in-law had wished on him, to find his own bearings and write to please that "self" which had never possessed any truly conscious existence? The whole tenor of this new life was to feminize Mark Twain, to make him feel that no loyalties are valid which conflict with domestic loyalties, that no activities are admirable which do not immediately conduce to domestic welfare, that private and familiar interests are, rightly and inevitably, the prime interests of man.

Eve's Diary, written by Mark Twain shortly after his wife's death, is said to figure their relationship: Adam there is the hewer of wood and the drawer of water, a sort of Caliban, and Eve the arbiter in all matters of civilization. "It has low tastes," says Beauty of this Beast. "Some instinct tells me that eternal vigilance is the price of supremacy." And how Mrs. Clemens exercised it! There is something for the gods to bewail in the sight of that shorn Samson led about by a little child who, in the profound somnolence of her spirit, was merely going through the motions of an inherited domestic piety. "Her life had been circumscribed," says Mr. Paine, "her experiences of a simple sort"; but she did not hesitate to undertake "the work of polishing and purifying her life companion. She had no wish to destroy his personality, to make him over, but only to preserve his best, and she set about it in the right way—gently, and with a tender gratitude in each achievement." To preserve his best! "She sensed his heresy toward the conventions and forms which had been her gospel; his bantering, indifferent attitude toward life—to her always so serious and sacred; she suspected that he even might have unorthodox views on matters of religion." That was before they were married: afterward, "concerning his religious observances her task in the beginning was easy enough. Clemens had not at that time formulated any particular doctrines of his own. . . . It took very little persuasion on his wife's part to establish family prayers in their home, grace before meals, and the morning reading of a Bible chapter."

Thus was reëstablished over him that old Calvinistic spell of his mother's, against which he had so vainly revolted as a child: preserving his "best," as we can see, meant preserving what fitted into the scheme of a good husband, a kind father and a sagacious man of business after the order of the Jervis Langdons of this world, for Olivia Clemens had never known any other sort of hero. "In time," says Mr. Paine, with a terrible unconscious irony, "she saw more clearly with his vision, but this was long after, when she had lived more with the world, had become more familiar with its larger needs, and the proportions of created things." It was too late then; the mischief had long been done. Mark Twain frightened his wife and shocked her, and she prevailed over him by an almost deliberate reliance upon that weakness to which he, the chivalrous Southerner—the born cavalier, in reality—could not fail to respond. Why did she habitually call him "Youth"? Was it not from an instinctive sense that her power lay in keeping him a child, in asserting the maternal attitude which he could never resist? He had indeed found a second mother now, and he "not only accepted her rule implicitly," as Mr. Howells says, "but he rejoiced, he gloried in it." He teased her, he occasionally enjoyed "shivering" her "exquisite sense of decorum"; but he, who could not trust his own judgment and to whom, consequently, one taboo was as reasonable as another, submitted to all her taboos as a matter of course. "I would quit wearing socks," he said, "if she thought them immoral."

It was, this marriage, as we perceive, a case of the blind leading the blind. Mark Twain had thrown himself into the hands of his wife; she, in turn, was merely the echo of her environment. "She was very sensitive about me," he wrote in his *Autobiography*. "It distressed her to see me do heedless things which could bring me under criticism." That was partly, of course, because she wished him to succeed for his own sake, but it was also because she was not sure of herself. We can see, between the lines of Mr. Paine's record, not only what a shy little provincial body she was, how easily thrown out of her element, how ill-at-ease in their journeyings about the world, but how far from unambitious she was also. It was for her own sake, therefore, that she trimmed him and tried to turn Caliban into a gentleman. Timid and ambitious as she was, having annexed him to herself she had to make him as presentable as possible in order to satisfy her own vanity before the eyes of those upon whose approval her happiness depended. . . . Imagine a European man of genius having to qualify, not as an individual, but as a member of a social order into which he had not been born! Charles Dickens never felt grateful to society because it tolerated the man who had once been a waif of the streets: Mark Twain, as Mr. Paine presents him, was always the barefoot boy among the gods.

Only in the light of this general subjugation of Mark Twain's character can we understand his literary subjugation. From the moment of his marriage his artistic integrity, already compromised, had, as a matter of fact, been irreparably destroyed: quite literally, as a man of letters, his honor rooted in dishonor stood and faith unfaithful kept him falsely true. He had accepted his father-in-law's financial assistance; he had bought his post on the Buffalo *Express;* in return, he had solemnly pledged the freedom of his mind. In these words of his Salutatory he made his pledge public:

Being a stranger it would be immodest for me to suddenly and violently assume the associate editorship of the Buffalo *Express* without a single word of comfort or encouragement to the unoffending patrons of this paper, who are about to be exposed to constant attacks of my wisdom and learning. But the word shall be as brief as possible. I only want to assure parties having a friendly interest in the prosperity of the journal that I am not going to hurt the paper deliberately and intentionally at any time. I am not going to introduce any startling reforms, nor in any way attempt to make trouble.... Such is my platform. I do not see any use in it, but custom is law and must be obeyed.

Never, surely, was a creative will more innocently, more painlessly surrendered than in those words; marriage had been, for Mark Twain's artistic conscience, like the final whiff of chloroform sealing a slumber that many a previous whiff had already induced. With that promise to be "good," to refrain from hurting "parties having a friendly interest in the prosperity" of his journal, the artist in Mark Twain had fallen into a final trance: anybody could manipulate him now. We have seen that his wife, who had become his chief censor, having no more independence of judgment than he, simply exposed him to the control of public opinion. This, in all matters of culture, meant New England, and especially Boston and accordingly to please Boston—impossible, terrifying task!—had become as obligatory upon Mark Twain as to please Elmira.

We have already observed the intellectual posture of Boston during the Gilded Age. Frigid and emasculate, it cast upon the presuming outsider the cold and hostile eye of an elderly maiden aunt who is not prepared to stand any nonsense. "Tomorrow night," writes Mark Twain, in one of his earlier letters, "I appear for the first time before a Boston audience—4,000 critics"; he was lecturing with Petroleum V. Nasby, and he tells how frightened Petroleum was before the ordeal. Fortunately, in a sense, for Mark Twain, he had, in Mr. Howells, a charitable sponsor, a charitable intermediary; but unfortunately for his genius Mr. Howells was no more independent than himself; Mr. Howells was almost as much the nervous and timid alien in Boston as Mrs. Clemens, and as the latter's natural ally and supreme authority in the task of shaping her husband, instead of dispelling Mark Twain's fears he simply redoubled them. Together, like two tremulous maids dressing the plebeian daughter of some newly-rich manufacturer in order to make her presentable for a court ball, they worked over him, expurgated him, trimmed him—to his own everlasting gratitude. To Mr. Howells he wrote: "I owe as much to your training as the rude country job-printer owes to the city-boss who takes him in hand and teaches him the right way to handle his art"; and of his wife he said: "I was a mighty rough, coarse, unpromising subject when Livy took charge of me . . . and I may *still* be to the rest of the world, but not to her. She has made a very creditable job of me." And no doubt that refining process was necessary.

If Mark Twain had been enabled to stand on his own feet, had been helped to discover himself as an artist, it would have resulted naturally from the growth of his own self-consciousness, his own critical sense. As it was, undertaken in behalf of a wholly false, external ideal and by people who had no comprehension of his true principle of growth, people who were themselves subservient to public opinion, it destroyed the last vestiges of his moral independence. There is a sorry tale about Mark Twain's neckties that is really symbolic of the process he was going through. It seems that long after his marriage he still continued to wear an old-fashioned Western string-tie which was the cause of great embarrassment to his family and his friends, an ever-present reminder that his regeneration was still incomplete. No one quite knew what to do about it till at last Howells and Aldrich boldly bought him two cravats and humored him, to his wife's infinite comfort, into wearing them. In this way the mysteries of a provincial gentility—provincial because it was without a sense of proportion—were kept constantly before his mind and he, the lovable victim of his own love, a Gulliver among the Lilliputians, a sleeping Samson, surrendered his limbs to the myriad threads of convention, yielded his locks to the shears of that simple Delilah his wife.

For what sort of taste was it that Mark Twain had to satisfy? Hardly a taste for the frank, the free, the animated, the expressive! The criticism he received was purely negative. We are told that Mrs. Clemens and her friends read Meredith "with reverential appreciation," that they formed a circle of "devout listeners" when Mark Twain himself used to read Browning aloud in Hartford. Profane art, the mature expression of life, in short, was outside Mrs. Clemens's circle of ideas; she could not breathe in that atmosphere with any comfort; her instinctive notion of literature was of something that is read at the fireside, out loud, under the lamp, a family institution, vaguely associated with the Bible and a father tempering the wind of King James's English to the sensitive ears and blushing cheek of the youngest daughter.

Her taste, in a word, was quite infantile. "Mrs. Clemens says my version of the blindfold novelette, *A Murder and a Marriage,* is 'good.' Pretty strong language for her," writes Mark Twain in 1876; and we know that when he was at work on *Huckleberry Finn* and *The Prince and the Pauper,* she so greatly preferred the latter that Mark Twain really felt it was rather discreditable of him to pay any attention to *Huckleberry Finn* at all. "Imagine this fact," he wrote to Howells; "I have even fascinated Mrs. Clemens with this yarn for youth. My stuff generally gets considerable damning with faint praise out of her, but this time it is all the other way. She is become the horse-leech's daughter, and my mill doesn't grind fast enough to suit her. This is no mean triumph, my dear sir." And shortly afterward he wrote to his mother:

> I have two stories, and by the verbal agreement they are both going into the same book; but Livy says they're not, and by George I she ought to know. She says they're going into separate books, and that one of them is going to be elegantly gotten up, even if the elegance of it eats up the publisher's profits and mine, too.

It was *The Prince and the Pauper,* a book that anybody might have written but whose romantic medievalism was equally respectable in its tendency and infantile in its appeal, that Mrs. Clemens felt so proud of: "nobody," adds Mr. Paine, "appears to have been especially concerned about Huck, except, possibly the publisher."

Plainly it was very little encouragement that Mark Twain's natural genius received from these relentless critics to whom he stood in such subjection, to whom he offered such devotion; for Mr. Howells, too, if we are to accept Mr. Paine's record, seconded him as often as not in these innocuous, infantile ventures, abetting him in the production of "blindfold novelettes" and plays of an abysmal foolishness. As for Mark Twain's unique masterpiece, *Huckleberry Finn,* "I like it only tolerably well, as far as I have got," he writes, "and may possibly pigeonhole or burn the MS. when it is done"; to which Mr. Paine adds: "It did not fascinate him as did the story of the wandering prince. He persevered only as the story moved him. . . . Apparently, he had not yet acquired confidence or pride enough in poor Huck to exhibit him, even to friends." And quite naturally! His artistic self-respect had been so little developed, had been, in fact, so baffled and abashed by all this mauling and fumbling that he could take no pride in a book which was, precisely, the mirror of the unregenerate past he was doing his best to live down.

Behold Mrs. Clemens, then, in the role of critic and censor. A memorandum Mark Twain made at the time when he and she were going over the proofs of *Following the Equator* shows us how she conceived of her task. It is in the form of a dialogue between them:

Page 1,020, 9th line from the top. I think some other word would be better than "stench." You have used that pretty often.

But can't I get it in *any*where? You've knocked it out every time. Out it goes again. And yet "stench" is a noble, good word.

Page 1,038. I hate to have your father pictured as lashing a slave boy.

It's out, and my father is whitewashed.

Page 1,050, 2nd line from the bottom. Change "breech-clout." It's a word that you love and I abominate. I would take that and "offal" out of the language.

You are steadily weakening the English tongue, Livy.

We can see from this that to Mrs. Clemens virility was just as offensive as profanity, that she had no sense of the difference between virility and profanity and vulgarity, that she had, in short, no positive taste, no independence of judgment at all. We can see also that she had no artistic ideal for her husband, that she regarded his natural liking for bold and masculine language, which was one of the outward signs of his latent greatness, merely as a literary equivalent of bad manners, as something that endangered their common prestige in the eyes of conventional public opinion. She condemned his writings, says Mr. Paine, specifically, "for the offense they might give in one way or another"; and that her sole object, however unconscious, in doing this was to further him, not as an artist but as a popular success, and especially as a candidate for gentility, is proved by the fact that she made him, as we observe in the incident of his father and the slave boy, whitewash not only himself but his family history also. And in all this Mr. Howells seconded her. "It skirts a certain kind of fun which you can't afford to indulge in," he reminds our shorn Samson in one of his letters; and again, "I'd have that swearing out in an instant," the "swearing" in this case being what he himself admits is "so exactly the thing Huck would say"—namely, "they comb me all to hell."

.   .   .   .

Mark Twain had come East with the only conscious ambition that Western life had bred in him, the ambition to succeed in a practical sense, to win wealth and fame. But the poet in him was still astir, still seeking, seeking, seeking for corroboration, for the frank hand and the gallant word that might set it free. We know this from the dim hope of liberation he had associated with the idea of marriage, and we can guess that his eager desire to meet "men of superior intellect and character" was more than half a desire to find someone who could give him that grand conception of the literary life which he had never been able to formulate, someone who could show him how to meet life in the proud, free way of the artist, how to unify himself and focus his powers. Well, he had met the best, the greatest, he had met the man whom the Brahmins themselves had crowned as their successor, he had met Mr. Howells. And in this man of marvelous talent, this darling of all the gods and all the graces, he had encountered once more the eternal, universal, instinctive American subservience to what Mr. Santayana calls "the genteel tradition." He had reached, in short, the heaven of literature and found it empty, and there was nothing beyond for the poet in him to seek.

Consider, if I seem to be exaggerating, the story of "Captain Stormfield's Visit to Heaven," which lay in Mark Twain's safe for forty years before he dared to publish it. That little tale was slight enough in itself, but he was always tinkering with it: as the years went on it assumed in his eyes an abnormal importance as the symbol of what he wished to do and was prohibited from doing. "The other evening," his little daughter Susy records in 1886, "as papa and I were promenading up and down the library, he told me that he didn't expect to write but one more book, and then he was ready to give up work altogether, die, or do anything; he said that he had written more than he had ever expected to, and the only book that he had been particularly anxious to write was one locked up in the safe downstairs, not yet published." He had begun it in 1868, even before he had issued *The Innocents Abroad,* the vast popular success of which had overlaid this tentative personal venture that he had been prevented, because of its "blasphemous" tendency, from pursuing. There was his true line, the line of satire—we know it as much from the persistence with which he clung to that book as from his own statement that it was the only one he had been particularly anxious to write; there was his true line, and he had halted in it for want of corroboration. And what was Mr. Howells's counsel? "When Howells was here last," writes Mark Twain to his brother Orion in 1878, "I laid before him the whole story without referring to the MS. and he said: 'You have got it sure this time. But drop the idea of making mere magazine stuff of it. Don't waste it. Print it by itself—publish it first in England—ask Dean Stanley to endorse it, which will draw some of the teeth of the religious press, and then reprint in America.' " There was the highest ideal, the boldest conception, of personal freedom, of the independence of the spirit, of the function of literature that Mark Twain had found in America. "Neither Howells nor I," he adds, "believe in hell or the divinity of the Savior, but no matter." No matter, no! The integrity of the spirit had become as indifferent to him as it was to the Gilded Age itself. He, this divided soul, had sought the great leader and had found only an irresponsible child like himself, a child who told him that you had to sneak off behind the barn if you wanted to smoke the pipe of truth.

Is it remarkable, then, that having found in the literary life as it shaped itself in industrial America every incentive to cower and cringe and hedge, and no incentive whatever to stand upright as a man—is it remarkable, I say, that Mark Twain should have relapsed into the easy, happy posture that came so natural to him in the presence of his wife, the posture of the little boy who is licensed to play the literary game as much as he likes so long as he isn't too rude or too vulgar and turns an honest penny by it and never forgets that the real business of life is to make hay in fame and fortune and pass muster, in course of time, as a gentleman? "Smoke?" he writes. "I always smoke from three till five on Sunday afternoons, and in New York, the other day, I smoked a week day and night. . . . And once or twice I smouched a Sunday when the boss wasn't looking. Nothing is half so good as literature hooked on Sunday, on the sly." Incorrigible naughty boy! He never dreams of asserting a will of his own; but doesn't he delight in his freedom from responsibility, isn't it a relief to be absolved from the effort of creating standards of his own and living up to them?

"A man is never anything but what his outside influences have made him," wrote Mark Twain, years later. "It is his human environment which influences his mind and his feelings, furnishes him his ideals, and sets him on his road and keeps him in it. If he leave that road he will find himself shunned by the people whom he most loves and esteems, and whose approval he most values." He who so willingly suppressed, at his wife's command, the first germ of a book he was to call his "Bible," a deistical note on God, who had formed the habit of withholding views which he thought would strike his neighbors as "shocking, heretical and blasphemous," who, in spite of his true opinions, spoke of himself in public to the end of his life as a Presbyterian, who had, in fact, like the chameleon which he said man was, taken the religious color of his environment, just as he had taken its social and financial color—had he not virtually ceased to feel any obligation to his own soul?

"If," he wrote, in *What Is Man?*, "if that timid man had lived all his life in a community of human rabbits, had never read of brave deeds, had never heard speak of them, had never heard anyone praise them nor express envy of the heroes that had done them, he would have had no more idea of bravery than Adam had of modesty, and it could never by any possibility have occurred to him to *resolve* to become brave. He *could not originate the idea*—it had to come to him from the *outside*."

The tell-tale emphasis of those italics! Is not that drab philosophy of Mark Twain's, that cumbrous chain of argument, just one long pathetic plea in self-extenuation?

1920

BRANDER MATTHEWS

IN AN AFTER-DINNER SPEECH which Mark Twain made in 1907 in London at the Savage Club, he protested against an interviewer's having made him say that a certain address was "bully," and he asserted that this distressed him, because "I never use slang to an interviewer of anybody else," adding that if he could not describe that address without using slang, he would not describe it at all. "I would close my mouth and keep it closed, much as it would discomfort me."

Possibly a few of those who heard Mark make this assertion, and probably more than a few of those who have read it in the volume in which his speeches are collected, may have been surprised, and perhaps a little inclined to wonder whether Mark was not here indulging in his customary humorous unveracity. Some of them may have recalled the slang which fell unbroken from the lips of Scotty Briggs when he was enlisting the services of the preacher for Buck Fanshawe's funeral.

But in saying that he never used slang to an interviewer or anybody else, Mark was only asserting what must be plain to every careful reader of his works and to everyone who has had the delight of hearing him tell a story. In the person of Scotty Briggs, who knew no other way of expressing himself, Mark could disclose his knowledge of the energetic and boldly imaginative speech of the unlettered Westerners:

"Mark Twain and the Art of Writing," from Harper's Monthly Magazine, *CXLI (October, 1920), 635-43. Copyright Nelson Macy, Jr., and reprinted by his permission.*

> Phrases such as camps may teach,
> Saber-cuts of Saxon speech.

In his own person, as Samuel L. Clemens, or in his assumed personality, as Mark Twain, he refrained from this well of English undefiled by pernicketty precisions, tempting as many of its vigorous vocables must have been to him, with his relish for verbal picturesqueness. He knew better than to yield to the easy allurement; and his English is as pure as it is nervous and direct and uncompromising. As he eschews slang, so he does not disfigure his pages with localisms, current only sectionally. He avoids dialectic peculiarities, however picturesque in themselves and however expressive. Of course, he lets his local characters express themselves in their local vernacular, and he took pride in the intimacy of his acquaintance with sectional vagaries of vocabulary. In an explanatory note, prefixed to *Huckleberry Finn,* he tells his readers that he has therein used a number of dialects:

to wit: the Missouri negro dialect; the extremest form of the backwoods Southwestern dialect; the ordinary "Pike County" dialect; and four modified varieties of this last. The shadings have not been done in a haphazard fashion, or by guesswork; but painstakingly, and with the trustworthy guidance and support of personal familiarity with these several forms of speech.

To a friend who had inquired as to his collaboration with Bret Harte in an unsuccessful and unpublished play, *Ah Sin,* he explained that they had talked out the plot and that he had played billiards while Bret wrote the play, adding: "Of course I had to go over it and get the dialect right. Bret never did know anything about dialect."

While Mark never conformed to the British standard, often insular, and sometimes parochial, he disclosed no individual aberrations either in vocabulary or in usage. The Americanisms he employs on occasion are all legitimate, in that they are what may be called American contributions to the language; and he enlists very few even of these.

With his sensitiveness to the form and color of words, he was acutely conscious of the many differences between our habitual speech and that of our kin across the sea. In a chapter, which was crowded out of *A Tramp Abroad* to find refuge later in a volume of his sketches, he tells us of an interview he had with an Englishman who complimented him on his English.

> I said I was obliged to him for his compliment—since I knew he meant it for one—but that I was not fairly entitled to it, for I did not speak English at all—I only spoke American.

Then he pointed out that he judged that even the educated classes in England had once dropped their h's in *humble* and *heroic* and *historic,*

> because your writers still keep up the fashion of putting *an* before those words, instead of *a*. This is what Mr. Darwin might call a rudimentary sign that an *an* was justifiable once and useful. . . . Correct writers of the American language do not put *an* before those words.

And he concluded by assuring his chance companion that,

> If I wanted to, I could pile up differences here until I not only convinced you that English and American are separate languages, but that when I speak my native tongue in its utmost purity an Englishman can't understand it at all!

This final statement is the extravagant whimsy of a humorist. Yet it is a fact that Mark spoke his native tongue in its utmost purity, which is why every Englishman could understand him. He spoke pure English, as free from obtruded Americanisms as from obsolete Briticisms, the English current on both shores of "the salt, unplumbed, estranging sea," the English of Defoe and Bunyan, of Franklin and Lincoln. He knew that English was his native tongue, a birthright and not a loan or a gift; and he was content with its ample resources, seeking always the exact noun and the inexorable adjective. As Mr. Howells has put it with his delicate felicity, Mark "used English in all its alien derivations as if it were native to his own air, as if it had come up out of American, out of Missourian ground;" and Mr. Howells has also pointed out that Mark had a "single-minded use of words, which he employs as Grant did to express the plain, straight meaning their common acceptance has given them, with no regard to their structural significance or their philological implications. He writes English as if it were a primitive and not a derivative language, without Gothic or Latin or Greek behind it, or German or French beside it." And he adds that the word Mark prefers is "the Abraham Lincolnian word, not the Charles Sumnerian; it is American, Western."

There is a superstition among those who have been educated beyond their intelligence that no man can be a master of English who does not possess Latin at least, and perhaps French also. But this absurdity is exploded by the vital vigor of Bunyan and Defoe, not less than by that of Franklin and Lincoln, Grant and Mark Twain. And the vitality of Mark's English was a gainer also by that fact that to him English was always a spoken tongue; he wrote as he talked; but then he was always as careful in his choice of words when he talked as when he wrote. He imparted to the printed page the vivacity of the spoken word, its swiftness and its apparently unpremeditated ease. His sentences never seemed labored, no matter how deeply they may have been meditated. In reading them they appear spontaneous; and, whatever the toil they may have cost him, they are not stained with the smoke of the casting or scratched with the mark of the file. Self-taught as he was, no apprentice to the craft of composition ever had a severer teacher. He so mastered the secrets of our stubborn tongue that he was able to write it as he spoke it, with precise accuracy and yet with flowing freedom.

In this Mark, all unwittingly (for he was never interested in the history of critical theories), was only acting on the principle laid down two and a half centuries ago by Vaugelas, the linguistic lawgiver of the French: "The rule is general and without exception, that what one does not say in speaking one ought never to say in writing." And again: "The greatest of all errors in the matter of writing is to think, as many do, that we must not write as we talk."

The same point had been made even earlier by the Italian Castiglione, in his once famous book on the *Courtier:*

> Writing is nothing but a form of speaking, which continues to exist after man has spoken, and is, as it were, an image of the words he utters. It is consequently reasonable to use greater diligence with a view to making what we write more polished and correct, yet not to do this so that the written words shall differ from the spoken, but only so that the best in spoken use shall be selected for our composition.

This is precisely what Mark trained himself to accomplish. He selected for his composition the best in spoken use. He profited by one of the advantages of writing as we speak, if only we are in the habit of speaking with due respect for the nobility of our tongue, that he did not cumber his pages with dead and gone words. Like every growing language, English has a host of words which have fallen into innocuous desuetude and are no longer understanded of the people. They may run off the pen of the pedantic, but they never fall from the lips of Mark Twain. He was a man of his own time, with no hankering after the archaic. His language is the living speech of those who have English for their mother-tongue, however scattered they may be on all the shores of all the seven seas.

In his *Autobiography,* from which only a few passages were published in his lifetime, Mark has told us that when he made the overland trip to Nevada (which he has described in *Roughing It)* he took with him Webster's unabridged Dictionary—an early testimony to his desire to spy out the secrets of the mother-tongue. It was a cumbrous impediment, and its carriage was costly, since the stage-coach charged extra baggage by the ounce. "And it wasn't a good dictionary, anyway—didn't have any modern words in it, only had obsolete ones that they used to use when Noah Webster was a child."

It must be noted also that Mark refrained from the employment of the newest words, the linguistic novelties which are on probation, as it were, which may in time win acceptance, but which for the moment are only colloquialisms, uncertain of their ultimate admission into the vocabulary as desirable citizens.

It was Mark's misfortune—in that it long delayed his recognition as a writer to be taken seriously—that he first won the favor of the public, in the United States and also in Great Britain with the *Innocents Abroad,* a book of robust humor, mirth-provoking and often rollicking in its extravagance. His readers thereafter looked into his successive volumes for the fun they were in search of, and, having found it, abundant and sparkling, they sought no further. If they had, they could not have failed to find other things also, not humorous, but grave and even pathetic. Yet even in the *Innocents Abroad,* which compelled their laughter, there are passages which ought to have arrested the attention of those who do not run as they read, passages which proved that Mark Twain was no mere clown, grinning through a horse-collar, and applying mechanically the formulas of John

Phoenix and Artemus Ward. There is, for example, the meditation before the Sphinx:

The great face was so sad, so earnest, so longing, so patient. There was a dignity not of earth in its mien, and in its countenance a benignity such as never anything human wore. It was stone, but it seemed sentient. If ever image of stone thought, it was thinking. It was looking toward the verge of the landscape, yet looking *at* nothing—nothing but distance and vacancy. It was looking over and beyond everything of the present, and far into the past. It was gazing out over the ocean of Time—over lines of century waves which, further and further receding, closed nearer and nearer together, and blended at last into one unbroken tide, away toward the horizon of remote antiquity. It was thinking of the wars of departed ages; of the empires it had seen created and destroyed; of the nations whose birth it had witnessed, whose progress it had watched, whose annihilation it had noted; of the joy and sorrow, life and death, the grandeur and decay, of five thousand slow revolving years. It was the type of an attribute of man—a faculty of his heart and brain. It was *Memory—Retrospection*—wrought into visible, tangible form. All who know what pathos there is in memories of days that are accomplished and faces that have vanished—albeit only a trifling score of years gone by— will have some appreciation of the pathos that dwells in those grave eyes that look so steadfastly back upon the things they knew before History was born—before Tradition had being—things that were, and forms that moved, in a vague era which even Poetry and Romance scarce know of —and passed one by one away and left the stony dreamer solitary in the midst of a strange new age, and uncomprehended scenes.

This description of a work of man must be companied by the description of a work of nature, contained in his second book of European travel, *A Tramp Abroad*. It is a vision of the Jungfrau, seen from Interlaken:

This was the mighty dome of the Jungfrau softly outlined against the sky and faintly silvered by the starlight. There was something subduing in the influence of that silent and solemn and awful presence; one seemed to meet the immutable, the indestructible, the eternal, face to face, and to feel the trivial and fleeting nature of his own existence the more sharply by the contrast. One had the sense of being under the brooding contempla- tion of a spirit, not an inert mass of rocks and ice—a spirit which had looked down through the slow drift of the ages, upon a million vanished races of men, and judged them; and would judge a million more—and still be there, watching, unchanged and unchangeable, after all life should be gone and the earth have become a vacant desolation.

In the writings of how many of the authors of the nineteenth century could the beauty and power of these passages be equaled? Could they be surpassed in any of them?

The Innocents Abroad was published in 1869 and *A Tramp Abroad* in 1879, and in the course of the decade which intervened between these books Mark was called up to speak at a dinner of the New England Society in New York. He chose as his topic the subject which forms the staple of our casual conversation, the weather, and never before had the demerits of the New England climate been delineated and denounced with such vigor and such veracity. Never before had Mark displayed more exuberantly the wealth of his whimsy. And then at the very end he made a plea in extenuation for the misdeeds of the culprit he had held up to derision.

But, after all, there is at least one thing about that weather (or, if you please, effects produced by it) which we residents would not like to part with. If we hadn't our bewitching autumn foliage, we should still have to credit the weather with one feature which compensates for all its bullying vagaries—the ice storm, when a leafless tree is clothed with ice from the bottom to the top—ice that is as bright and clear as crystal; when every bough and twig is strung with ice-beads, frozen dew-drops, and the whole tree sparkles cold and white, like the Shah of Persia's diamond plume. Then the wind waves the branches and the sun comes out and turns all those myriads of beads and drops to prisms that glow and burn and flash with all manner of colored fires, which change and change again with inconceivable rapidity from blue to red, from red to green, and green to gold—the tree becomes a spraying fountain, a very explosion of dazzling jewels; and it stands there the acme, the climax, the supremest possibility in art or nature, of bewildering, intoxicating, intolerable magnificence.

Only by quotation is it possible to indicate the sustaining dignity of Mark's thought, his interpreting imagination, the immeasurable range of his vocabulary, the delicate precision of his choice of words, and the certainty of his construction. To the three passages already chosen for this purpose, it is impossible not to append a fourth, taken from one of the last papers that he penned with his own hand—the account of the death of his youngest daughter, Jean, only four months before he was himself to die. It was written at intervals, after he was awakened on the morning before Christmas by the sudden announcement, "Miss Jean is dead!" and during the days that intervened until she was laid away by the side of her mother, her brother, and her elder sister. He did not write it for publication; it was too intimate for that; but he told his future biographer that if it was thought worthy, it could appear as the final chapter in the *Autobiography,* whenever that should at last be printed. In these broken paragraphs, set down from hour to hour while he was stunned by the blow, he attains to the severest simplicity—the sincere simplicity of the deepest feeling. The selections must be few and brief:

> Jean lies yonder, I sit here; we are strangers under our own roof; we kissed hands good-by at this door last night—and it was forever, we never suspecting it. She lies there, and I sit here—writing, busying myself, to keep my heart from breaking. How dazzling the sunshine is flooding the hills around! It is like a mockery.
>
> Seventy-four years twenty-four days ago. Seventy-four years old yesterday. Who can estimate my age today? . . .
>
> Would I bring her back to life if I could do it? I would not. If a word would do it, I would beg for strength to withhold the word. And I would have the strength; I am sure of it. In her loss I am almost bankrupt, and my life is a bitterness, but I am content: for she has been enriched with the most precious of all gifts—that gift which makes all other gifts mean and poor—death.

It is not a little curious that few of those who have written about Mark Twain have called attention to his mastery of style, and that even fewer have paid any attention to the essays and the letters in which he himself discussed the art of writing. Perhaps this is just as well, since his own work has been judged free from any bias aroused by his criticism of other men's writing. It may have been a disadvantage to Howells and Henry James and Robert Louis Stevenson that they approved themselves as critics as well as novelists, and that they were frank in expressing their opinions and in formulating their theories about the art of fiction and the art of writing; and it may be that the reticence in regard to these matters observed by Hawthorne and Hardy and Kipling is wiser. Mark's ventures into criticism are not many, but they are significant; and they shed light upon his own artistic standards.

There is illumination, for example, in one of the maxims of Pudd'nhead Wilson's Calendar: "As to the Adjective: when in doubt, strike it out." It would be useful to have that stamped in gold on the border of the blotting-pad of many a man of letters. And there are other remarks equally suggestive, scattered through his letters and through his essays on Howells as a master of English, on "Fenimore Cooper's Literary Offenses" and "In Defense of Harriet Shelley."

The predisposing condition which led Mark to take up his pen in defense of Shelley's wife was his manly detestation of insinuating insincerity; and the exciting cause was his perusal of Dowden's unfortunate biography of her husband. Mark was moved to wrath, as well he might be, by Dowden's special pleading, by his maneuvers to whiten Shelley by blackening Shelley's wife. Mark begins by a characterization of Dowden's style:

> Our negroes in America have several ways of entertaining themselves which are not found among the whites anywhere. Among these inventions of theirs is one which is particularly popular with them. It is a competition in elegant deportment. . . . A cake is provided as a prize for the winner in the competition. . . . One at a time the contestants enter, clothed regardless of expense in which each considers the perfection of style and taste, and walk down the vacant central space and back again. . . . All that the competitor knows of fine airs and graces he throws into his carriage, all that he knows of seductive expression he throws into his countenance. . . . They call it a cake-walk. The Shelley biography is a literary cake-walk. The ordinary forms of speech are absent from it. All the pages, all the paragraphs walk by sedately, elegantly, not to say mincingly, in their Sunday best, shiny and sleek, perfumed, and with *boutonnières* in their buttonholes; it is rare to find even a chance sentence that has forgotten to dress.

From this expressive characterization it is plain that Dowden had a liking for what Kipling has described as "the Bouverie-Byzantine style, with baroque and rococo embellishments," and that Mark Twain did not share this liking. He detested pretense and pretentiousness. Affectation in all its myriad aspects was ever abhorrent to him, and what he most relished in an author was a straightforward concreteness of presentation. We may be sure that he would have approved Brunetière's assertion that, "A good writer is simply one who says all he means to say, who says only what he means to say, and who says it exactly as he meant to say it."

It was the false tone and the unfair intent of Dowden's book which compelled Mark to his merciless exposure. In his less carefully controlled essay on "Fenimore Cooper's Literary Offenses," he impales the author of The Leather Stocking Tales for the verbal inaccuracies not infrequent in Cooper's pages. Mark declares that the rules for good writing require that

> an author shall *say* what he is proposing to say, not merely come near it; use the right word, not its second cousin; eschew surplusage; not omit necessary details; avoid slovenliness of form; use good grammar; and employ a simple and straightforward style.

He insists that all seven of these rules, of these precepts for correct composition, "are coldly and persistently violated in *The Deerslayer* tale."

A little later in his searching criticism Mark becomes more specific. He tells us that

> Cooper's word-sense was singularly dull. When a person has a poor ear for music he will flat and sharp right along without knowing it. He keeps near the tune, but it is *not* the tune. When a person has a poor ear for words, the result is a literary flatting and sharping; you perceive what he is intending to say, but you also perceive that he doesn't *say* it. This is Cooper. He was not a word-musician. His ear was satisfied with the *approximate* word.

Even an ardent admirer of the broad, bold pictures of life in the green forest and on the blue water painted in *The Last of the Mohicans* and in *The Pilot* cannot but admit that there is not a little justice in Mark's disparaging criticism. Cooper is not a word-musician; he sometimes flats and sharps, and he is often content when he has happened on the approximate term. But the seven rules here cited, while they cast light on Cooper's deficiencies, also illuminate Mark's own standards of style. He was annoyed by Cooper's occasional carelessness in the use of words, as many other readers must have been; but Mark is more annoyed than most of these other readers because his own practice had made him inexorable in precision. He himself was never satisfied with the approximate word; he never flatted or sharped; he had a word-sense that was always both acute and alert.

Although he never prepared a paper on Walter Scott's literary offenses, Mark held that the author of *Guy Mannering* had been guilty of verbal misdemeanors as heinous as those of the author of

The Last of the Mohicans. And in a letter that he wrote to me in 1903 he asked a series of questions which he obviously held to be unanswerable:

Are there in Sir Walter's novels passages done in good English— English which is neither slovenly nor involved? Are there passages whose English is not poor and thin and commonplace, but of a quality above that? Did he know how to write English, and didn't do it because he didn't want to? Did he use the right word only when he couldn't think of another one, or did he run so much to wrong because he didn't know the right one when he saw it?

Here again the loyal lover of *Quentin Durward* and of *The Heart of Midlothian* cannot deny that there are inaccuracies and inelegancies in Scott's flowing pages, and quite enough of them to make it a little difficult to enter a general denial of all these piercing queries. Scott did not take his fiction over-seriously. He was, as Carlyle put it bluntly, "improvising novels to buy farms with." His style, like his construction, is sometimes careless, not to call it reckless. Mark had trained himself to be careful and to take delight in the dexterities of verbal adjustment, and this had made him intolerant of the verbal untidiness, so to term it, perhaps not so frequent in Scott as in Cooper, but far too frequent in both of them, even if their works had major merits which Mark was led to overlook in his disgust at their minor lapses from rhetorical propriety.

Besides calling attention to these linguistic deficiencies, Mark takes occasion in the essay on Cooper and in the letter on Scott to express his dislike for their stories, merely as stories. He holds that Cooper violated the rules which require that "a tale shall accomplish something and arrive somewhere;" that "the episodes of a tale shall be necessary parts of the tale, and shall help to develop it;" that "the personages in a tale shall be alive, except in the case of corpses, and that always the reader shall be able to tell the corpses from the others;" and that "the personages in a tale, both dead and alive, shall exhibit a sufficient excuse for being there." He asks whether Scott has "personages whose acts and talk correspond with their characters as described by him?" Whether he has "heroes and heroines whom the reader admires, admires and knows *why?*" Whether he has "funny characters that are funny, and humorous passages that are humorous?" And he asserts that

It is impossible to feel an interest in these bloodless shams, these milk-and-water humbugs. And, oh, the poverty of the invention! Not poverty in inventing situations, but poverty in furnishing reasons for them.

Here we come face to face with one of Mark's most obvious limitations as a critic of literature—he is implacable in applying the standards of today to the fiction of yesterday. Despite their occasional slovenliness of diction and their constant heaping up of adventure upon adventure, Scott and Cooper could create individual characters, standing upright on their own feet and dominating the situations in which they are immeshed. But both of these bold storytellers did this in their own fashion, in the fashion of their own time, for they knew no other; and they could not foresee that their methods would be demoded in fivescore years. Mr. Howells was right when he declared that thè art of fiction is a finer art now than it was only half a century ago. Of course it is, and so is the art of the drama and the art of painting also. And equally, of course, this declaration carries with it no implication that the artists of the present are mightier than the masters of the past. There were giants in those days, as we all know, but these giants were not armed and equipped with the weapons of precision now available for men of only ordinary stature. The state of the art—whichever this art may be, fiction or drama or painting—is never stationary; and its processes are continually modified and multiplied.

One explanation for Mark's error of judgment is probably that he is a realist, with all the realist's abiding abhorrence for romanticism, wilful, arbitrary and highflown, for its striving for vivid external effects, and for the departure from veracity which this seeking entails. He so detested the attitude of Scott and Cooper, he was so painfully annoyed by their frequent failure to pierce below the surface that he blinded himself to their major merits, to the outstanding qualities which make them majestic figures in the history of fiction, however old-fashioned their way of telling a story and however blundering their use of language. But this explanation will not serve to elucidate the reason for his hatred of Jane Austen's novels. She was also a realist and a humorist—and her style is not open to the strictures which Scott and Cooper invite by their haste in composition. Yet he once wrote to a friend that he had often wanted to criticize Jane Austen, but her books madden me so that I can't conceal my frenzy from the reader, and therefore I have to stop every time I begin. Every time I read *Pride and Prejudice* I want to dig her up and beat her over the skull with her own shin-bone!

There is no denying the vernacular vigor of this whimsical ebullition. Mark knew well enough what he did not like; but why didn't he like Jane Austen? And the answer is far to seek. Perhaps it is that Jane Austen is a miniaturist of exquisite discretion, not a mural painter—because she molds Tanagra figurines and not the Winged Victory, because her little miracles of delicate observation seemed to him only the carving of cherry-stones. Her field is limited and her vision, keen as it is, is restricted, whereas Mark was wont to survey the full spectroscope of American life—that spectroscope which may seem at times to be almost a kaleidoscope. It may be, however, that the explanation lies a little deeper in the difference between the clever spinster of Winchester and the robust humorist of Hannibal, Missouri; it may be that with Mark's ingrained democracy he was outraged by Jane's placid and complacent acceptance of a semi-feudal social organization, stratified like a chocolate layer-cake, with petty human fossils in its lower formations.

It is only fair to note that Mark never wrote a criticism of Jane Austen, although he once went out of his way (in *Following the Equator*) to speak of her disparagingly. He expressed his desire to desecrate her grave only in a letter to an intimate, familiar with his imaginative exaggeration. In the same letter he confessed that he had no right to criticize books, because he could not keep his temper. "I don't do it, except when I hate them." He hated Dowden's biography of Shelley, and for good reason, since it is intellectually dishonest. He persuaded himself that he hated Cooper's *Deerslayer,* and admirers of The Leather Stocking Tales must admit that he had a case, even if he does not win a verdict from the jury.

Once, and once only, was he moved to criticism, not by hate, but by love, by a sincere appreciation of the superb craftsmanship of a fellow-practitioner of the art of fiction. His unbroken friendship with Howells is one of the most salient in all the long history of literature, worthy to be set by the side of those of Molière and Boileau, Goethe and Schiller, Emerson and Carlyle. It endured cloudless for twoscore years, and its full significance will not appear until the letters they interchanged are collected and published. Four years before he died Mark wrote a brief essay on Howells. It is a study of style, of Howells's command over the language, of the characteristics which combine to make Howells one of the indisputable masters of our stubborn speech.

For forty years his English has been to me a continual delight and astonishment. In sustained exhibition of certain great qualities—clearness, compression, verbal exactness, and unforced and seemingly unconscious felicity of phrasing—he is, in my belief, without his peer in the English-writing world. . . . There are others who exhibit those great qualities as greatly as does he, but only by intervaled distributions of rich moonlight, with stretches of veiled and dimmer landscape between; whereas Howells's moon sails cloudless skies all night and all the nights.

Mark finds in Howells's writing the very virtue which he failed to find in Cooper's (who worked, it must again be pointed out, more than fourscore years earlier).

In the matter of verbal exactness Mr. Howells has no superior, I suppose. He seems to be almost always able to find that elusive and shifty grain of gold, the *right word*. Others have to put up with approximations more or less frequently; he has better luck. To me, the others are miners working with the gold-pan—of necessity some of the gold washes over and escapes; whereas, in my fancy, he is quicksilver raiding down a riffle —no grain of metal stands much chance of eluding him.

And then Mark gives us an explanation certain to be quoted again and again in our future manuals of composition:

A powerful agent is the right word; it lights the reader's way and makes it plain; a close approximation to it will answer, and much traveling is done in a well-enough fashion by its help, but we do not welcome it and applaud it and rejoice in it as we do when *the* right one blazes out on us. Whenever we come upon one of those intensely right words in a book or a newspaper the resulting effect is physical as well as spiritual, and electrically prompt; it tingles exquisitely around through the walls of the mouth and tastes as tart and crisp and good as the autumn-butter that creams the sumac-berry.

These quotations reveal Mark's own standards of style as sharply as they illuminate Howells's practice. And this quotation, the last of all, imposes itself because it exemplifies Mark's own mercurial clutch on the right word:

As concerns his humor, I will not try to say anything, yet I would try, if I had the words that might approximately reach up to its high place. I do not think anyone else can play with humorous fancies so gracefully and delicately and deliciously as he does, nor has so many to play with, nor can come so near making them look as if they were doing the playing themselves and he was not aware they were at it. For they are unobtrusive and quiet in their ways and well conducted. His is a humor which flows softly all around about and over and through the mesh of the page, pervasive, refreshing, health-giving, and makes no more show and no more noise than does the circulation of the blood.

Did any humorist ever praise another with a more absolute understanding and with a more certain insight into the essence of the best humor?

1920

GAMALIEL BRADFORD

MARK TWAIN is generally known to the world as a laugher. His seriousness, his pathos, his romance, his instinct for adventure are all acknowledged and enjoyed. Still, the mention of his name almost always bring a smile first. So did the sight of him.

There is no doubt that he found the universe laughable and made it so. The ultimate test of the laughing instinct is that a man should be always ready to laugh at himself. Mark was. The strange chances of his life, its ups and downs, its pitiful disasters, sometimes made him weep, often made him swear. But at a touch they could always make him laugh. "There were few things that did not amuse him," writes his biographer, "and certainly nothing amused him more, or oftener, than himself." One brief sentence sums up what he was never tired of repeating: "I have been an author for twenty years and an ass for fifty-five."

And he not only saw laughter when it came to him: he went to seek it. He was always fond of jests and fantastic tricks, made mirth out of solemn things and solemn people, stood ready, like the clown of the circus, to crack his whip and bid the world dance after him in quaint freaks of jollity, all the more diverting when staid souls and mirthless visages played a chief part in the furious revel.

On the strength of this constant sense and love of laughter many have maintained that Mark was one of the great world-humorists, that he ranks with Cervantes and Sterne and the Shakespeare of *As You*

"Mark Twain," from Atlantic Monthly, *CXXV (April, 1920), 462-73.* ©*1920 by The Atlantic Monthly Company; reprinted by permission.*

Like It and *Twelfth Night,* as one who was an essential exponent of the comic spirit. With this view I cannot wholly agree. It is true that Mark could find the laughable element in everything; true also that he had that keen sense of melancholy which is inseparable from the richest comedy. Few have expressed this more intensely than he has. "Everything human is pathetic. The secret source of humor itself is not joy, but sorrow. There is no humor in heaven." Yet the very extravagance of expression here suggests my difficulty. Somehow in Mark the humor and the pathos are not perfectly blended. The laughter is wild and exuberant as heart can desire, but it does not really go to the bottom of things. Serious matters, so-called serious matters, are taken too seriously; and under the laughter there is a haunting basis of wrath and bitterness and despair.

To elucidate this, it is necessary to examine and follow the process and progress of Mark's thinking. In early years, he himself admits, he thought little—that is abstractly. His mind was active enough, busy enough, and, as we have seen, his fancy was always full of dreams. But he let the great problems alone, did not analyze, did not philosophize, content to extract immense joviality from the careless surface of life, and not to probe further. Even the analysis of laughter itself did not tempt him. In this he was probably wise, and he maintained the attitude always. "Humor is a subject which has never had much interest for me." Indeed, the analysis of humor may be safely left to those gray persons who do not know what it is. But much of the jesting of Mark's youthful days is so trivial that it distinctly implies the absence of steady thinking on any subject. Not that he was indifferent to practical seriousness. Wrong, injustice, cruelty could always set him on fire in a moment. There was no folly about his treatment of these. But at that stage his seriousness was busy with effects rather than with causes.

Then he acquired money and leisure and began to reason on the nature of things. This late dawning of his speculative turn must always be remembered in considering the quality of it. It accounts for the singular gaps in his information about simple matters, for the impression of terrific but not very well guided energy which comes from his intellectual effort. It accounts for the sense of surprise and novelty in his spiritual attitude, which Mr. Howells has so justly pointed out. He seems always like a man discovering things which are perfectly well known to trained thinkers, and this gives an extraordinary freshness and spirit to his pronouncements on all speculative topics. When he grew aware of his reasoning powers, he delighted in them. His shrewd little daughter said of him, "He is as much of a philosopher as anything, I think." He was a philosopher by inclination, at any rate. He loved to worry the universe, as a kitten worries a ball of yarn. Perhaps this seemed to make up in a small way for the worries the universe had given him. He loved to argue and discuss and dispute and confute, and then to spread over all bitterness the charm of his inextinguishable laughter. His oaths and jests and epigrams convulsed his interlocutors, if they did not convince them.

As to his theoretical conclusions, it may be said that they were in the main nihilistic. But before considering them more particularly, it must be insisted and emphasized that they were wholly theoretical and did not affect his practical morals in the least. Few human beings ever lived who had a nicer conscience and a finer and more delicate fulfilment of duty. It is true that all his life he kept up a constant humorous depreciation of himself in this regard. If you listened to his own confessions, you would think him the greatest liar in existence, and conclude that his moral depravation was equaled only by his intellectual nullity. This method is often effective for hiding and excusing small defects and delinquencies. But Mark needed no such excuse. What failings there were in his moral character were those incident to humanity. As an individual, he stood with the best.

The most obvious instances of his rectitude are in regard to money. In spite of his dreams and speculative vagaries, he was punctiliously scrupulous in financial relations, his strictness culminating in the vast effort of patience and self-denial necessary to pay off the obligations of honor which fell upon him in his later years. But the niceness of his conscience was not limited to broad obligations of this kind. "Mine was a trained Presbyterian conscience," he says, "and knew but the one duty—to hunt and harry its slave upon all pretexts and all occasions." He might trifle, he might quibble, he might jest; but no one was more anxious to do what was fair and right, even to the point of overdoing it. "I don't wish even to seem to do anything which can invite suspicion," he said, as to a matter so trivial as taking advantage in a game.

And the moral sense was not confined to practical matters of conduct. Human tenderness and kindliness and sympathy have rarely been more highly developed than in this man who questioned their existence. The finest touch in all his writings is the cry of Huck Finn when, after a passionate struggle between his duty to society and his duty to friendship, he tears the paper in which he proposed to surrender the nigger, Jim, and exclaims, "All right, then, I'll *go* to hell." And Mark himself would have been perfectly capable, not only of saying he would go, but of going.

As he loved men, so he trusted them. In the abstract, judging from himself, he declared they were monsters of selfishness, greedy, deceitful, treacherous, thoughtful in all things of their own profit and advantage. In the individual, again judging from himself, he accepted them at their face value, as kindly, self-sacrificing, ready to believe, ready to love, ready to help. Being himself an extreme example, both in skeptical analysis and in human instinct, he often fell into error and trusted where there was no foundation to build on.

In consequence, his actual experience went far to justify his skeptical theories, and he presents another example, like Swift, like Leopardi, of a man whose standard of life is so high, who expects so much of himself and of others, that the reality perpetually fails him, and excess of optimism drives him to excess of pessimism. For example, his interesting idealization or idolatry of Joan of Arc, his belief that she actually existed as a miracle of nature, makes it comprehensible that he should find ordinary men and women faulty and contemptible enough compared with such a type.

It is not the place here to analyze Mark's speculative conclusions in detail. They may be found theoretically elaborated in *What Is Man?* practically applied in *The Mysterious Stranger* and the *Maxims of Pudd'nhead Wilson,* and artistically illustrated in *The Man Who Corrupted Hadleyburg* and innumerable other stories. They may be summed up as a soulless and blasting development of crude evolutionary materialism, as best manifested in the teachings of Robert Ingersoll. Man's freedom disappears, his best morality becomes enlightened selfishness, his soul is dissipated into thin air, his future life grows so dubious as to be disregarded, and the thought of death is tolerable only because life is not. The deity, in any sense of value to humanity, is quite disposed of; or, if he is left lurking in an odd corner of the universe, it is with such entire discredit that one can only recall the sarcasm of the witty Frenchman: "The highest compliment we can pay God is not to believe in him."

In all this perpetually recurrent fierce dissection of the divine and human one is constantly impressed by the vigor and independence of the thinking. The man makes his views for himself; or since, as he repeatedly insists, no one does this, at least he makes them over, rethinks them, gives them a cast, a touch that stamps them Mark Twain's and no one else's, and, as such, significant for the study of his character, if for nothing more.

On the other hand, if the thinking is fresh and vigorous, one is also impressed and distressed by its narrowness and dogmatism. Here again the man's individuality shows in ample, humorous recognition of his own weakness, or excess of strength. No one has ever admitted with more delightful candor the encroaching passion of a preconceived theory. I have got a philosophy of life, he says, and the rest of my days will be spent in patching it up and "in looking the other way when an imploring argument or a damaging fact approaches." Nevertheless, the impression of dogmatism remains, or, let us say better, of limitation. The thinking is acute, but does not go to the bottom of things. The fundamental, dissolving influence of the idealistic philosophy, for instance, is not once suggested or comprehended. This shows nowhere more fully than in the discussion of Christian Science. Everything is shrewd, apt, brilliant, but wholly on the surface.

The effect of the bitter and withering character of Mark's thought on his own life was much emphasized by the lack of the great and sure spiritual resources that are an unfailing refuge to some of us. He could not transport himself into the past. When he attempted it, he carried all the battles and problems of today along with him, as in *A Connecticut Yankee in King Arthur's Court*. He had not the historical feeling in its richest sense. Art also, in all its deeper manifestations, was hidden from him. He could not acquire a love for classical painting or music, and revenged himself for his lack of such enjoyment by railing at those who had it. Even nature did not touch great depths in him, because they were not there. He felt her more theatrical aspects—sunsets, ice-storms. Her energy stimulated a strange excitement in him, shown in Twitchell's account of his rapture over a mountain brook. I do not find that he felt the charm of lonely walks in country solitude.

It is on this lack of depth in thinking and feeling that I base my reluctance to class Mark with the greatest comic writers of the world. His thought was bitter because it was shallow; it did not strike deep enough to get the humble tolerance, the vast self-distrust, that should go with a dissolving vision of the foundations of the individual universe. His writing alternates from the violence of unmeaning laughter to the harshness of satire that has no laughter in it. In this he resembles Molière, whose Scapins are as far from thought as are his Tartuffes from gayety. And Mark's place is rather with the bitter satirists, Molière, Ben Jonson, Swift, than with the great, broad, sunshiny laughers, Lamb, Cervantes, and the golden comedy of Shakespeare.

Indeed, no one word indicates better the lack I mean in Mark than "sunshine." You may praise his work in many ways; but could anyone ever call it merry? He can give you at any time a riotous outburst of convulsive cachinnation. He cannot give you merriment, sunshine, pure and lasting joy. These are always the enduring elements of the highest comedy. They are not the essential characteristics of the work of Mark Twain.

But perhaps this is to consider too curiously. The total of Mark's work affords other elements of interest besides the analysis of speculative thought, or even of laughter. Above all, we Americans should appreciate how thoroughly American he is. To be sure, in the huge mixture of stocks and races that surrounds us, it seems absurd to pick out anything or anybody as typically American. Yet we do it. We all choose Franklin as the American of the eighteenth century and Lincoln as the American of the nineteenth. And most will agree that Mark was as American as either of these.

He was American in appearance. The thin, agile, mobile figure, with its undulating grace in superficial awkwardness, suggested worlds of humorous sensibility. The subtle, wrinkled face, under its rich shock of hair, first red, then snowy white, had endless possibilities of sympathetic response. It was a face that expressed, repressed, impressed every variety of emotion known to its owner.

He was American in all his defects and limitations. The large tolerance, cut short with a most definite end when it reached the bounds of its comprehension, was eminently American. The slight flavor of conceit, at least of self-complacent satisfaction, the pleasant and open desire to fill a place in the world, whether by mounting a platform at just the right moment or wearing staring white clothes in public places, we may call American with slight emphasis, as well as human.

But these weaknesses were intimately associated with a very American excellence, the supreme candor, the laughing frankness which recognized them always. Assuredly no human being ever more abounded in such candor than Mark Twain. He confessed at all times, with the amplitude of diction that was born with him, all his enjoyment, all his suffering, all his sin, all his hope, all his despair.

And he was American in another delightful thing, his quickness and readiness of sympathy, his singular gentleness and tenderness. He could lash out with his tongue and tear anything and anybody to pieces. He could not have done bodily harm to a fly, unless a larger pity called for it. He was supremely modest and simple in his demands upon others, supremely depreciative of the many things he did for them. "I wonder why they all go to so much trouble for me. I never go to any trouble for anybody." The quiet wistfulness of it, when you know him, brings tears.

Above all, he was American in his thorough democracy. He had a pitiful distrust of man; but his belief in men, all men, was as boundless as his love for them. Though he lived much with the rich and lofty, he was always perfectly at home with the simple and the poor, understood their thoughts, liked their ways, and made them feel that he had been simple and poor himself and might be so again.

He was not only democratic in feeling and spirit, he was democratic in authorship, both in theory and practice. Hundreds of authors have been obliged to write for the ignorant many, for the excellent reason that the cultivated few would not listen to them. Perhaps not one of these hundreds has so deliberately avowed his purpose of neglecting the few to address vast masses as Mark did. The long letter to Mr. Andrew Lang, in which he proclaims and explains this intention, is a curious document. Let others aim high, he says, let others exhaust themselves in restless and usually vain attempts to please fastidious critics. I write for the million, I want to please them, I know how to do it, I have done it. "I have never tried in even one single instance to help cultivate the cultivated classes. . . . I never had any ambition in that direction, but always hunted for bigger game—the masses. I have seldom deliberately tried to instruct them, but have done my best to entertain them. To simply amuse them would have satisfied my dearest ambition at any time."

It is hardly necessary to dwell upon the weak points in this theory. Whatever Mark, or anyone else, professes, it cannot be questioned that he prefers the approbation of the cultured few, when he can get it. Moreover, it may easily be maintained that the many in most cases take their taste from the few; and if this does not hold with a writer's contemporaries, it is unfailing with posterity. If a writer is to please the generations that follow him, he can do it only by securing the praise of those who by taste and cultivation are qualified to judge. In other words, if Mark's works endure, it will be because he appealed to the few as well as to the many.

However this may be, there can be no question that Mark reached the great democratic public of his own day and held it. To be sure, it is doubtful whether even he attained the full glory of what he and Stevenson agreed to call "submerged authorship," the vast acceptance of those who are wept over at lone midnight by the shop-girl and the serving-maid. But his best books—*Tom Sawyer, Huckle-berry Finn, Life on the Mississippi, The Prince and the Pauper*—may justly be said to belong to the literature of American democracy; and the travel books and many others are not far behind these.

In view of this fixed intention to appeal to the masses and to affect the masses, it becomes an essential part of the study of Mark's career and character to consider what his influence upon the masses was. He talked to them all his life, from the platform and from the printed page, with his sympathetic, human voice, his insinuating smile. What did this talk mean to them, how did it affect them, for good or for evil?

In the first place, beyond a doubt, enormously for good. Laughter in itself is an immense blessing to the weary soul—not a disputable blessing, like too much teaching and preaching, but a positive benefit. "Amusement is a good preparation for study and a good healer of fatigue after it," says Mark himself. And amusement he provided, in vast abundance, muscle-easing, spirit-easing.

Also, he did more than make men laugh, he made them think, on practical moral questions. He used his terrible weapon of satire to demolish meanness, greed, pettiness, dishonesty. He may have believed, in the abstract, that selfishness was the root of human action, but he scourged it in concrete cases with whips of scorpions. He may have believed, in the abstract, that men were unfit to govern themselves, but he threw scorn biting as vitriol on those who attempted to tyrannize over others.

Finally, Mark's admirers insist, and insist with justice, that he was a splendid agent in the overthrow of shams. He loved truth, sincerity, the simple recognition of facts as they stand, no matter how homely, and with all his soul he detested cant of all kinds. "His truth and his honor, his love of truth, and his love of honor, overflow all boundaries," says Mr. Birrell. "He has made the world better by his presence." From this point of view the praise was fully deserved.

Yet it is just here that we come upon the weakness. And if Mark made the world better, he also made it worse—at any rate, many individuals in it: for, with the wholesale destruction of shams, went, as so often, the destruction of reverence, "that angel of the world," as Shakespeare calls it. The trouble was that, when Mark had fairly got through with the shams, there was nothing left. One of his enthusiastic admirers compares him to Voltaire. The comparison is interesting and suggestive. Voltaire, too, was an enormous power in his day. He wrote for the multitude, so far as it was then possible to do it. He wielded splendid weapons of sarcasm and satire. He was always a destroyer of shams, smashed superstition and danced upon the remains of it. But Voltaire was essentially an optimist and believed in and enjoyed many things. He enjoyed literature, he enjoyed glory, he enjoyed living; above all, he believed in and enjoyed Voltaire. When Mark had stripped from life all the illusions that remained even to Voltaire, there was nothing left but a naked, ugly, hideous corpse, amiable only in that it was a corpse, or finally would be.

Mark himself frequently recognizes this charge of being a demolisher of reverence, and tries to rebut it. I never assault real reverence, he says. To pretend to revere things because others revere them, or say they do, to cherish established superstitions of art, or of morals, or of religion, is to betray and to deceive and to corrupt. But I never mock those things that I really revere myself. All other reverence is humbug. And one is driven to ask, what does he really revere, himself? His instinctive reverence for humanity in individual cases is doubtless delicate and exquisite; but in theory he tears the veil from God and man alike.

To illustrate I need only quote two deliberate and well-weighed utterances of his riper years. How could you wither man more terribly than in the following?

A myriad of men are born; they labor and sweat and struggle for bread; they squabble and scold and fight; they scramble for little mean advantages over each other; age creeps upon them; infirmities follow; shames and humiliations bring down their prides and their vanities; those they love are taken from them and the joy of life is turned to aching grief. The burden of pain, care, misery, grows heavier year by year; at length ambition is dead; pride is dead; vanity is dead; longing for release is in their place. It comes at last,—the only unpoisoned gift earth ever had for them,—and they vanish from a world where they were of no consequence, where they have achieved nothing, where they were a mistake and a failure and a foolishness; where they have left no sign that they have existed—a world which will lament them a day and forget them forever.

For those who thus envisaged man there used to be a refuge with God. Not so for Mark. Man deserves pity. God—at least, any God who might have been a refuge—deserves nothing but horror and contempt. The criticism is, to be sure, put into the mouth of Satan; but Satan would have been shocked at it: he was not so far advanced as Mark:—

A God who could make good children as easily as bad, yet preferred to make bad ones; who could have made every one of them happy, yet never made a single happy one ... who mouths justice and invented hell —mouths mercy and invented hell—mouths Golden Rules, and forgiveness multiplied by seventy times seven, and invented hell; who mouths morals to other people and has none himself; who frowns upon crimes, yet commits them all; who created man without invitation, then tries to shuffle the responsibility for man's acts upon man, instead of honorably placing it where it belongs, upon himself; and finally, with altogether divine obtuseness, invites this poor, abused slave to worship him.

Can it be considered that doctrines such as this are likely to be beneficial to the average ignorant reader of democracy, or that the preacher of them made the world wholly better by his presence? It is true that they do not appear so openly in Mark's best-known books, true that the practical manliness and generosity of Tom and Huck largely eclipse them. Yet the fierce pessimism of Pudd'nhead Wilson stares at the reader from the popular story of that name and from the equally popular *Following the Equator,* and even in the history of Tom and Huck the hand that slashes reverence is never far away.

The charge of evil influence fretted Mark as much as that of irreverence. He defends himself by denying that there is such a thing as personal influence from doctrines. Our happiness and unhappiness, he says, come from our temperament, not from our belief, which does not affect them in the slightest. This is, of course, gross exaggeration, as the story of Mark's own life shows again and again. One can perhaps best speak for one's self. It took years to shake off the withering blight which Mark's satire cast for me over the whole art of Europe. For years he spoiled for me some of the greatest sources of relief and joy. How many never shake off that blight at all! Again, in going back to him to write this portrait, I found the same portentous, shadowing darkness stealing over me that he spread before. I lived for ten years with the soul of Robert E. Lee, and it really made a little better man of me. Six months of Mark Twain made me a worse. I even caught his haunting exaggeration of profanity. And I am fifty-six years old and not very susceptible to infection. What can he not do to boys and girls of sixteen?

It is precisely his irresistible personal charm that makes his influence overwhelming. You hate Voltaire; you love Mark. In later years a lady called upon him to express her enthusiasm. She wanted to kiss his hand. Imagine the humor of the situation—for Mark. But he accepted it with perfect dignity and perfect tender seriousness. "How God must love you!" said the lady. "I hope so," answered Mark gently. After she had gone, he observed as gently and without a smile, "I guess she hasn't heard of our strained relations."

How could you help being overcome by such a man and disbelieving all he disbelieved? When he clasps your hand and lays his arm over your shoulder and whispers that life is a wretched, pitiable thing, and effort useless, and hope worthless, how are you to resist him?

So my final, total impression of Mark is desolating. If his admirers rebel, declare this utterly false, and insist that the final impression is laughter, they should remember that it is they, and especially Mark himself, who are perpetually urging us to take him seriously. Taken seriously, he is desolating. I cannot escape the image of a person groping in the dark, with his hands blindly stretched before him, ignorant of whence he comes and whither he goes, yet with it all suddenly bursting out into peals of laughter, which in such a situation, have the oddest and most disconcerting effect.

Yet, whatever view you take of him, if you live with him long, he possesses you and obsesses you; for he was a big man and he had a big heart.

1930

VERNON LOUIS PARRINGTON

AS WHITMAN contemplated the feeble literature purveyed by the worshipers of the genteel he asked with some irritation: "What is the reason in our time, our lands, that we see no fresh local courage, sanity, of our own—the Mississippi, stalwart Western men, real mental and physical facts, Southerners, etc., in the body of our literature?" That was in 1870 and the answer was at hand in the person of Mark Twain. Here at last was an authentic American—a native writer thinking his own thoughts, using his own eyes, speaking his own dialect—everything European fallen away, the last shred of feudal culture gone, local and western yet continental. A strange and uncouth figure in the eyes of Thomas Bailey Aldrich, yet the very embodiment of the turbulent frontier that had long been shaping a native psychology, and that now at last was turning eastward to Americanize the Atlantic seaboard. Yet in spite of a rare vein of humor, the outcropping of a rich and whimsical imagination, he made his way slowly to polite recognition. For years he was regarded by authoritative critics as little more than a buffoon, an extravagant fun-maker with a broad streak of western coarseness; and it was not till near the end, when he had long been an international figure, that the culture of the East accepted him. It was Howells then who pronounced him "the sole, the incomparable, the Lincoln of our literature . . . the very marrow of Americanism."

"The Backwash of the Frontier — Mark Twain," abridged from Main Currents in American Thought, *III, ©1930 by Harcourt, Brace, & World, Inc.; renewed 1958 by Vernon L. Parrington, Jr., Louise P. Tucker, and Elizabeth P. Thomas. Reprinted by permission of the publishers.*

Just as that judgment was at the time, it needs qualification now. The marrow of Americanism is not the same substance from generation to generation. The outer environing life of a people works itself slowly into the bones and brings about subtle changes. Mark Twain was indubitably an embodiment of three centuries of American experience—frontier centuries, decentralized, leveling, individualistic; but the Americanism that issued from them came to its flower and was quickly succeeded by another kind as the fields of experience were re-plowed by industrialism and sowed to a different grain. Mark Twain was the child of a frontier past—as Lincoln was, as the Gilded Age was—and the America of today could no more breed him than it could breed Lincoln, or Greeley, or Whitman; his Americanism was the reflection of an environment that is no longer ours, in the slack folk-ways of the frontier that we have outgrown. Child of the Southwest in its early boom days, he was cradled in profitless schemes and nourished on dreams of vast potential wealth. The frontier spirit was an effervescence in his blood and golden expectations flung their mirage over the drab reality. As a boy he took impress from a kindly, ignorant, slave-holding, Calvinistic village world, and he quitted the slattern village life to plunge into the picturesque traffic of the Mississippi in the boom days when every river pilot drove his boat full steam ahead. Then the Far West of silver mines and the Golden Gate took him in hand—a gambling, romantic, optimistic frontier, feverish with flush times, "a beggar's revel of potential millionaires without the price of a square meal." And finally this buoyant, irreverent adolescent was taken in hand by the Far East: by New England respectability in the persons of Olivia Langdon of Elmira, William Dean Howells of Cambridge, Twitchell and Warner of Hartford; and by New York in the persons of Carnegie and Gilder and Whitelaw Reid and Henry H. Rogers, to be made over into a man of the world.

Such were his origins and his schooling. All his life he remained a boy, with the imitativeness of youth, and yet with something deep within him that cherished its own integrity. Quick to take color from his environment and at home in crowds, he lived nevertheless in the solitude of his own heart. Acutely conscious of his rough western ways, he admired the culture of the Langdons and the refined art of Howells, and he wanted to be approved by them. A kinsman of Beriah Sellers, he delighted in the great barbecue and wanted to carve great portions for himself, to heap up his plate as others were doing. His reactions to experience were always emotional. He was not a Walt Whitman to penetrate curiously to the core of his own being and grow thence outwardly, content to wait till the world came round to him. He loved to make a splurge, to be talked of, to be in the public eye, to live on an ample scale; he accepted the world's standards and wished to be measured by them. It was characteristic of the frontier. Wanting other standards, the frontier measured success by obvious material standards. Its aggressive individualism was never spiritual or intellectual or cultural. So with all his heritage of generations of frontier individualism he never achieved an intellectual or spiritual unity, an untroubled conscious integrity, as Emerson did and Whitman did. He never was at home in the world of catholic thought, but all his life he suffered from the petty inhibitions of his origins. He could not throw off the frontier—its psychology and its morality were too deeply intertwined with his primitive self; and the result was a harassing inner conflict that left him maimed.

Yet with all his shortcomings—because of them indeed—Mark Twain is an immensely significant American document. He is a mirror reflecting the muddy crosscurrents of American life as the frontier spirit washed in, submerging the old aristocratic landmarks. To know Mark Twain is to know the strange and puzzling contradictions of the Gilded Age. With unconscious fidelity he reveals its crudity, its want of knowledge, discipline, historical perspective; its intellectual incapacity to deal with the complexities of a world passing through the twin revolutions of industrialism and science. And he reflects with equal fidelity certain other qualities that go far to redeem the meanness: a great creative power; an eager idealism, somewhat vague but still fine; a generous sympathy; a manly independence that strove to think honestly; a passionate hatred of wrong and injustice and an honest democratic respect for men as men. A significant if not an unsoiled or heroic document!

That in his later years an impassable gulf opened between Mark Twain and his generation, that the buoyant humorist of the seventies ripened into the bitter satirist of the nineties, is a matter that has been much remarked upon. The fact is clear enough but the explanation is not so clear. In part no doubt—as Van Wyck Brooks has pointed out—the change resulted from a thwarting of the creative artist by a disastrous surrender to the ideals of the Gilded Age; in part, also, it was the inevitable toll exacted by the passing years. A humane and generous spirit cannot long watch with indifference the motley human caravan hastening to eternity—cannot find food for laughter alone in the incredible meanness and folly of men cheating and quarreling in a wilderness of graves. Tenderness, chivalry, love of justice, are poor bucklers to withstand the blows of fate, and Mark Twain had little skill in defense. The humorist like the poet is sensitively responsive to life and the scars multiply fast. Endowed with a nature not unlike Swift's in its fierce rage at inhumanity, not unlike Sir Philip Sidney's in its romantic chivalry, he was not a stoic to endure with equanimity. He was foredoomed to suffer vicariously. The comment he wrote Howells in 1899 throws a white light on the man. "I have been reading the morning paper," he said. "I do it every morning—well knowing that I shall find in it the usual depravities and basenesses and hypocrisies and cruelties that make up civilization, and cause me to put in the rest of the day pleading for the damnation of the human race."

Yet granting so much, and granting also a morbid conscience that harassed him with self-condemnation—"What a man sees in the human race is merely himself in the deep and honest privacy of his own heart"—it still remains true that the bleakness of his later years was due in part, at least, to the insubstantial dwelling he chose to live in. The architects of the Gilded Age were jerry-builders, and Mark Twain found his jerry-built house a poor protection against the winter winds. It was perhaps not greatly his fault that he built so flimsily. He was too willing to be caught in the web of material things. He could not reach out for companionship with the great earth. Hamlin Garland in a bleak Dakota shack found help and comfort in the philosophy of Taine, but Mark Twain could not get outside his own skin. He could not break a path through the provincialism of his environment. He was held prisoner to his own thoughts and his only release was through the window of imagination. When harassed beyond endurance he sought release in writing that hid the evidence of his rebellion. What would Livy say, what would the American public say, if they knew he had come to deny all the tribal gods!

There is no more pathetic figure in American literature than Mark Twain, alone and solitary amid the blatant American crowd, living in a dreary wash of speeches and banquets, spinning the threads of a rebellious philosophy out of his own bowels, unaware of what others were spinning, regarding himself as a dangerous fellow and stowing away in his strong-box intellectual bombs that he thought too explosive for the Gilded Age to play with. In his intellectual isolation he could not take the measure of his speculations and he did not realize how common were such conclusions—that his own generation indeed, under the tutelage of the physical sciences, was fast drifting in the same direction, and that the clouds of pessimism were obscuring for many the brighter horizons of an earlier day. If he had known Henry Adams as intimately as he knew Henry H. Rogers, very likely his eyes would have been opened to many things that would have done him good. As it was he knew only that his speculations ran counter to the formal creed of his middle-class neighbors and friends. To deny the dogmas of the conventional orthodoxy and in the face of a smug optimism to assert a mechanistic pessimism, was an unpleasant business that he would have avoided if he could.

But he couldn't avoid it wholly, and in that fact is to be found the thread that runs through his later life, giving to it such unity and coherence as it possessed. It is this: here was a thoroughly honest mind, that hated all sham and quackery and humbug, and a singularly warm heart, that hated all wrong and cruelty and injustice; and this honest mind and chivalrous heart, deceived and led astray by the mass *mores,* espoused and defended such fragments of ideals, such bits of truth, as he came upon in his solitary brooding, until driven from one stronghold after another he came to doubt the adequacy of all strongholds and took refuge in a black pessimism— God is a malignant being, the universe is a machine, and man is a creature of determinism. It was a fierce and stark reaction from the emotionalism of the fifties—from Beecher's God of love and Whitman's religion of democracy. His earlier loyalty to half-gods had brought him at last to deny all the gods. And so a maimed giant, stumbling and uncertain, he made such way as he could; and his journeyings wrung from him many a fierce comment that his generation did not understand.

When the milk of western humor curdled in his veins, a Mark Twain emerged who was a puzzle to the Gilded Age. A humorist who was a good Republican and business man, the Gilded Age could understand; but a satirist who launched his shafts at sacred things—at evangelical religion, the Republican party, the government at Washington, the damned human race itself—it could not understand. The professional fun-maker had outgrown his audience. Expecting the familiar exaggeration, they accounted his bitterest sally a characteristic whimsy, and laughed when he commented bitterly on "this plodding sad pilgrimage, this pathetic drift between the eternities," or when he exclaimed, "Everything human is pathetic. The secret source of Humor is not joy but sorrow. There is no humor in heaven." But the significant thing is that in the end the tyrannizing *mores* did not conquer, they did not destroy him wholly; but such convictions as he had hewn from puzzling experience, however bleak or repellent they might be, he clung to firmly, desperately, and at last flung them in the face of the Gilded Age that had kept him prisoner.

The slow drift of Mark Twain's thought from humor to satire—it smacks of Philistinism to call it progress with its many false alarums and excursions and its huge frontier wastefulness—is plain enough to anyone who will take the trouble to chart his course. Roughly it falls into definite stages: the swaggering gayety of western youth in *Innocents Abroad* and *Roughing It*—the mood of flush times, down-grade with the brakes off; then a gay plunge into satire in *The Gilded Age;* then the West recalled in middle life—*Tom Sawyer, Life on the Mississippi, Huckleberry Finn*—living over again a youth that is gone; then an excursion into the Middle Ages—*The Prince and the Pauper* and *A Connecticut Yankee in King Arthur's Court*—a romantic flare-up of the democratic passions of the Enlightenment; then the search for the ideal in *Joan of Arc*—the dream of the perfect woman, the Domnei of James Branch Cabell; and finally *The Mysterious Stranger* and *What Is Man?*—a fierce satire of disillusion, the cry of an idealist who realizes at last how greatly he has been cheated by his dreams.

That he should have begun by burlesquing life was itself a broad sign of his frontier origins. Since the first crossing of the Allegheny Mountains a swaggering extravagance of speech had been the hallmark of the Westerner. In part this swagger was an unconscious defense-mechanism against the drabness of frontier life, and in part it was the spontaneous expression of new experiences in an untrammeled world, the spirit of wilderness-leveling. Its procreative source would seem to have been the Ohio River where the rough flatboatmen bequeathed the Mike Fink legend to literature; and it expanded in the huge Davy Crockett hoax—a hoax that would have tickled the ribs of Mark Twain had he traced its genesis and progress, as a colossal example of how the damned human race loves to be humbugged. It developed further in Gus Longstreet's *Georgia Scenes* with its grotesque Ransy Sniffle—sorriest of backwoods heroes, too mean-spirited to ruffle like Canebrake Davy; and in Joseph Baldwin's *Flush Times of Alabama and Mississippi,* with its greasy frontier blackguard, Colonel Simon Suggs.

This earliest backwoods humor had been done in realistic colors and bears the impress of authenticity. But the school that succeeded —John Phoenix, Artemus Ward, Petroleum V. Nasby—quickly conventionalized the technique, relying on burlesque, tall lying, distorted spelling, genial philosophy. The picaresque strain was softened and perverted by deliberate human-interest touches—a better case must be made out for the untutored children of nature. It was this humor that Mark Twain inherited, and he enriched it with a wealth dug from his own large and generous nature. An incorrigible idealist, as all great humorists must be, he recreated some of the earlier types, translating Colonel Simon Suggs into Colonel Sellers, and Ransy Sniffle into Huck Finn. It was a glorious transformation, but the result lacked something of the soiled reality of the earlier blackguards. Yet underneath his idealism was a generous deposit of the common mud of life. The spirit of Mike Fink was never far from Mark Twain. It haunted him like an evil genius, refusing to be exorcised by Olivia Clemens, and it found vent in sly literary sprees that begot offspring to be handed about furtively and chuckled over by the sons of Adam; but for the most part it was kept in strict subjection to the proprieties of Elmira and Hartford. . . .

He had opened [in *The Gilded Age*] another door to his genius and discovered the satirist. There lay the real Mark Twain. But the wares of the satirist were not in demand at the barbecue, so he closed the door and fell to purveying what the public wanted. *Tom Sawyer* was in part a malicious thrust at the Sunday School tale, and in part a whimsical pronouncement of the natural rights of the small boy. But it is in *Huckleberry Finn*—the one great picaresque tale of the frontier—that the western philosophy of Mark Twain, a philosophy that derives straight from the old naturistic school, crops out most sharply. It is a drama of the struggle between the individual and the village *mores,* set in a loose picturesque framework, and exemplifying the familiar thesis that the stuff of life springs strong and wholesome from the great common stock. Huck Finn is a child of nature who has lived close to the simple facts of life, unperverted by the tyrannies of the village that would make a good boy of him. He had got his schooling from the unfenced woods, from the great river that swept past him as he idly fished, from the folk-tales of negroes and poor whites, from queer adventures with Tom Sawyer; and from such experiences he had got a code of natural ethics. Then he found himself on the raft with Jim the runaway nigger, and his little pagan soul felt the stirrings of the problem of right and wrong. The village code and the natural code clashed and the conflict was terrifying. The village code warned him that hell yawned for one who helped a slave escape, and the human code warned him that betrayal was a blackguardly thing. With the fear of hell upon him he wrote to Miss Watson, and then his sense of the kindliness of Jim, the honest humanity under the black skin, rose up in fierce protest.

It was a close place. I took [the letter] up, and held it in my hands. I was a-trembling, because I'd got to decide, forever, betwixt two things, and I knowed it. I studied for a minute, sort of holding my breath, and then says to myself:

"All right, then, I'll *go* to hell"—and tore it up.

It was awful thoughts and awful words, but they was said. And I let them stay said; and never thought no more about reforming.

It was a triumph over the sacred tribal law of conformity—the assertion of the individual will in opposition to society—and it reveals the heart of Mark Twain's philosophy. The rebel Huck is no other than the rebel Mark Twain whose wrath was quick to flame up against the unrighteous customs and laws of caste. If men were only honest realists—that is, if they were men and not credulous fools—how quickly the stables might be cleansed and life become decent and humane. If only the good brains could be segregated and trained in a real "man-factory," the history of civilization might become something the angels need not weep over as they read it. It all comes back to an honest realism that in accepting fact will clear away the superstitious fogs in which men have floundered and suffered hitherto. The one sacred duty laid on every rational being is the duty of rebellion against sham—to deny the divinity of clothes, to thrust out quack kings and priests and lords, to refuse a witless loyalty to things. This creed of the rebel is written all through Mark Twain's later work, edging his satire and lending an Emersonian note to his individualism. . . .

It is in *A Connecticut Yankee in King Arthur's Court*—a curious medley, half philippic and half farce—that Mark Twain's passion for justice rises to white heat. The book has been grossly misunderstood. It is not an attack on chivalry—at least not primarily; it is rather an attack on thirteen centuries of reputed Christian civilization that under pretense of serving God has enslaved and despoiled the children of God. The keen satire is given point and edge by the long tragic perspective. Thirteen centuries heavy with sorrow and misery and frustrated hopes—a meaningless succession of foolish and futile generations, wandering in fogs of their own brewing, hag-ridden by superstitions, deceived and exploited by priest and noble, with no will to be free—here is a perspective to correct our callow enthusiasms, our revolutionary hopes! Why indeed should we expect men to possess the will to freedom, seeing that each generation is molded after the likeness of the past and none has been free? There is change, advance, and recession, but the story of the generations is no more than a "sad drift between the eternities," without purpose or meaning. In the brain of the Connecticut Yankee are secrets hidden from the children of King Arthur's time—a curious ability to use the forces of nature, some glimmerings of social justice. But to what purpose have Hartford and the nineteenth century used their knowledge? It is a world of slaves still as it was in King Arthur's day. The human animal cannot lift himself to heaven by his own bootstraps, and heaven will not stoop to lift him. For a "clammy atmosphere of reverence, respect, deference," it has substituted smartness, vulgarity, irreverence.

As one slips back and forth between the two worlds the satire takes on vaster perspectives; it cuts deep into all civilizations, for all alike are sham, all have issued from the conquest of man's native intelligence by his superstitions that are too useful to his masters to be dissipated. Clearly in Mark Twain's philosophy of history the hopes of the Enlightenment are fading. Passionately dedicated to the program of the Enlightenment—freedom, individuality, humanitarianism, democracy—his faith in reason, free will, progress, was burning low, in presence of the historical record. The determinism that lurked at the bottom of John Locke's psychology, unperceived by the French idealists, was revealing itself to Mark Twain and he was already trimming his sails to the chill winds blowing from the outer spaces of a mechanistic cosmos.

More immediately of course *A Connecticut Yankee* is an attack on the aristocratic romanticism of Sir Walter. There is little loitering in the great hall—except to comment on the coarseness of the knights and ladies—and much poking about in unlovely secret places where one comes upon a rare collection of human animals thrust away in the *oubliettes* or pigging together in mean huts. Few chapters in American literature are so noble in their *saeva indignatio,* so beautiful in their stern simplicity, as certain sketches of the king's progress through his realm—not a royal progress but a peasant's. There are no tears in them, they go far beyond that. The scene in the smallpox hut where the wife is glad her husband and daughters are dead—they are either in heaven or hell, it makes little difference, for they are no longer in Britain and so are happy; and the scene of the young mother hanged for stealing a piece of cloth of an ell's length or so, hanged that property in Britain might be safe—such pictures reveal how far he had traveled from the days of *Roughing It.* He was no longer a good Federalist-Whig concerned about exploitation and the safeguards of property. Although he voted the Republican ticket he made merry over the tariff and he frankly hated the dominant Republican property-consciousness. Like Lincoln he was for the man rather than the dollar when the rights of the two clashed. In these later years he was steadily drifting to the left, on the side of the social underling, sympathetic with those who do the work of the world. "He never went so far in socialism, as I have gone," said Howells, "if he went that way at all . . . but from the first he had a luminous vision of organized labor as the only present help for workingmen. . . . There was a time when I was afraid that his eyes were a little holden from the truth; but in the very last talk I heard from him I found that I was wrong, and that this great humorist was as great a humanist as ever."

It is good for an American to read *A Connecticut Yankee*—and *Joan of Arc* as well; for in them is a flame that sears and shrivels the mean property-consciousness which lays a blight on every civilization. In the peasant girl of Domrémy, the rapt mystic led by her Voices, Mark Twain found his ideal, the lily that bloomed out of the muck of medieval times; and as he contemplated her life and work he was lifted to the plane of worship. She had waged heroic warfare against the embattled lies and shams and treacheries of a sordid age, and that she should have died at the stake was inevitable. What other reward was to be expected from bishops and kings and suchlike spawn of the devil? Not till the people grow to manhood can any savior help them, and in that day they will need no savior but themselves. . . .

No Bayard ever did his devoir more knightly to his lady than Mark Twain to Joan, finding in the noble drama of her life the romance he had not found at Arthur's court. The knights of the Round Table were "but ghosts fighting in the fog," but Jeanne D'Arc was human and lovable and divine. And then the outlet through which his idealism had found release slowly closed in, and he was left alone with his comfortless speculations. What profits it to rail at the damned human race when man has about as much chance for happiness as a blind puppy in a sack? The bitter lot of humanity is due not to institutions alone or chiefly, it is a part of the mad plan of a bleak mechanical universe. For Mark Twain the solid earth was dissolving, leaving only a rack behind. It is futile to lament. A sympathetic heart, indeed, is the last and bitterest irony—for why weep over an evil exhalation! *"Life itself is only a vision, a dream. . . . Nothing exists save empty space—and you."* . . . So, like Cabell, Mark Twain asserts that man must build within and by letting his dreams flow out create for himself such shelter as he can against the chill of the eternal void. A flea on the epidermis of earth, nevertheless he is thought and thought is deathless. To such a conclusion did the buoyant youth of *Roughing It* arrive in the dun twilight years. *The Mysterious Stranger* is only *Tom Sawyer* retold in the midnight of his disillusion. What an ending for a child of the Gilded Age! In his youth a complete frontiersman, with vast potential wealth within him, he hewed and hacked at his genius, working the easiest veins, exploiting the most accessible resources, wasting much to cash in on a little. And when in the end the fool's gold turned to ashes in his mouth, as a frontiersman still he pursued his way alone, a solitary pioneer exploring the universe, seeking a homestead in an ironical cosmos, until overwhelmed by the intolerable solitude he made mock at all the gods. What a commentary on the Gilded Age!

1931

CONSTANCE ROURKE

IT IS A MISTAKE to look for the social critic—even *manqué*—in Mark Twain. In a sense the whole American comic tradition had been that of social criticism; but this had been instinctive and incomplete, and so it proved to be in Mark Twain. Like the earlier humorists he was rich in notation; from *Roughing It* to *The Gilded Age* he contrived to enclose the color of a period with a thousand details of manner, ambition, lingo. But as he turned toward the inclusive or penetrative view he was invariably blocked by some preposterous extravagance that seemed to mount visibly before his eyes. He was primarily a *raconteur,* with an "unequaled dramatic authority," as Howells called it. He was never the conscious artist, always the improviser. He had the garrulity and the inconsequence of the earlier comic story-tellers of the stage and tavern; and his comic sense was theirs almost without alteration.

He summed this up, as they had never done, in "How to Tell a Story." "The humorous story is American, the comic story is English, the witty story is French. The humorous story depends for its effect upon the *manner* of telling; the comic story and the witty story upon the matter." He had defined the native quality which he had made his own. His stories were oral and histrionic: manner was everything. "The humorous story is told gravely; the teller does his best to conceal the fact that he even dimly suspects that there is

"Facing West from California's Shores" from American Humor: A Study of the National Character, *©1931 by Harcourt, Brace, & World, Inc.; renewed 1959 by Alice D. Fore. Reprinted by permission of the publishers.*

anything funny about it." Here was the tradition for the mask, and for the long procession of dull-looking unlikely oracles. "The humorous story is strictly a work of art, high and delicate art, and only an artist can tell it; but no art is necessary in telling the comic and witty story, anybody can do it." Even the touch of national exaltation was familiar. But the art was hardly high and delicate, as Mark Twain proved by an illustration that was a vast oral practical joke, inducing the jolt of surprise through fright.

Born in the precise era when the American comic sense was coming to its first full expression, in 1835, Mark Twain had grown up in a small town on the Mississippi, in a region where the Crockett myth had taken shape and the tall tale had grown in stature. As a young printer he must have read newspapers of St. Louis and New Orleans that overflowed with the familiar comic narratives; he must have caught the full impact of that spirit of burlesque flourishing so broadly up and down the Great Valley. He could remember—as his tales of the Mississippi show—a crowd of wayward figures given to comedy, troupers, minstrels, itinerant preachers, wandering adventurers from the other side of the world: the variegated lot of migrants who could be seen anywhere in that period moving along the river or toward the plains.

In the compact encirclement of California with its renewal of pioneer life these elements flooded to the surface. Every essential aspect of his talent became articulate there; even his lecturing began in the West, the lecturing which was not truly lecturing at all but the old, spacious form of the theatrical monologue. His first two conspicuous efforts were hoaxes, in the vein which had become familiar thirty years before: after the gory "Dutch Nick Massacre" came "The Petrified Man," which wore the old air of mythology, and permitted only the slowest recognition of the fact that the fabulous relic had its thumb to its nose. The tale which first gave him nation-wide fame, "The Jumping Frog of Calaveras," called by Howells "one of his most stupendous inventions," was in fact a tall tale current in California before Mark Twain went there. His Colonel Sellers of later years seems to have been modeled on a slight sketch of the rascally Simon Suggs impersonating an opulent Colonel Witherspoon of Kentucky: Suggs too had soared like a kite as his fancy was loosed.

Again and again Mark Twain went back to that era of the river boatmen which had been a vanishing era in his youth. "I remember the annual procession of mighty rafts that used to glide by Hannibal when I was a boy—an acre or so of white, sweet-smelling boards in each raft. . . . I remember the rude ways and tremendous talk of their big crews, the ex-keelboatmen and their admiringly patterning successors." Some of the talk he reproduced in *Life on the Mississippi*. The Child of Calamity discoursed on the nutritiousness of Mississippi water, and declared that a man who had drunk it could grow corn in his stomach if he wanted to, and that as compared to the water of the Mississippi that of the Ohio was as nothing. "You look at the graveyards: that tells the tale. Trees won't grow worth shucks in a Cincinnati graveyard, but in a Sent Louis graveyard they grow upwards of eight hundred feet high. It's all on account of the water the people drunk before they laid up. A Cincinnati corpse don't richen the soil any."

That grotesque naturalism which had often approached ancient myth lived again briefly in such glimpses, here recalling—as in caricature—the legend of the buried Osiris, from whose body sprang the growing stalk of the corn. Once more through Mark Twain those antiphonal and primitive self-descriptions of the river boatmen were heard, which at their best gave a gross effect of poetic ritual. "Whoo-oop! bow your neck and spread, for the kingdom of sorrow's coming! Hold me down to the earth, for I don't feel my powers a-working! Whoo-oop! I'm a child of sin, *don't* let me get a start! Smoked glass, here, for all! Don't attempt to look at me with the naked eye, gentlemen! When I'm playful I use the meridians of longitude and the parallels of latitude for a seine and drag the Atlantic ocean for whales! I scratch my head with the lightning and purr myself to sleep with the thunder! When I'm cold, I bile the Gulf of Mexico and bathe in it; when I'm thirsty I reach up and suck a cloud dry like a sponge; when I range the earth hungry, famine follows in my tracks! Whoo-oop! Bow your neck and spread! I put my hand on the sun's face and make night on the earth; I bite a piece out of the moon and hurry the seasons; I shake myself and crumble the mountains! Contemplate me through leather—don't use the naked eye!"

Yankees had come to the Mississippi; Mark Twain could render the dialogue of two old Yankees bargaining over lots in the graveyard as well as any of the Yankee actors. He turned to the Yankee fable, shaping this anew in *Innocents Abroad,* which came into new and startling life, since the account was factual. The voyage of the *Quaker City* might even be called epochal, when the persistence is recalled with which the American had viewed himself in relation to the parent nations. Here at last, in this voyage of 1869, was the American exodus faintly foretold in earlier years by such creatures of the American fancy as Sam Slick and Sam Patch.

Turning to the European past an habitual and dedicated eye, Mark Twain found on this trip what a century-old and composite American, nurtured on the Yankee fables, could be expected to find, not only that its monuments were decayed, but that the European was a dastardly fellow for the most part, however the circumstance might arouse laughter in the genial newcomer. That the ancestral European had been cringing was proved by the attitude of famous artists of the past toward princely patrons. Even European topography was inferior. "It is popular to admire the Arno. It is a great historical creek with four feet of water in the channel and some scows floating around." Mark Twain followed the cult of newness like a thousand comic prophets and serious exhorters who had gone before him. He preferred copies of masterpieces to the originals because they were brighter. In a dozen forms he repeated the old assurance that American manners need not be mended. The American could do no fundamental wrong, because he was good. The American had always been good, in the native fancy; he had always been innocent in relation to the European.

For the first time on any substantial scale Mark Twain pictured the American within the European scene. He might have drawn this provincial and untutored traveler against the accumulated riches of ages, with satire and pathos. Perhaps the theme was too new for a truly spacious approach: Mark Twain was himself one of the innocent invaders, without distance, and without perspective. But he seems to have been hampered at the outset by the old formula. He took the trip and wrote the book as though off on an inevitable tangent, when he left California. He circled around the same theme in *A Tramp Abroad;* he repeated it broadside in *A Connecticut Yankee at King Arthur's Court.* "The boys all took a flier at the Holy Grail now and then." "You can't throw too much style into a miracle. It costs trouble, and work, and sometimes money; but it pays in the end." "No soap, no matches, no looking-glass—except a metal one, about as powerful as a pail of water!" Again he took pot-shots at art. He scorned tapestries. "As for proportions, even Raphael himself couldn't have blotched them more formidably, after all his practice on those nightmares they call his 'Celebrated Hampton Court Cartoons.' Raphael was a bird. We had several of his chromos: one was his 'Miraculous Draught of Fishes,' where he puts in a miracle of his own—puts three men into a canoe which wouldn't have held a dog without upsetting. I always admired to study R's art, it was so fresh and unconventional."

In the history of the old fable these three pieces by Mark Twain stand as monuments. As the last migration westward surged toward the Pacific another smaller and more transient movement had begun toward Europe. Even in the early '50's American travelers had begun to announce their judgments on the European scene, sometimes with an acrid humor, sometimes with rapture. A considerable number began a private "pillage of the past," bringing home copies of the masterpieces, marbles, tapestries. This migration had been halted by the Civil War, but it continued in force as soon as the War was over. By the end of the '60's the long and serious quest for European culture was well under way.

The reaction of Mark Twain to this phenomenon was foreordained, steeped as he was in the native tradition and entirely untutored. As a boy he might have seen it enacted on some small western stage, establishing the image. The basic fable grew rigid in his mind, as it had grown rigid for many other Americans. The new cultural migration was contrary to an established figment. So thousands uproariously laughed at the attack and upset and triumph of these latter-day versions, enjoying the rough and tumble the more because they too, many of them, had stood perplexed before masterpieces.

The talent of Mark Twain was consistently a pioneer talent. He showed touches of that abysmal melancholy which had led the boatmen of the Ohio and the Mississippi and the miners of California to drift into lonesome ditties; he struck out, as they did, into a wild burlesque. His obscenity was also of the pioneer piece. The sentimental strain that had been thinly interwoven with the rough tirades of the pioneer appeared in his *Joan of Arc*. Emotion he seldom revealed except in travesty; one of his favorite forms of comedy was to create the semblance of an emotional scene, beguiling the reader or hearer into the belief that this might be true, then puncturing it. Thin-skinned, so sensitive that he could hardly endure a joke turned against himself, he showed the quick revulsions, the neurotic explosive-ness, which for long had broken forth into a long-winded comic vein. His fun was often half perplexity, like a revolt from crowding circum-stance with no secure base anywhere: the theme of perplexity enters into his humor again and again, in his hoaxes, in his yarns, in *Inno-cents Abroad*. The savage note sounded, with the crackling weakness of the sardonic, like the inevitable outcome of the romantic mood gone wrong. A great repository, he caught the mood of disillusion-ment that followed the Civil War.

Mark Twain achieved scale, with the gusty breadth astir in the country as the Pacific was reached. *Huckleberry Finn* belongs within the scope of that epical impulse which had taken shape in the '50's: it has indeed a cumulative epical power as its main story branches off in innumerable directions under the stress of an opulent improvisa-tion. In this book Mark Twain gave to the great flood of the Missis-sippi its elementary place in the American experience, with the river as a dominating fantasy, with the small human figures as prototypes of those untethered wanderers who had appeared so often on the popular horizon. Even *The Gilded Age,* in spite of its divided pur-pose and shambling approaches, takes on something of the same scale, moving toward the encompassment of a period and a people. Mark Twain could never yield to the mode of satire in this book, but fell back continually upon the vast burlesque that had belonged to earlier years and was his heritage. Colonel Sellers was the epitome of those earlier strollers who were fakers and believers with unbounded confidence in fantasies—himself a fantasy of the first magnitude, embodying that perennial unworldliness which mixed so oddly with prosaic qualities in the native character. He too looked afresh at the world every morning and saw a new empire. If he was not the fabu-lous single figure toward which the national types had tended to merge, his stride was great; he was accepted throughout the nation as its own.

In the end Mark Twain's scope was nation-wide, because of the quality of his imagination, because of the regional elements which he freely mixed, the Yankee with the Californian, the backwoodsman with both of these. The wide reach may be unimportant for judgments of intrinsic quality, but its significance may be great among a people seeking the illusive goal of unity and the resting-place of a tradition. Through Mark Twain the American mind resumed many of its more careless and instinctive early patterns. The sense of legend was continued or restored, or at least the high comic legend again commanded the native fancy. The patterns might have been richer patterns; and Mark Twain's accent of a tense relationship with the older countries may seem deplorable; and much of his comic display has gone the transient way of comedy: he both gained and lost by a primitive vigor and by his adherence to the spoken and theatrical. But all these elements—the tense relationship with the rest—had long since joined in the making of the native character: to have abandoned or lost them would have meant an essential violence and disintegration.

1932

V. F. CALVERTON

WHILE WALT WHITMAN should be described as the first American poet, Mark Twain must be credited with being the first American prose writer of any importance. Both men were products of the frontier force, which . . . was not something that was confined to its own region; it was a force that swept abroad in the land; gathering energy from its source, it arose like an intellectual typhoon, spiralling this way and that as it acquired momentum, and scattering itself in a myriad fragments as it spread. Even Europe felt its impact. Chateaubriand responded to it, and wrote his novel, *Atala,* in reaction to its magnificence; the European masses responded in an intenser fashion, picked up their belongings, abandoned the countries of their birth, and, spellbound by the promise it held forth, were drawn by its suction into the centre of its influence. Few American writers of the day were not shaken by its presence. Only Whitman, however, in the East, . . . absorbed the fulness of its impact, and, overwhelmed by the magnitude of its power and the magnificence of its promise, transmuted it into poetic form. Twain, on the other hand, did not have to absorb its impact; its impact was part of his native heritage; it lived in his spiritual bloodstream. With him its influence was not derivative but fundamental. He expressed it in his person, exhaled it in his words, voiced it in his philosophy. In short, he became its dynamic symbol in literature.

"The Frontier Force," from The Liberation of American Literature *(New York: Charles Scribner's Sons, 1932), pp. 319-28. Reprinted by permission of the publishers.*

Beginning as a pure frontier product, reeling off in his prose all the spontaneity of that region, its hilarious gaieties and irresponsible enthusiasms, he ended in the East as a convinced pessimist and dyspeptic philosopher not less desperate in his despairs than Leopardi. In a way, he was the Charlie Chaplin of American literature. Ever eager, especially in his latter days, to be a Hamlet, he was forced to remain a Falstaff. There were, thus, two Mark Twains and not one, and those who have tried to interpret the contradictions in his character have tripped up very often by their failure to see that this dichotomy in his personality had as much to do with the environment as with the immediate conflict of his soul. The youthful Mark Twain, the Mark Twain of the West, the avatar of the frontier, who loved pilots, and miners, and the common run of people, who felt himself part of the region he described, and who in humorous form gave life to those people and to that region—that Mark Twain was an optimist, a lover of life, a devotee of the soil and of the country which he cherished with such childish pride. The other Mark Twain, the older Mark Twain, the Mark Twain of the East, the Mark Twain who was successful, had lost the optimism and zest, had lost the faith of his youth. The America that he saw growing up about him was not the America of his dream. The promise of the frontier had begun to grow stale. The era of the trusty boatmen had vanished. Industry had overcome the nation, and subdued the land and those who had once controlled it. Before he wrote *What Is Man* and *The Mysterious Stranger,* America had already "snatched the Philippines," as he remarked in an article, and "stained the flag." Indeed, there was little left of the America which he once loved. Nothing expressed his disillusionment more completely than his conversation with Tchaikoffsky, the Russian revolutionist, who appealed to him to address a mass meeting:

I told him what I believed to be true: that our Christianity which we have always been so proud of—not to say so vain of—is now nothing but a shell, a sham, a hypocrisy; that we have lost our ancient sympathy with oppressed peoples struggling for life and liberty; that when we are not coldly indifferent to such things we sneer at them, and that the sneer is about the only expression the newspapers and the nation deal in with regard to such things; that his mass meeting would not be attended by people entitled to call themselves representative Americans, even if they may call themselves Americans at all; that his audiences will be composed of foreigners who have suffered so recently that they have not yet had time to become Americanized and have their hearts turned to stones in their breasts; that these audiences will be drawn from the ranks of the poor, not those of the rich; that they will give and give freely, but they will give from their poverty and the money result will not be large. I said that when our windy and flamboyant President conceived the idea a year ago of advertising himself to the world as the New Angel of Peace, and set himself the task of bringing about the peace between Russia and Japan and had the misfortune to accomplish his misbegotten purpose, no one in all this nation except Doctor Seaman and myself uttered a public protest against this folly of follies. That at that time I believed that that fatal peace had postponed the Russian nation's imminent liberation from its age-long chains indefinitely—probably for centuries; that I believed at that time that Roosevelt had given the Russian revolution its death-blow and that I am of that opinion yet.

Carking psychological conflicts and heart-shaking tragedies too had come upon Twain, and embittered his personal outlook. To have remained the same man, then, to have retained the same philosophy, through all those vicissitudes of change, would have been impossible for any but the most insensitive personality.

The Mark Twain we are interested in, however, the Mark Twain who is important to American literature, is the early Mark Twain, the Mark Twain who was the author of *Innocents Abroad, The Gilded Age,* and *Huckleberry Finn,* and not the older Mark Twain, the Mark Twain who was the author *What Is Man* and *The Mysterious Stranger. What Is Man,* for example, voicing the disenchantment of spirit that overcame him toward the end of his life, is a revealing philosophic exercise but nothing more. Its literary significance is infinitesimal. *Huckleberry Finn,* on the other hand, expressing the philosophy of his earlier life, and carrying within it the seeds of his own experience and the spirit of his native environment, is a significant fiction. Indeed, its literary importance has increased instead of decreased with the years. Representing the younger Mark Twain who meant more to American literature than the older, and representing the America which at that time was the most American, *Huckleberry Finn* stands out not only as Twain's best work but also as one of the few *American* classics.

While Mark Twain had less difficulty in attaining recognition in America than Walt Whitman, it was not until the twentieth century, when the colonial complex broke down in the rising tide of nationalistic impulse, that he became appreciated for what he really was. In the nineteenth century he was viewed as a "funny man," a superb humorist, a literary burlesquer. Acclaimed far and wide for his fun-making proclivities, for his skill in evoking laughter, he was seldom considered in a serious vein, as an artistic genius or literary force. When he mounted a platform, people began to laugh before he started to speak. Nothing that he said was taken seriously. Although William Dean Howells, possibly because of his own mid-western rearing, early appreciated the significance of Twain's literary genius, there were few others in the East who esteemed it at its true value. It was Howells, in fact, who said to Twain: "You have already written the longed-for Great American Romance, though nobody seems to know it—and you will do it again. *What stupendous fame you would have if you were only a foreigner!*" Henry L. Mencken described excellently Twain's fate in the nineteenth century when he observed that "with only his books to recommend him, (Twain) would probably have passed into obscurity in middle age; it was in the character of a public entertainer, not unrelated to Coxey, Dr. Mary Walker and Citizen George Francis Train, that he wooed and won the country. The official criticism of the land denied him any solid literary virtue to the day of his death." Only in the twentieth century was Twain's fame esteemed at its real worth. Van Wyck Brooks found Twain significant enough to write one of his best books about him: *The Ordeal of Mark Twain,* and Waldo Frank was moved to call Huckleberry Finn "the American epic hero," and to declare that "the soul of Mark Twain was great."

The Americanness of Twain was scorned in the nineteenth century just as that of Whitman was scorned. In the case of Twain there was no sexual candor to be feared or shunned, for, as Twain has recorded, his wife edited every line he wrote and removed from his work every passage that bordered on the salacious. The main objection to his work was that it was not in the English tradition. It was American in its humor, American in its slang idiom, American in its frontier spirit. In every way it violated the canons of good taste which England had established. It hugged close to the soil of its native land instead of to that of the mother country. It expressed the barbarous, inchoate, spontaneous spirit of the American people instead of the refined, elegant, dignified spirit of the English literary code.

Innocents Abroad, which sold over thirty-one thousand copies within the first six months of its publication, was, perhaps, the first *American* work of prose to appear in this country. Few books have voiced the spirit of the frontier, which represented at that time the only part of the country where the colonial complex did not predominate, as clearly and as challengingly as *Innocents Abroad.* Like Whitman, Twain sensed in democracy, democracy in the frontier form, the distinguished characteristic of America. But it was not democracy that stopped at the ballot. It was democracy that ran through the whole course of life, permeating economics as well as politics, art as well as science. When he went abroad he poked fun at European art and culture, satirized the masters, preferred copies of the masterpieces to the originals, and sneered at the fake idolatry of the old which dominated European civilization. He preferred the new, the American. And yet his contempt was not based on the sheer prejudice of the barbarian. His opposition to European art was founded upon his democratic bias. "We visited the Louvre," he wrote, " . . . and looked at its miles of paintings by the old masters. Some of them were beautiful, but at the same time they carried such evidences about them of the cringing spirit of those great men that we found small pleasure in examining them. Their nauseous adulation of princely patrons was more prominent to me and chained my attention more surely than the charms of color and expression which are claimed to be in the pictures. Gratitude for kindness is well, but it seems to me that some of those artists carried it so far that it ceased to be gratitude, and became worship. If there is a plausible excuse for the worship of men, then by all means let us forgive Rubens and his brethren." In another place, he continued in the same vein but with added bitterness. "And who painted these things? Why Titian, Tintoretto, Paul Veronese, Raphael—none other than the world's idols, the old masters."

"Andrea del Sarto glorified his princes in pictures that must save them forever from the oblivion they merited, and they let him starve. Served him right. Raphael pictured such infernal villains as Catherine and Marie de Medici seated in heaven and conversing familiarly with the Virgin Mary and the angels (to say nothing of higher personages), and yet my friends abuse me because I am a little prejudiced against the old masters—because I fail sometimes to see the beauty that is in their productions. I cannot help but see it, now and then, but I keep protesting against the grovelling spirit that could persuade those masters to prostitute their noble talents to the adulation of such monsters as the French, Venetian, and Florentine princes of two and three hundred years ago, all the same . . .

"I am told that the old masters had to do these shameful things for bread, the princes and potentates being the only patrons of art. If a grandly gifted man may drag his pride and his manhood in the dirt for bread rather than starve with the nobility that is in him untainted, the excuse is a valid one. It would excuse theft in Washingtons and Wellingtons, and unchastity in women as well."

What are these moral judgments of art but the pure product of the ideology of the frontier? The frontier with its petty bourgeois psychology believed in the free man, the freedom of the individual man from the tyranny of aristocrats as well as plutocrats. It believed in itself, as we have said, it believed in its own principles and potentialities. It did not want to be tied on to Europe. It refused to be overawed by an adoration of the old. It was at one with Mark Twain in his remarks upon European people and places; it shared his dislike for tapestries and his scorn for venerated sites and vistas. Its spirit spoke in Twain's carping description of the Arno as "a great historical creek with four feet of water in the channel and some scows floating around." Only an American, too, could have made Twain's famous reflection upon the Grand Duomo of Florence—"a vast pile that has been sapping the purses of her citizens for five hundred years, and is not nearly finished yet."

Innocents Abroad, then, was not the result of a sudden outburst of distemper by an American who was at once irritated and amused by the European things he saw. It was an individual outgrowth of a whole social philosophy. Back in earlier days, when he was associated with *The Californian,* the literary journal which Charles Henry Webb had established and with which Bret Harte was connected for a time, Twain had begun the work which later found more coherent form in *Innocents Abroad.* In his first pieces in *The Californian,* he had started making fun of art, had ridiculed the opera, and had even gone so far as to satirize science. And, above everything else, in all his writing there he had early revealed his preference for the language of the people to the language of the dictionary. Indeed, in true frontier

style, he had shown, in an imaginary discussion with a miner, the folly
and futility of dictionary-diction as an instrument of human com-
munication.

In *The Gilded Age,* which Twain wrote in collaboration with
Warner, he turned his attention immediately to America, and
launched a vigorous attack upon the political corruption in the nation.
Twain's picture of how Congress was controlled, and how votes were
bought and sold, combined with his ironic preface celebrating the
achievements of our "ideal commonwealth," made his volume into
one of the most challenging of the time. From beginning to end it
stung with satire. "We send many missionaries to lift up the benighted
races of other lands," the authors dryly observed, "how much cheaper
and better it would be if those people could only come here and drink
of our civilization at its fountain-head." *The Gilded Age* was one of
the earliest and best embodiments of the petty bourgeois philosophy of
the frontiersman in his struggle against the corrupting influence of the
class in power. In fact, *The Gilded Age* was the precursor of those
many attacks upon the exercise of power, which were to be made by
the novelists and politicians of later generations. It anticipated in its
way the novels of Frank Norris and Herbert Quick and the political
protests of William Jennings Bryan and Robert M. La Follette. Its
humor was of that biting, realistic variety which stabbed at the same
time that it entertained. In *The Gilded Age* appeared evidences of
that bitterness which later on was to dominate Twain's philosophy.
The situation which Twain attacked in that book, however, was
soon to become hopeless of cure, for within little more than a decade
the West was to be controlled by the railroads and enslaved by the
financial forces of the East.

At no time, except perhaps when he became so obsequious over
the Oxford degree that was bestowed upon him, did Twain desert his
forthright petty bourgeois point of view; at no time did he "sell out"
his philosophy to the upper bourgeoisie of the East. In the twentieth
century, if he had lived until our day, it is even likely that he might
have joined in with Dreiser and taken a communistic stand. But living when he did, when all of America, even its labor movement,
was dominated by a petty bourgeois instead of a proletarian psychology, the petty bourgeois position was the most advanced one of his
type could take. To such as Twain it often seemed the stand of the

revolutionary. In *Roughing It* he sarcastically condemned the American practice of not mining "the silver ourselves by the sweat of our brows and the labor of our hands, but to *sell* the ledges to the dull slaves of toil and let them do the mining." He was always enthusiastic about the French Revolution, and even defended the Terror without hesitation. His condemnation in *Life on the Mississippi* of the influence of Sir Walter Scott upon the South was of the same petty bourgeois strain:

> Then comes Sir Walter Scott with his enchantments, and by his single might checks this wave of progress, and even turns it back; sets the world in love with dreams and phantoms; with decayed and degraded systems of government; with the silliness and emptiness, sham grandeurs, and sham chivalries of a brainless and worthless long vanished society.

Twain at least sought to make his philosophy inclusive. He tied up his art with his politics. "I have never tried in even one single instance to help cultivate the cultivated classes," he wrote in defense of his treatment of the English upper classes in *A Yankee at The Court of King Arthur,* "I was not equipped for it, either by native gifts or training. And I never had any ambition in that direction, but always hunted for bigger game—the masses." Even in *Huckleberry Finn,* the virtues extolled are those of the petty bourgeois frontiersman. Huck is a western lad, embodying the independent, dare-devil spirit of the region, a rapscallion type contemptuous of rules and regulations, scornful of Sunday-school and even of civilization— scornful of everything but himself and what he regards as right. Huck, an epic embodiment of the frontier in knee-pants, sticks by himself in defiance of what others think, in defiance even of institutions and all the moral paraphernalia of the conventional world.

1933

GRANVILLE HICKS

WHEN *The Innocents Abroad* appeared in 1869, sweeping into such popular favor as few American books had enjoyed, Samuel Clemens could scarcely ignore his destiny: however often he might try to rebel, he was committed to a literary career. *The Innocents Abroad,* taken together with the stories and sketches he had previously written, made it easy to identify the tradition with which Mark Twain was, by temperament, experience, and literary aims, identified. Unlike Harte, whose earliest impressions, whose education, whose impulse to write had come in the East, he was part of the Southwestern frontier, and he naturally expressed himself in the forms that that frontier had evolved. The tall story, the expletive-studded rhetoric, and the practical joke of the Mississippi deck-hand, or the transcontinental stage-driver, or the Nevada miner were familiar to his ear and satisfying to his sense of humor. In stories and songs, handed on by word of mouth, persistently modified, often adapted to suit historical figures, the Southwest had given birth to a rich folklore. Some of this lore had found its way into print in *The Autobiography of David Crockett,* Baldwin's *Flush Times of Alabama and Mississippi,* Longstreet's *Georgia Scenes,* and similar works. Its spirit and many of its mannerisms entered into the lectures and books of Petroleum Nasby, Josh Billings, and Artemus Ward. At

"A Banjo on My Knee," from The Great Tradition *(New York: The Macmillan Co., 1933), pp. 38-49. Reprinted by permission of the publishers.*

its worst it relied on purely verbal humor and forced exaggeration; at its best it derived from sharp observation and expressed the courage and buoyancy of self-reliant adventurers.

The honesty of *The Innocents Abroad,* its informality, its freedom from affected humility—everything, in short, that distinguishes it from the travel books of conventionally educated tourists—may be attributed to the frontier spirit. On the other hand, the book's weaknesses are the weaknesses of the tradition from which it stemmed. The frontier was, obviously, provincial, and it is provincialism that vitiates *Innocents Abroad.* Much as Mark Twain might boast of his indifference to the guide-books and his refusal to make their standards his standards, he was very much at their mercy, and his record suggests that, like the typical tourist, he was confused, a little frightened, and more than a little unhappy. For any sympathetic penetration of the spirit of other races he was quite unprepared, and his soul rendered homage most readily to the kind of spectacle that could be interpreted in statistical terms. Long before the journey was over his supply of quips ran low, for they were less the natural response of a fresh and unspoiled spectator than the stock-in-trade of the newspaper funny man; and his pathetic recourse, time after time, to remarks about dirt or relics or guide-books, betrays the inadequacy of his equipment for the experiences he was passing through. The latter part of the book, with its mixture of swaggering skepticism and senseless credulity, its pumped-up piety for home consumption, and its monotonous narrative so eloquent of the writer's weariness, must have revealed, even to Mark Twain himself, that the literary life made greater demands upon intellect and imagination than, at that point, he could conceivably measure up to.

The frontier tradition, as all this suggests, could offer a writer no more than a start; but it was a good start, a start in the right direction. At the basis of western humor lay a gift for accurate observation and shrewd characterization—for realism, in other words. Longstreet defended the minuteness of detail in *Georgia Scenes,* and Crockett spoke of "the many small and, as I fear, uninteresting circumstances" of his narrative. They need not have apologized; every frontier tale, no matter how tall, relied on just such concrete observations. This realism not only gave point to exaggerations; it appealed in its own right to men whose lives depended on their ability to use their eyes. And Mark Twain was capable of it, as the early stories show even more fully than *Innocents Abroad*. Here was a virtue worth cultivating, a quality that could enrich our literature. But before the primitive realism of the frontier could take literary shape, even at the hands of a Mark Twain, a long course of discipline was necessary.

He seems to have known that something was wrong, and he was not unwilling to accept the guidance of those who might be able to remedy his deficiencies. Indeed, he was, if anything, too submissive for his own good, for his humility led him to believe, however uneasily, in the standards of eastern gentility. In Honolulu Anson Burlingame had prescribed "refinement of association" and "companionship among men of superior intellect and character": "Never affiliate with inferiors; always climb." Circumstances helped Mark Twain to obey the admonition. As if it were not enough for him to attach himself to Henry Ward Beecher, Charles Dudley Warner, and Thomas Bailey Aldrich, he became engaged to Olivia Langdon, a former invalid and a paragon of the accepted virtues of the Victorian era in eastern America, who celebrated their betrothal by helping him to prune away the crudities of *Innocents Abroad*. By the time he had settled in Hartford, tasted the joys of respectable wealth, and won recognition in England as well as at home, he had delivered himself into the hands of the genteel tradition. It could not suppress his inborn genius, but neither could it develop that genius, shape it, summon forth all its potentialities, conduct it to a leval on which it could richly function. Could the genteel writers encourage Mark Twain's realism when they were themselves both less courageous and less keen-sighted than he? Could they help him to understand American life when they persistently ignored the forces that were shaping it? No, they could correct his grammar and chasten his exuberance, but they could give him no inkling of what it might mean, to a man with his talents and his experience, to be an American author in the Gilded Age.

Because there was so little in his own preparation, and so little in the intellectual life of his time, to guide him, Mark Twain could never satisfy himself that a literary career adequately expressed the powers that he felt within him. It is no wonder, then, that he was restless, considered a variety of vocations, speculated constantly, undertook scores of books that he never finished, and prosecuted in most dilatory fashion the writing of such books as, often under financial pressure, he deigned to complete. It is no wonder that, as he more than once confessed, the joys of literature never equaled the pride he had felt when he mastered the shoals and windings of the Mississippi. Yet he did continue to write. After *Innocents Abroad* came *Roughing It,* a better book and a stronger testimony to the potentialities of frontier realism. The year after its publication, that is, in 1873, he wrote *The Gilded Age* with Charley Dudley Warner —a strange collaboration with strange results. And then, three years later, came *Tom Sawyer,* in which he showed the possibilities, good and bad, of a return to the scene of his childhood. Thrice in the course of the next twenty years he returned to the Mississippi Valley for material—in *Huckleberry Finn, Life on the Mississippi,* and *Pudd'nhead Wilson.* The four books of Missouri life, together with his principal piece of satire, *A Connecticut Yankee in King Arthur's Court,* and his major adventure in romanticism, *Joan of Arc,* are his chief contribution to American literature.

He continued to write, and we should be considerably the poorer if he had failed to do so. But it is doubtful if he ever achieved all that he had given promise of doing or really deserved the high rank that was so readily accorded him. There is, it is at least clear, no one of his books that is wholly satisfactory, no one of his books that is quite so good as, while reading the opening chapters, one expects it to be. *Tom Sawyer,* at the outset, is not merely a glamorous evocation of the romance that boyish enthusiasm lends to life; it is a fine and subtle portrayal of the Missouri frontier. Yet it ends in the tawdry melodrama of conventional juvenile fiction. In the same way in *Huckleberry Finn,* after moving passages that celebrate the joys of loafing on a gently floating raft, after the swift narrative of the Shepherdson-Grangerford feud and the shooting of Boggs, after the robust humor of the episode of the Royal Nonesuch, comes the tedious and labored account of the rescue of Jim. We need not prolong the list, but who can forget the painfulness of the latter chapters of *Life on the Mississippi,* those commonplace notes on river towns, after the glorious record that, in the first part of the book, the author gives of his own river days? In book after book, after the most brilliant kind of beginning, Mark Twain crawls with undisguised weariness of soul to the closing page.

The imagination that can seize, as his so often and so effectively did, upon some trifling incident and catch its implications, is not necessarily an imagination equipped for the sustained development of a major theme. The literary attributes that lend brilliance to a descriptive paragraph or a brief narrative are not always able to maintain an entire novel upon a consistently high level. For what Mark Twain wanted to do, for the creation of a record of American life, for the expression of his own personality and experience, something was lacking. He had seen enough, and he could write, when he was at his best, much more eloquently than those contemporaries who rebuked him for his barbarism. But the imaginative power that sees hidden relations among the fragments observation reveals, that takes the fragments and shapes them into a whole, that builds toward some towering climax—that power was denied him.

Like Bret Harte and like the majority of his contemporaries, Mark Twain made no attempt to come to terms with the world in which he lived. Except *The Gilded Age*—and the exception is important enough to be given detailed consideration later, though it merely confirms our conclusions—not one of his major fictions concerns itself with the movements and events of American life in the latter half of the nineteenth century. For four of his books he made use, as has already been noted, of materials that belonged to his frontier childhood. In his principal satire he struck out against the evils of feudalism, evils that either had disappeared or were far less important than the sins of American industrialism. To disclose most fully the romantic and idealistic side of his nature, he told the story of the martyred Joan.

Yet it will not be maintained that Samuel Clemens was a recluse, sheltered from the hopes and fears of his contemporaries. He was, on the contrary, in the thick of current economic and political developments, participating as an investor in mechanical progress, occasionally raising his voice in presidential campaigns, making friends with Napoleons of finance as readily as with fellow-authors. The expansiveness that sent him seeking after fortune, the boundless optimism with which he sought it—these were of the essence of the American character in those giddy days. He knew what was happening in contemporary America, and he felt all that Americans were feeling; and yet for purposes of literature he looked back on a different kind of life. Life was so much simpler in the Missouri of the forties and fifties, and in a way so much finer. If there was poverty, no one realized it. If there was a caste system, there was no bitter competition on a pecuniary level. If there were the fearful dogmas of Presbyterianism, there were also the games of youth and the dances, songs, and stories. If there were crudity and violence in the village, there was beauty in the woods and on the river. And it was a world Mark Twain knew and understood and in which he had once had a recognized place. When he returned to that world, he escaped from the strain of conventional society, from the fear of treachery, from the everlasting demand for money. So strong was the temptation that it could have been resisted only if he had mastered, for literary purposes, the complex life of industrial America as he had mastered life on the Mississippi. If he had understood, if he had been at home in, the world of his own social interests, his own investments, his own ambitions, he might have written about it. The frontier humorist and realist might have become a great social novelist.

If we point out what Mark Twain might have become, it is neither to disparage the work he actually did nor to pass moral judgment upon him. But there is significance in our analysis because it was only by developing as a realist that he could develop at all. If such development was impossible, as it probably was, our regret must be the keener. For the alternative was stagnation. In minor ways Mark Twain made progress, but he never transcended the limitations of his tradition. And insofar as he failed to cultivate the realistic elements in that tradition, he was forced to rely on the humorous elements. He was, and knew he was, merely an entertainer.

As an entertainer he could scarcely be expected to regard the literary life as a serious enterprise. It is no wonder that he filled *Innocents Abroad* with surefire gags; that is what, so far as he knew, he was supposed to do. It is no wonder that he catered in *Tom Sawyer* to as wide a variety of tastes as possible, that he introduced in *Huckleberry Finn* devices the success of which he had tested. That he allowed burlesque to weaken the satire of the *Connecticut Yankee*. At times he willingly accepted the role of entertainer, but there were moments when he conceived of playing a nobler part. One night during the lecture tour he made with George W. Cable, he turned to his companion and said, "Oh, Cable, I am demeaning myself. I am allowing myself to be a mere buffoon. It's ghastly. I can't endure it any longer." Are we to suppose that he never recognized the resemblance between his functions as lecturer and his functions as author?

This awareness, however vague, of his failure to fulfil himself was expressed with peculiar force in his bitter condemnation of his lack of independence. Self-reliance, the great frontier virtue, always stood at the top of Mark Twain's hierarchy of values. When he wrote *Innocents Abroad,* the "cringing spirit" of the great painters seemed to him utterly contemptible: "Their nauseous adulation of princely patrons was more prominent to me and chained my attention more surely than the charms of color and expression which are claimed to be in the pictures." But a few years later, declaring that the river pilot was "the only unfettered and entirely independent human being that ever lived in the earth," he added this comment: "Writers of all kinds are manacled servants of the public. We write frankly and fearlessly, but then we 'modify' before we print." This became, indeed, a favorite theme in conversations and private letters. "For seven years," he said, "I have suppressed a book which my conscience tells me I ought to publish," and added, with bitter irony, "Yes, even *I* am dishonest." In an article, written in 1885 but first published in his autobiography, he listed "certain sweet-smelling sugar-coated lies current in the world," first of all the belief "that there is such a thing in the world as independence: independence of thought, independence of opinion, independence of action."

Obviously there is some connection between his shame at his lack of independence and his recognition of his status as a writer, and both of these facts have something to do with his growing pessimism. When he began life he shared the optimism of the time and place in which he was born, the frontiersman's confidence that he can enforce his will upon the surrounding world. Neither the loss of his position as river pilot nor his failure to make a fortune in Nevada seems to have diminished his hopes. Only after success of a kind had come to him, after he had seen much of life in the Gilded Age, did doubt and despair overtake him. And the character of his pessimism indicates something of its origin. The naive joy that the sophomoric philosopher of *What Is Man?* takes in attacking the conception of freedom of the will is more closely related to the need for self-justification than it is to any fundamental understanding of determinism. The insistence on the chaotic meaninglessness of life perfectly reflects the author's bewilderment. "Byron despised the race," he said, "because he despised himself. I feel as Byron did, and for the same reason." The faith the frontier had nurtured was being destroyed, and its destruction was all the more rapid because the frontier itself was disappearing. By a different process Mark Twain learned the lesson that hunger and homelessness were teaching so many settlers in the West: the era of pioneer self-reliance had ended. The world that had given him birth and had nurtured him—not only as a man but also as a writer—was dying, and in the world that was taking its place neither the man nor the writer could feel at home.

The buoyant spirit that the frontier had created could not be wholly subdued; to the end jovial moods alternated with the hours of fury and despair, and the cynic of Stormfield could be transformed into the beaming idol of public gatherings. But, much as he might relish the approval of his contemporaries and expand in its warmth, at heart he knew what it was worth. When, at the end of his life, a friend said that he must be pleased with the constant evidences of popular affection, he gently answered, "Yes, they have liked to be amused." He had amused a nation; what more had he done? A good deal more, of course, but a good deal less than, all things considered, he had given promise of doing.

1937

WALTER BLAIR

IT IS IMPOSSIBLE, of course, to discover any author who furnishes a better climax to a consideration of American humor than Mark Twain. It would also be difficult to discover any author who furnishes better opportunities for a summary. For Mark Twain was trained as a writer in the old Southwest during the days of the flowering of its humor; his first recovered published sketch appeared in a comic periodical published in Boston by a writer of Down East humor; he rose to fame as a literary comedian, and his masterpieces were created in the field of local color.

No one in the early days of Clemens's fame would have argued against the assertion that he emerged to prominence as a literary comedian, or, as the phrase had it, "a funny man." The reviewer in the *Nation* found in *Innocents Abroad* (1869) "all the prominent characteristics of our peculiar school of humorists—their audacity, their extravagance and exaggeration." A few years later, Howells was noting "the grotesque exaggeration and broad irony" of *Roughing It* (1872), which, as a scholar has recently asserted, "was looked upon as a funny book, of the journalistic sort." Other books which followed did not change the opinion of a number of critics about his proper classification: in 1891, Professor Beers of Yale thought it proper to mention him as one of a group including Artemus Ward,

"Mark Twain," from Native American Humor 1800-1900 *(New York, 1937), pp. 147-67. ©1966 by Chandler Publishing Company, San Francisco, and reprinted with permission.*

Nasby, Billings, Kerr, and Nye, "the most eminent by all odds" of them, but much like Ward:

> Mark Twain's drolleries have frequently the same air of innocence and surprise as Artemus Ward's, and there is a like suddenness in his turns of expression, as where he speaks of "the calm confidence of a Christian with four aces." If he did not originate, he at any rate employed very effectively that now familiar device of the newspaper "funny man," of putting a painful situation euphemistically, as when he says of a man who was hanged that he "received painful injuries which terminated in his death." He uses to the full extent the American humorist's favorite resources of exaggeration and irreverence. An instance of the former quality may be seen in his famous description of a dog chasing a coyote, in *Roughing It,* or in his interview with the lightning-rod agent. . . .

"He was often very funny," remarked Barry Pain, in 1910, "and he knew every trick of the trade."

He did, indeed; going through his pages one may discover any number of the devices of the literary comedians—in abundance in his earlier works and scattered through his later ones—puns, malapropisms, misquotations of the Bible or the classics (like the famous mistreatment of Shakespeare in *Huckleberry Finn),* sentences which juxtapose incongruities, understatements. Sometimes, as in Chapter XVII of *A Tramp Abroad,* a series of comic sentences huddled together on a page:

> . . . a most prodigious fire-breathing dragon used to live in that region, and made more trouble than a tax collector. He was as long as a railway train. . . . [comic similes] His breath bred pestilence and conflagration, and his appetite bred famine. [Exaggeration] He ate men and cattle impartially, and was exceedingly unpopular. [Anticlimax and understatement]. . . . So the most renowned knights came from the four corners of the earth and retired down the dragon's throat one after the other. [Anticlimax]

The manner was unmistakable in such passages. Too, he assumed for purposes of humor, like the doctor in *Innocents Abroad,* and like typical funny men, the character of what Mark called "an inspired idiot." "The most conspicuous intellectual trait of Mr. Clemens," observed an English critic, "seems to me to be an almost preternatural shrewdness, thinly veiled under the assumption of simplicity. . . ."

On the lecture platform, he assumed the manner of the conventional comic lecturer, acting out the customary role. A member of the audience attending his first lecture described:

> His slow deliberate drawl, the anxious and perturbed expression of his visage, the apparently painful effort with which he framed his sentences, and, above all, the surprise that spread over his face when the audience roared with delight or rapturously applauded the finer passages. . . .

The commentator went on to say that this was something previously entirely unknown, original; but that seems doubtful, for every part of the description applied equally well to Ward on the lecture platform.

It seems quite possible, in fact, that Mark learned a great deal about the art of the humorous lecture from Ward. He cited Ward as a great artist in "the dropping of a studied remark apparently without knowing it" and in the handling of the pause, and on at least one occasion, he suggested before a lecture: "Would you mind, now, just to please me, letting me introduce myself, as Artemus used to do?"

Understandably, therefore, it became conventional to suggest that Mark learned from Ward not only the way to speak but also the way to write humorously. "The imitation is discoverable," suggested Robert Ford, "in the joke forms peculiar to both. Each writer . . . begins in a serious—or apparently serious—mood, and produces his comic effects—or the best of them—by giving the most ludicrous and unexpected turns to his sentences." Conceivably, he might have cited such a passage as this, written by Clemens when, above the pseudonym of Thomas Jefferson Snodgrass, he used the sort of cacography employed by Ward:

> It mought be that some people think your umble sarvent has "shuffled off this mortal quile" and bid an eternal adoo to this subloonary atmosphere—nary time. He ain't dead, but sleepeth. That expreshun are figerative, and go to signerfy that he's pooty much quit scribblin.

Place alongside this a passage by Ward:

> Gentz—Hears two you old fellers . . . I spose you have bin a wonderin whare upon arth the undersined was . . . and prehaps the sollum thawt has struck you that i had taken my departer from this mundane spear and as Hamleck sez, "Shoveled orf this mortal Koil," and seazed two be no moore. Likeliz not yu hav bin temptid moren once to rite a obitchuary . . . But surs my time hasent arrovan yet.

The resemblance is unmistakable. But if there is any influence here, it is Clemens who is the tutor; for the Snodgrass letter appeared April 10, 1857, and the Ward letter is dated "May the 25 18&58." It is probable, however, that neither author particularly influenced the writings of the other. Both were following a well established tradition in American humor. But though there is probably no literal indebtedness on Mark's part to Ward, Clemens owes much to the method of the literary comedians.

His debt to Down East humor may, similarly, be one merely to tradition; though a closer relationship with an individual work seems highly possible. The first printed sketch by Sam Clemens which has been discovered appeared in the *Carpet-Bag,* edited by B. P. Shillaber, in the issue of May 1, 1852, in the same issue which contained a Partington paper detailing the mischievous activity of Ike Partington in school. This humorous paper was well known in the West: it had two agents in St. Louis; it was widely quoted by river town newspapers; it was a permanent exchange of the Hannibal *Journal,* into which some of its jests were copied. Sam Clemens, printer's devil, may have put some of them in type, or later, when the Partington books appeared, he may have read one or two of them.

At any rate, when Clemens, in *Tom Sawyer,* portrayed the amusing Aunt Polly, a better feminine characterization than any created by his Southwestern humorous predecessors, he drew one quite reminiscent of Shillaber's Mrs. Partington. There is a physical resemblance. One who looks at a picture of Shillaber's heroine is immediately struck by the fact that she looks exactly like Aunt Polly. The fact must have been noted by someone in 1876, for, inexplicably, labeled "Contentment" and presumably representing Tom's aunt, the pleasing illustration which had revealed the dame in *The Life and Sayings of Mrs. Partington* (1854) turned up in the first edition of *Tom Sawyer* on page 274. But the resemblance is more than physical. Like Aunt Polly, Ruth Partington was a widow, burdened with the task of caring for an orphaned nephew. Like Aunt Polly, it develops in the series of books about her, she cared for the boy's health by administering frequent doses of patent medicine in which she had great faith. Aunt Polly, said Mark, "was one of those people who are infatuated with patent medicines." Mrs. Partington had said of such nostrums: ". . . there's so much virtue in 'em that everybody . . . will be made over new, and there'll be no excuse for dying. . . ." Aunt Polly had trouble because doctors changed their treatments frequently. So with Ike's aunt. "Things change so," she complained, "that I don't know how to subscribe for any disease now-a-days."

Mrs. Partington and Aunt Polly, both Calvinists, believed that they should sternly punish their nephews for their frequent mischievous adventures. (Ike, like Tom, had a particular flare for torturing cats.) Often, though, both tender-hearted women failed to do their duty, and then rebuked themselves. And typically both Tom and Ike pulled the wool over the eyes of their innocent aunts:

"Dear me," said she [Mrs. Partington], dropping into a chair, "I am afraid your predestination will not be a good one, if you go on so; and little boys who tease their aunts don't go to heaven, by a great sight." Ike was much subdued by this, and taking advantage of her momentary abstraction and three doughnuts, he whistled for Lion and went out to play.

. . . she [Aunt Polly] took him [Tom Sawyer] into the closet and selecting a choice apple, delivered it to him, along with an improving lecture upon the added virtue and flavor a treat took to itself when it came without a sin through virtuous effort. And while she closed with a happy Scriptural flourish, he "hooked" a doughnut. Then he skipped out.

Since these traits of Mrs. Partington are thus faithfully reproduced in depiction of Aunt Polly, it may seem rather surprising that Mark told his biographer that Tom's aunt was really a portrayal of the author's mother. The statement was probably, so far as Mark's recollection went, quite true. But one sentence in the biography by Paine makes one wonder how accurate Mark's recollections were. Speaking of his mother's tenderness, he said: "She would drown the young kittens, when necessary, but warmed the water for the purpose." It makes one wonder because, in 1854, Shillaber had recorded that Ike's aunt, confronted with a similar unpleasant chore, prepared for its performance by pouring hot water in the tub to take the chill off. "It would be cruel," she said, "to put 'em in stone-cold." Such repetition may have been an example of fiction appropriated to autobiography, like the Davy Crockett story which Clemens appropriated to himself or Crockett's own use of "Georgia Theatrics" from Longstreet's volume. The details of the portrait of Tom's aunt may have been an example of the sort of "unconscious plagiarism" which caused Mark to borrow from Holmes. The whole resemblance may have been a coincidence. It is impossible to say. The conclusion must be, however, that Mark here, as elsewhere, had links with the traditions of the pre-war Down East humor.

But most important of all was the influence in Mark's writing of the humor of the old Southwest. He grew up with that humor. It adorned the newspaper and periodical exchanges which came to his brother's newspaper, for which he set type. He heard oral versions of it in Hannibal where he lived as a boy and on the river steam-boats where he worked as a young man. It followed him to the Pacific Coast, where it was published, sometimes in its old forms, sometimes in newly adapted forms, in the newspapers. To it, he was greatly indebted. Specifically, perhaps, in general, certainly, he was indebted to Crockett, Longstreet, and those who followed them. Passages in Mark's writings time after time are reminiscent of this older Southwestern humor. A paragraph in *Tom Sawyer* which tells how Tom behaved when a fellow student stole his sweetheart offers an example. Tom rehearsed, alone, the defiant remarks he would make upon meeting his rival. And, says Mark:

. . . he went through the motions of thrashing an imaginary boy—pummeling the air, and kicking and gouging. "Oh, you do, do you? You holler 'nough, do you? Now, then, let that learn you!" And so the imaginary flogging was finished to his satisfaction.

The humor of the paragraph is, of course, exactly the same as that in Longstreet's "Georgia Theatrics," wherein another imaginative youngster ruthlessly had licked an imaginary opponent. Mark as an old man told his biographer that he had known *Georgia Scenes* for a long time. Did he recall the book when he wrote the passage? Did he, perhaps, recall oral tellings of the same tale? Regardless of how this question is answered, it must be conceded that the paragraph and its point derive from the Longstreet tradition. Many passages show that he turned to the same materials as did the earlier humorists, looking at those materials with the same attitudes, and using the same patterns and methods.

So far as material went, Mark's "Dandy Frightening the Squatter," the *Carpet-Bag* tale of 1852, might be regarded as a mosaic of materials earlier used. It told of a fop outwitted by a rustic: the theme had inspired a Kentucky almanac story as early as 1828. The rustic called the swaggering dude's bluff when threatened with physical violence: the same theme had been developed by J. M. Field in a tale published in *A Quarter Race in Kentucky* (1846) and in Field's *The Drama in Pokerville* (1847). The sketch told how a man went ashore from a steamboat to manhandle an inhabitant: the situation had been unfolded, with variations, in a volume published in 1851, and Clemens's tale was, in plot, very like one going the rounds of newspapers just before his yarn was published. Hints for the passage about Huck's trip to the circus might have come to Mark from tales by W. T. Thompson, G. W. Harris, or Richard Malcolm Johnston. G. W. Harris might have suggested, in one of his sketches, the more refined episode about the boys in the loft who played jokes on the teacher in Chapter XXI of *Tom Sawyer*. The passage in *Innocents Abroad* in which Clemens scornfully recorded that Lake Como was not nearly as wide as the Mississippi and that the Italian lake would seem a "bedizened little courtier" in the "august presence of Lake Tahoe" and the passage about the Arno being "a historical creek with four feet of water . . . a very plausible river if they would pump some water into it" were definitely foreshadowed in 1841, by T. B. Thorpe, when he remarked: "Imagination in Europe is not up to reality in America. . . . The 'Big Bear of Arkansas,' if he should see the Thames, would designate it as 'that creek, thar.' " Mark's explanation that his whole career was affected by his having a contagious disease revealed the same sort of comic thinking which led Madison Tensas to assert that *his* whole career depended on the fact that when Tensas was ten years old, a young woman wore "No. 2 shoes, when common sense and the size of her foot whispered 'fives.' " Perhaps, as Mr. DeVoto suggests, Mark was specifically indebted to other passages in the writings of Field, Thompson, Hooper, and Sol Smith. However, whether his indebtedness was specific in any particular instance or not, there is no denying that in many passages of his works the subject matter and the attitudes of Mark Twain are definitely in the tradition of Southwestern humor.

The greatest gift of Southwestern humor to Mark, however, was the gift of a narrative method. This method is evident in his "Jumping Frog" story of 1865. The tale was an old one when he told it, even then "a classic of the mining-camps, rehearsed around campfires and in convivial gatherings." It had been told, with variations, of course, at least twice in California newspapers. But when Mark told that tale, he made it his own, and he made it his own because he applied to its telling the very effective framework technique whose efficacy had been discovered by numerous writers for the *Spirit of the Times*. Only one previous incarnation of a version of the yarn—so far as is known—had employed that technique, and significantly, that telling of the story had appeared in Porter's paper. In Mark's story, Simon Wheeler, "fat and bald-headed," with "an expression of winning gentleness," was given the honor of unfolding the narrative, which was repeated in Simon's own words—words which revealed the way his mind worked, the way he looked on life, the way he imagined. The technique—in its use of various types of incongruity, in its revelation —was in essentials exactly the technique of T. B. Thorpe's "Big Bear of Arkansas," of the Sut Lovingood yarns, of dozens of frontier masterpieces.

It was a technique which Mark fully appreciated. In "How to Tell a Story," he cited as a beautiful example a tale thus told by Riley "in the character of a dull-witted old farmer." The way of telling it, he noted, revealed the character of the narrator perfectly: "The simplicity and innocence and sincerity and unconsciousness of the old farmer are perfectly simulated, and the result is a performance which is thoroughly charming and delicious. This is art—and fine and beautiful, and only a master can compass it . . . ." Such a technique, Clemens pointed out to Joel Chandler Harris, was responsible for what was best in the Uncle Remus stories. Harris had modestly protested that "the matter and not the manner . . . attracted public attention and won the consideration of people of taste in the North . . . ." Mark scoffed at the notion:

My dear Mr. Harris,—You can argue *yourself* into the delusion that the principal life is in the stories themselves and not in the setting; but you will save labor by stopping with that solitary convert, for he is the only intelligent one you will bag. In reality the stories are only alligator pears—one merely eats them for the sake of the salad-dressing. Uncle Remus is most deftly drawn, and is a lovable and delightful creation; he, and the little boy, and their relations with each other, are high and fine literature, and worthy to live, for their own sakes; and certainly the stories are not to be credited with *them*. But enough of this; I seem to be proving to the man that made the multiplication table that twice one are two.

He appreciated the framework. He appreciated, too, the monologue revealing character whether it was enclosed in a framework or not. Hence, as many testify, he could, by appreciative reading, make crystal-clear the obscure monologues by Robert Browning. Hence he could create *Huckleberry Finn,* in which every paragraph revealed the yarn-spinner's character.

Clemens could assume, for the length of an essay, or for part of a book, or for a platform appearance, the role of a literary comedian; but essentially, all his life long, he was a teller of humorous anecdotes in the manner of Southwestern humorists, usually in a framework of description or narration. Mr. DeVoto properly characterized the technique when he said:

He took the humorous anecdote, combined it with autobiographical reminiscence, and so achieved the narrative form best adapted to his mind. . . . *The Innocents Abroad* is Mark's discovery of the method. . . . Descriptive passages interrupt the narrative from time to time but its steady progress is accomplished by means of stories. . . . The same framework produces *Roughing It, A Tramp Abroad, Life on the Mississippi,* and *Following the Equator.*

The picaresque method—the method with emphasis upon anecdotal narrative—developed in Southwestern humor was the art which he could best appreciate and employ. Of the larger patterns of fictional form created by a Nathaniel Hawthorne or a Henry James he might be unaware, but he knew, as he said, "that a man might tell that Jumping Frog Story fifty times without learning how to tell it."

Like Richard Malcolm Johnston, therefore, Clemens was a Southwestern humorist whose abilities were properly appreciated and encouraged in the period of flourishing local color writing. He climbed to his first fame, of course, as a literary comedian; but there was something in the spirit of the times, something in addition to the appreciation of his comedy, which brought appreciation of what he had to offer. Consider the case of J. Ross Browne (1821-1875), his predecessor, a man whose earlier life ran a course parallel to the life of Clemens. In *Yusef* (1853) and in *Adventures in the Apache Country* (1869), this author, whose attitudes and artistry were shaped by very similar currents to those which molded Mark's artistry, wrote books which had all the tricks of humor, all the journalistic appeals of Mark's very similar *Innocents Abroad* and *Roughing It.*

But Browne won slight recognition and dropped out of sight, while Mark not only succeeded sensationally but also forged ahead to write his masterpieces. Probably Browne could have written nothing like those masterpieces, but unlike Clemens, he was never urged to try. Those masterpieces quite conceivably were encouraged by the appreciation of Mark Twain as a local colorist. As early as 1872, Howells was calling attention to the admirable depiction of life in Nevada discoverable in *Roughing It*. The local color of *Life on the Mississippi* won for it the honor of serial publication in the *Atlantic*. The phrases used by Howells in praising *Tom Sawyer* were duplicated, in substance, in dozens of reviews of local color depictions: the book gave, he said, "incomparably the best picture of life in that region as yet known to fiction." It is noteworthy that *The Adventures of Huckleberry Finn* was published at what Professor Pattee called "the high tide" of "the greatest flood of dialect literature that America has ever known," along with a surge of such writings which made the years 1883 and 1884 memorable. By 1897, a critic was announcing that Clemens deserved fame, not because he was a great humorist or because he was a great artist but because:

He has recorded the life of certain southwestern portions of our country, at one fleeting stage in their development, better than it is possible it will ever be done again. . . . His tenacious memory . . . microscopic imagination, and his real interest in the serious side of life make his pictures . . . both absolutely accurate and surprisingly comprehensive.

Many of his attitudes were those of the local colorist. He looked back to a time in the past which seemed to him particularly charming, lovingly re-creating its details from memory. He wanted to be accurate in giving the flavor of those idyllic days. His accuracy, typical in the 1880's, extended, so far as he could make it extend, to even the recording of the dialects of the section. And in his depictions there were elements of tenderness far more characteristic of the local colorists than of the earlier humorists.

Mark Twain, in short, who as a personality could not help but be a humorist, as a literary artist whose works were channeled by such currents, could not help but be an American humorist. His works are, in a sense, a summary of nineteenth-century native American humor. They are a climax, as well, to its development.

They had, to be sure, its faults; but more important, in their best passages, they revealed the development of its artistry in the works of a genius.

His sins, which were many, were likely to be those of a literary comedian. He sometimes strained for too many laughs and therefore got none, assuming unnatural poses of idiocy, pouring out too many sentences hopefully constructed to create hilarity, forcing his materials into forms too fantastic to be amusing, allowing burlesque and caricature to intrude even into the pages of his best books. In the earlier books, only occasional passages hinted at his real abilities. But his sins diminished, though they did not disappear, as he moved from the role of the literary comedian to the accomplishment of a literary artist—in passages (for his greatness must be perceived in passages, or not at all) in *The Gilded Age, Tom Sawyer, Huckleberry Finn, Pudd'nhead Wilson, Life on the Mississippi,* and the underrated *Tom Sawyer Abroad.*

In the best parts of these volumes, more richly than any earlier humorist, he revealed background. Farm and woodland—the natural setting—had been vividly depicted in *The Biglow Papers;* the country folk at work and play had moved through the background of the writings of such diverse humorists as Seba Smith and G. W. Harris; and W. T. Thompson had explored the value of a community as a background. In Mark's pages, the scenic background was faultlessly described; and folk toiling and frolicking, whole communities as well as individuals, came to life. The dwellings of the characters, only slightly appreciated by earlier humorists—the unforgettable Grangerford interior or "the House Beautiful" of Chapter XXXVIII of *Life on the Mississippi,* for example—minutely described, offered a new kind of delight.

His characterization, too, in his best anecdotal pieces of narration, marked a culmination. Smith, Lowell, Shillaber, Mrs. Whitcher, Thompson, Hooper, and G. W. Harris, and others each might create one, two, or three animated humorous characters, but Mark could throng his pages with laughable figures who breathed the breath of life. He could make them exist vividly through many pages, as he did with Huck, Tom, Jim, Colonel Sellers and Pudd'nhead Wilson, or he could give them vital creation in a few phrases as he did, in a few pages of *Huckleberry Finn,* when he depicted Boggs,

Colonel Sherburn, and the village loafer who re-enacted the killing of Boggs. Or he could sketch them quickly in a framework, and then let them talk so revealingly that their mere way of telling a story made them intimate acquaintances of the reader. Mark Twain accomplished a wide range of character portrayal visioned but not achieved by earlier humorists.

But Mark, like those who preceded him in humor, was not only a fictionist: he was, in addition, a humorous fictionist. Satire of mankind in general and of American mankind in particular flashed as brilliantly on his best pages as it had in the pages of Seba Smith, James Russell Lowell, Johnson J. Hooper, and Petroleum V. Nasby. Like the humorous group of the Southwest, he recognized and developed the comedy of hilarious situation, writing with such high spirits that his most successful narratives had an exuberant zestfulness. Like most American humorists, he knew and exploited the incongruities between learned language and the vernacular. Like them, too, he realized the possibilities of laughter created by contrasts between realistic passages and fantastic ones, winning even greater success than they had because of his greater skill in perceiving, imagining, and recording what was essentially the same sort of detail. His gorgeous imagination made possible the recording of the fanciful flights of the Mississippi raftsmen, Jim Baker, and Huckleberry Finn, all perfectly in character and all wildly delightful.

His genius showed itself, too, in the creation of that type of poetry with which American humor had experimented since the beginning—the poetry of folk speech. "He imparted to the printed page," said Brander Matthews, "the vivacity of the spoken word, its swiftness and its apparently unpremeditated ease." Matthews referred to passages written by Clemens in his own character; but, even more notably, perhaps, the same quality was imparted to spoken dialogue. No signs of laborious phrasing were evident in the drawling speech of Simon Wheeler, Jim Baker, or Huck Finn—they just talked. But their talk, it should be noted, had the precision, the imagination, of poetic art: almost every critical word was exactly the right one, nearly every phrase reproduced the rhythms of conversation and evoked the most effective imagery for purposes of laughter. And the daringly chosen verbs, the metaphors, the conceits—verbal devices used often enough by the earlier humorists—were shaped by Mark's artistry to lift the boldly colored talk of his characters, at its best, to new heights of splendor.

American humor, then, gave Mark Twain his materials, his methods, and his inspiration. His success was merely the working out of its attempted achievements on the level of genius. Its master-piece, as well as Mark Twain's, was *Huckleberry Finn*.

1938

DeLANCEY FERGUSON

NO AMERICAN critical theory has taken deeper root than Mr. Van Wyck Brooks's thesis that Mark Twain was a thwarted satirist whose bitterness toward the damned human race was the fruit of a life-long prostitution of his talents. Despite the counter-attacks of Bernard DeVoto and others, it flourished everywhere from the London *Times Literary Supplement* to the last semester paper turned in by an English major at the University of Middletown. Past question, it is picturesque and dramatic, but—as Braxfield said of the clever chiel who would be none the worse for a hanging—it would be better if it were supported by a few facts.

A new interpretation of a great writer cannot have too many facts to stand on. The books published by the man himself or his literary executors are not enough; one must study him in his unguarded moments, in the letters withheld from his biography and in the first drafts of his books. Had Mr. Brooks thus studied Mark Twain, he would have found out many things. But he could not have written his book.

If a writer either consciously or unconsciously withholds anything of himself in his public utterances, traces of the buried talents are bound to show in the early drafts that are not yet groomed and sleeked for print. If nothing appears there which is not in the finished book, then the author is not censored, either by himself, his wife, or his literary advisors.

"Huck Finn Aborning," from the Colophon, *III, n.s. (Spring, 1938), 171-80. Reprinted by permission of the publishers.*

Everyone, including Mr. Brooks, agrees that *Huckleberry Finn* is Mark Twain's masterpiece. Written at the height of his creative power, it includes all he had to say, for good and ill, of the Mississippi world of his boyhood. Mr. DeVoto, while rejecting the Brooks thesis, admits it is impossible to pass final judgment on Mark Twain as an artist until we know, among other things, what was deleted from the early drafts of *Huck,* and why. For here, if Mark Twain had any more to say about the damned human race than he admitted to print, is where he would have said it.

It speaks little for the enterprise of the critics that a large part of the original manuscript of *Huck Finn* has for the past fifty years lain in the Buffalo Public Library without attracting the least notice. Its author gave it to James Fraser Gluck of Buffalo in 1886; soon afterward Mr. Gluck gave it to the library, along with a lot of other literary documents. It has been there ever since, most of the time on public exhibition.

True, the manuscript represents a little less than three-fifths of the book. Beginning in the middle of Chapter XII, it extends to the end of Chapter XIV, resumes at Chapter XXII, and is complete from there on. (The manuscript chapters are not numbered, and the few signs of divisions seldom coincide with those in the book.) Nevertheless, incomplete as it is, it is fully representative. Some strong scenes are missing, among them the Shepherdson-Grangerford feud, the camp-meeting, and the shooting of Boggs, but it includes the attempt to lynch Col. Sherburn, "The Royal Nonesuch," the whole Wilks episode, and Huck's struggle with his conscience over surrendering Jim. The presence of the weak Tom Sawyer chapters at the end is offset by the absence of those at the beginning.

Furthermore, it is genuinely the *original* manuscript, not a specially revised fair copy. Though it bears no printer's marks, it must be the text from which the book was set up, for it includes the original title-page, with the author's instructions to the printer, and similar instructions are written here and there in the margins. Without counting the innumerable differences in punctuation, the manuscript contains more than nine hundred textual changes, ranging from single words to whole paragraphs added or deleted, and shows, moreover, several distinct layers of correction, done at different times. Some changes were made at first writing, or almost immediately afterward; others indicate the direction taken in rejected passages not now in the manuscript; still others must have been made in proof. Besides these, a number of penciled marginalia show a critical reading intermediate between first composition and proofs.

But whatever their date, nature, or extent, all the revisions are the same sort. They are not the excision of scathing passages which Mrs. Clemens or Howells would disapprove of, neither are they the dilution of grim realism to make it meat for babes. They are the work of a skilled craftsman removing the unessential, adding vividness to dialog and description, and straightening out incongruities. Not more than two or three of the lot are the sort Olivia Clemens is reputed to have insisted on, and these two or three are so trifling that Mark may well have made them himself, without his wife's orders.

The only clear evidence of change of plan in the main section of the story will scarcely hearten the believers in censorship. When Huck and Tom arrived at Silas Phelps's plantation their creator originally intended them to find there a boy and a girl about their own age, named Phil and Mat. Fragmentary deleted passages, on renumbered pages, show that Mark Twain had developed this idea as far as where Tom passes himself off as Sid. Huck had confided Tom's impending arrival to Phil and Mat. But about that time Mark plainly realized that Tom and Huck, unaided, were going to furnish quite as many complications as the story would hold. He destroyed the older children, leaving only the brood of youngsters who were too small to share in the excitement. But he neglected to revise downward the ages of Silas and Sally (at first called Ruth) Phelps, who therefore appear in the book as somewhat elderly for the parents of so young a family.

So far, then, as the surviving manuscript shows, the general plan was little altered. Most of the changes are of detail. Thus when Huck and Jim visit the wrecked steamboat, Huck talks down Jim's fears by pointing out the untold riches, in five-cent cigars and other things, of steamboat captains. This whole long speech was added overleaf in the manuscript, to replace the unimaginative sentence, "Steamboat captains is always rich, and have everything they want, you know." Some of the best phrases were inserted in proof. The King's "soul-butter and hogwash" was only "humbug and hogwash" in the manuscript. Later on, when the King has "to brace up mighty quick, or he'd 'a squashed down like a bluff bank that the river has cut under," the simile was an afterthought. In the manuscript he merely "kerflummoxed." Again, the mob tears down Sherburn's fence, and begins "to roll in like a wave." When the Colonel appears with his shotgun, the book says, "The racket stopped, and the wave sucked back." For the last phrase, the manuscript has only "the crowd fell back." In the next paragraph, the book says, "Then pretty soon Sherburn sort of laughed; not the pleasant kind, but the kind that makes you feel like when you are eating bread that's got sand in it." This replaces, "not the kind of laugh you hear at the circus, but the kind that's fitten for a funeral—the kind that makes you feel crawly."

Many substitutions are dramatic. The first thoughts may be picturesque, but are out of character. Huck's summing up of Mary Jane Wilks was first, "She was the best girl that ever was! and you could depend on her like the everlasting sun and the stars, every time." The speech might have fitted the mouth of the Playboy of the Western World, but not Huck's. It was changed in proof to, "She was the best girl I ever see, and had the most sand." A sentimental reference to "the big friendly river stretching out so homelike before us" was deleted entirely. Huck, telling Jim of the ways and works of kings, at first said that Henry VIII made each wife tell him a tale every night, "and he kept that up till he had hogged a thousand and one tales that way, and then he got out a copyright and published them all in a book, and called it Domesday Book—which was a good name and stated the case. Of course most any publisher would do that, but you wouldn't think a king would. If you didn't know kings." But copyright is outside Huck's range of knowledge. Mark Twain, author and publisher, had taken his place. The passage was struck out of the proofs.

Remarks, again, might be right in character, but wrong in tone. Some of the more serious persons tended at first to orate in the style of Drury Lane melodrama. Col. Sherburn's speeches are full of passages like the one here italicised: "Because you're brave enough to tar and feather poor friendless cast-out women that come along here *lowering themselves to your level to earn a bite of bitter bread to eat, did it fool you into thinking you had courage enough to lay your hands on a MAN?"* And when Dr. Robinson denounces the King and Duke as impostors, his oration originally wound up thus:

> He is the thinnest of thin impostors—has come here with a lot of empty names and facts which he picked up somewhere; and you weakly take them for *proofs,* and are assisted in deceiving yourselves by these thoughtless unreasoning friends here, who ought to know better. Mary Jane Wilks, you know me for your friend, and your honest and unselfish friend. Now listen to me: cast this paltry villain out—I beg you, I beseech you to do it. Will you?

As any reader of Victorian novels knows, this was a natural literary idiom in the 1870's. But even if Dr. Robinson had really talked that way, it was not the natural idiom for Huck to report him in.

Another sort of revision marks the King's two speeches, "all full of tears and flapdoodle," over Peter Wilks's coffin. Their permanent form, like the immortal phrase which introduces them, was an afterthought. They were first written in direct discourse, thus:

> Friends, good friends of the deceased, and ourn too, I trust—it's indeed a sore trial to lose him, and a sore trial to miss seeing him alive, after the wearisome long journey of four thousand miles; but it's a trial that's sweetened and sanctified to us by this dear sympathy and these holy tears; and so out of our hearts we thank you, for out of our mouths we cannot, words being too weak and cold. May you find such friends and such sympathy yourselves, when your own time of trial comes, and may this affliction be softened to you as ourn is today, by the soothing ba'm of earthly love and the healing of heavenly grace. Amen.

In this speech and its companion, every phrase in the draft is carried over into the final text, but the indirect reporting, by implying compression from much greater length, immeasurably heightens the effect. It also gives Stephen Leacock, who says that Mark Twain never could convey the idea of prolixity except by getting prolix, something to ponder.

For still other effects, entire situations are expanded or reduced. Apparently almost the whole plan of the Wilks auction and its consequences came to Mark Twain as he wrote. After reporting the sale of the slaves, he at first went on with merely, "Next day was auction. They sold off the girls' house, and the tanyard and the rest of the property, but the prices wasn't the very highest." He immediately struck this out, and developed the narrative much as it stands in the book. Mark's invention, like most people's, did not always run smooth. Some passages, such as the chapter recording Huck's efforts to warn Mary Jane of impending trouble with the King and the Duke, have as many as twenty or twenty-five textual changes on a single page of print; at other times, whole pages of the book stand unchanged from the manuscript. There is no relation between the level of the work and the number of changes: Tom's arrival at the Phelps's is almost as much revised as Huck's interview with Mary Jane, and more than the attempted lynching of Sherburn.

Earlier in the Wilks episode, at the opening of Chapter XXVI, Mark originally began:

Well, when they was all gone the king asked Mary Jane how they was off for spare rooms, and she said they had two; so he said they could put his valley in the same bed with *him*—meaning me. He said in England it warn't usual for a valley to sleep with his master, but in Rome he always done the way the Romans done, and besides he warn't proud, and reckoned he could stand Adolphus very well. Maybe he could; but I couldn't a stood *him,* only I was long ago used to sleeping with the other kind of hogs. So Mary Jane showed us all up, and they was plain rooms but nice.

Here again deletion was immediate. Huck's nocturnal prowls, and his hiding the Wilks gold, would have been impossible had he slept in the same room with the King. This, like the auction passage, shows Mark composing as he went along, with only the vaguest general plan in mind.

In the earlier adventure on the wrecked steamboat some changes are in the manuscript; others were not made until the proofs. At first writing, when Huck and Jim board the wreck, "rip comes a flash of lightning out of the sky, and shows us a skiff tied to the skylight pretty close beyond the door, for all that side was under water." This was struck out at once; it destroyed both the surprise of discovering the ruffians on the boat and the suspense when the raft went adrift. But later in the chapter the manuscript elaborates the plans of Bill and Jake for silencing their treacherous companion, Jim Turner. They are going to gag him, to keep him quiet till the wreck breaks up and drowns him. Bill objects,

"But s'pose she *don't* break up and wash off?"

"Well, we can wait the two hours, can't we? *Then*, if the thing don't work, it'll still be long enough befo' daylight, and we'll come back and do the *next* best thing—tie a rock to him and dump him into the river."

"All right, then: come along and less gag him."

And later, when the ruffians come out just as Huck and Jim are getting away in the skiff, a wail from Turner calls them back to replace the gag he has worked loose. In the book, all references to the gagging disappear, apparently because it merely complicated the action without intensifying it.

In this same episode appears the first of the marginalia indicating critical revision between first writing and sending to press. When Huck cuts the skiff loose, his creator has penciled in the margin, "Provide him with a knife." This reminder is no doubt what allowed Huck to find, among the junk in the wrecked house floating down river in Chapter IX, "a bran-new Barlow knife worth two bits in any store."

Several such notes appear on the pages telling of the flight after the Wilks fiasco. When the crooks are plotting to sell Jim, the Duke, says Huck, "found fault with every little thing, and he even cussed Jim for being a fool and keeping his blue paint and King Leer clothes on, and made him take them off and wash himself off; and yet it warn't no fault of Jim's, for nobody hadn't ever told him he might do it." This passage is scored through, and a note says, "This is lugged—shove it back yonder to where they escape lynching and regain raft." But Mark failed to shove it, and so never told how or when Jim shed his "sick Arab" make-up. But the next note was acted on. When Huck, trying to find what the scoundrels have done with Jim, arrives at the Phelps's, a penciled note says, "Has good clothes on." Consequently, in the previous chapter, when Huck leaves the raft, the book has him putting on his store clothes, instead of "some old rough clothes" that he wore in the manuscript. There also, when he is going ashore in the canoe, one note says, "The skiff being new and worth advertising;" another, "Go back and [*sink* deleted] burn the skiff when they escape lynching;" a third, on the next leaf, "Go back and put on old clothes after escape from lynching." All these were finally ignored. So were a couple during Tom's elaborate schemes to free Jim. Where Tom instructs Huck about famous escapes, his author added in the margin, "Edmond Dantes," but let the book text stand as "them prisoners in the bottom dungeon of the Castle Deef." In the next chapter, when the boys are working in Jim's shack, a note says, "They always take along a lunch." But no change was made, and so far as the book reveals they carried on their night work without extra nourishment.

Most interesting of all is the note on the leaf which describes the King's make-up in "The Royal Nonesuch." It is the single word, scored through, "scandalous." Here, if anywhere, we might expect censorship. No one acquainted with fraternity initiations and other gatherings where Greek phallic comedy survives, has ever been in doubt as to the sort of show the King provided for the male population of Bricksville, Arkansas. Mark's canceled comment shows that he knew it was dangerous ground; the text shows exactly how much censorship he—or possibly Olivia—exercised. One phrase is deleted: the King originally "said he judged he could caper to their base instincts; 'lowed he could size their style." The title of the "play" is changed: throughout the manuscript it is "The Burning Shame" instead of "The Royal Nonesuch." The description of the King's makeup is modified in two places. In the manuscript he is "stark naked;" in the book merely "naked." The next sentence was first, "And—but I won't describe the rest of his outfit, because it was just outrageous, although it was awful funny." In the book Huck says, "And—but never mind the rest of his outfit; it was just wild, but it was awful funny." Out of the vast laboring mountain of charges that Mark Twain was a blighted Hemingway emerges this tiny and ineffectual mouse. If this was the utmost he suffered in revising what by implication is probably the bawdiest passage he ever conceived for publication, he was one of the freest authors who ever lived, instead of one of the most repressed.

The complete list of other changes which were, or may have been, made for decorum's sake bears out the impression from "The Royal Nonesuch." "Drunk," used twice in one paragraph, becomes "tight" and "mellow." Kings "hang," instead of "wallow," round the harem. "Rotten eggs" is changed to "sickly eggs," but since "rotten cabbages" stands in the same line, the change may be mere avoidance of repetition. The smells "too various" for Huck in the book were "too rancid" in the manuscript, and "the signs of a dead cat being around" replace "the smell of a dead cat." In several other places Mark's second thought modified his unhappy fondness for seeking humor in death, decay, and viscera. Jim, made up as the sick Arab, "didn't only look like he was dead, he looked considerably more than that." It may be doubted if realism would have gained much had the phrase been let stand as "he looked like he was mortified." It would be a questionable improvement to describe unappetizing meat as "a hunk of your old cold grandfather" instead of the "hunk of old cold cannibal," which again was second thought. And is it any better to say your conscience "takes up more room than a person's bowels" instead of "all the rest of a person's insides?"

A very few alterations considered the feelings of the churchly. Huck first said that the King rigged out in his store clothes looked as if "he had walked right out of the Bible;" this was changed to "the ark," but he still might be "old Leviticus himself." "Judas Iscarott" is softened to "Judas;" the king looks up towards the sky instead of the Throne. Two of Tom's jibes are altered, "mild as a Sunday School" becoming "mild as goose-milk," and "Sunday-schooliest ways" becoming "infant-schooliest." On the other hand, when Huck trusts "to Providence to put the right words in [his] mouth when the time come," Mark changed "Providence" to "luck" in the manuscript, but restored the original reading in the proofs. And once he inadvertently wrote "damn," but immediately changed it to "dern."

In the Wilks episode, the manuscript allows the King and Duke to be a trifle more goatish towards Mary Jane and her sisters than the book does. The description of their welcome by the girls originally included this:

Soon as he could, the duke shook the hairlip, and sampled Susan, which was better looking. After the king had kissed Mary Jane fourteen or fifteen times, he give the duke a show, and tapered off on the others.

When Huck is getting Mary Jane away as the show-down approaches, he asks, "Do you reckon you can face your uncles, and take your regular three or four good-morning smacks?" The earlier passage was deleted, and this one softened. The motive is obviously artistic, not prudish. Mary Jane is a heroine, Huck's ideal of spirited young womanhood. The canceled passages are esthetically out of key with his feelings towards her.

Out of all the hundreds of changes, just one deletion is sincerely to be regretted as a masterly sample of Mark Twain's invective. When the scoundrels quarrel after the Wilks fiasco, the Duke's denunciation of the King originally ended as here italicised: "You wanted to get what money I'd got out of the 'Burning Shame' and one thing or another, and scoop it *all, you unsatisfiable, tunnel-bellied old sewer!*" Mark may have canceled it himself, without his wife's help, but it is the sole instance in the entire manuscript which gives her critics a chance to score, and they had better make the most of it.

In short, the Mark Twain who emerges from this study is a man of letters practising his art, a humorist who knows what he is doing and making the most of his materials. Of the thwarted Swift invented by Mr. Brooks and his followers there is not a trace. Mark Twain didn't write humor because his wife forced him to prostitute his genius; he wrote it because he was Mark Twain.

1942

BERNARD DeVOTO

IN SEVERAL LETTERS and in Mark Twain in Eruption Mark Twain has described his episodic method of working on his books. He customarily kept half a dozen literary projects under way, taking up whichever he found most stimulating and working on it till the going got difficult or his enthusiasm slackened, then laying it aside till the "tank" filled up and he could begin on it again with renewed energy. The intervals might be brief but were sometimes very long: during the 1890's he went back to several manuscripts which he had laid away in the '70's and there is one manuscript in the Mark Twain Papers to which he returned after thirty years. Most of his books show signs of having been thus sporadically composed. It is the way of inspiration, the way of genius if you like, but it is not the way of a conscientious literary workman. It resulted in some of the most brilliant improvisations in American literature—and in some of the most painful disharmonies in Mark's books. And it is one reason why we cannot determine just when he began to write The Adventures of Tom Sawyer. . . .

Mark began writing the book as we now know it in either 1873 or 1874 (on the whole, the latter seems the likelier year), and on July 5, 1875, told Howells that he had finished it. His episodic

"The Phantasy of Boyhood: Tom Sawyer," from Mark Twain at Work (Cambridge: Harvard University Press, 1942), pp. 3-24. Reprinted by permission of the publishers. Modified version of introduction to Tom Sawyer (New York: Limited Editions Club, 1939).

method of composition shows in the book's handsome indifference to minutiae. Judge Thatcher's appearance as Judge Fletcher in a middle section has been mentioned. This was rectified in the manuscript but a confusion in the relationships and residence of the Thatcher family survives in the book. The Judge ends by swallowing Lawyer Thatcher, whom he is visiting when he first appears, and by the end of the book is a permanent resident of St. Petersburg, though half-way through it his home is still Constantinople, which had originally been called Coonville in the manuscript. (He is still in St. Petersburg in *Huckleberry Finn,* but his daughter Becky has become Bessie.) Mr. Dobbins's school is larger at the ceremonies of graduation than when we first see the classes reciting. Tom's enchanted summer is similarly elastic: the season is not yet over when the Widow Douglas gives her party for the boys, but if you count the weeks that have elapsed since the Fourth of July you will find that autumn should be well along. There are other incongruities, inconsistencies, and loose ends. They do not matter at all but they are the sort of thing that Arnold Bennett had in mind when he called Mark Twain "the divine amateur." Bennett was a type-specimen of the professional writer, whose pride of craft it is to leave nothing undigested, to tie all knots and sandpaper all joints till the parts are perfectly fitted in a whole. Mark Twain was at times superior to and always incapable of such discipline. He had the discipline of daily work and the sterner discipline that made his prose one of the great styles of English, but he lacked the discipline of revision and the discipline that makes a writer uneasy until his material has been completely thought through into form. That lack is his greatest defect as an artist; it is rather less evident in *Tom Sawyer* than in most of his novels but sometimes it shows clearly.

Finishing his book, Mark was eager to submit it to his arbiter and censor, Howells. The letter of July 5, 1875, asks Howells to read it "and point out the most glaring defects"—and Mark is then of the opinion that "It is *not* a boy's book, at all. It will only be read by adults. It is only written for adults." Howells's summer plans deferred his reading and there was no hurry, for both the English and American publishers were awaiting a more favorable time for publication. An amanuensis copy of the manuscript (now privately owned) was prepared, and this is the one which Howells read the following

November and on which he made his annotations. On November 21, he wrote to Mark:

> I finished reading *Tom Sawyer* a week ago, sitting up till one A.M., to get to the end, simply because it was impossible to leave off. It's altogether the best boy's story I ever read. It will be an immense success. But I think you ought to treat it explicitly *as* a boy's story. Grown-ups will enjoy it just as much if you do; and if you should put it forth as a study of boy character from the grown-up point of view, you'd give the wrong key to it. I have made some corrections and suggestions in faltering pencil, which you'll have to look for. They're almost all in the first third. When you fairly swing off, you had better be left alone. The adventures are enchanting. I wish *I* had been on that island. The treasure-hunting, the loss in the cave, it's all exciting and splendid. I shouldn't think of publishing this story serially. Give me a hint when it's out, and I'll start the sheep jumping in the right places.
>
> I don't seem to think I like the last chapter. I believe I would cut that.

Mark wrote at once (November 23) "As to that last chapter, I think of just leaving it off and adding nothing in its place. Something told me that the book was done when I got to that point— and so the strong temptation to put Huck's life at the Widow's into detail, instead of generalizing it in a paragraph was resisted." The meaning of this is cloudy but the present stilted "Conclusion" has been added to the amanuensis copy in Mark's own hand, and that may indicate that there was another chapter—that *Adventures of Huckleberry Finn* began prematurely in *Tom Sawyer*.

Illness kept Mark from making revisions until January, when, on the 18th, he wrote to Howells:

> There was never a man in the world so grateful to another as I was to you day before yesterday, when I sat down (in still rather wretched health) to set myself to the dreary and hateful task of making final revision of *Tom Sawyer*, and discovered, upon opening the package of MS that your pencil marks were scattered all along. This was splendid, and swept away all labor. Instead of *reading* the MS, I simply hunted out the pencil marks and made the emendations which they suggested. I reduced the boy battle to a curt paragraph; I finally concluded to cut the Sunday school speech down to the first two sentences, leaving no suggestion of satire, since the book is to be for boys and girls [his opinion has changed since July]; I tamed the various obscenities until I judged that they no longer carried offense. So, at a single sitting I began and finished

a revision which I supposed would occupy 3 or 4 days and leave me mentally and physically fagged out at the end. [Mark's conception of revision shows in this estimate.]

Most of Howells's suggestions can still be made out in the margins of the amanuensis copy. Mark seems to have adopted all of them, but there are fewer than the letters suggest. At the end of Chapter III, Howells writes, "Don't like this chapter much. The sham fight is too long. Tom is either too old for that or too young for [word or words lost]. Don't like the chaps in [word or words lost]." Obediently Mark cuts some three hundred words from the sham battle, much to its improvement. (He missed one word, however, which remained a meaningless vestige in all editions of the book till 1939. Tom rode a broomstick horse in that battle, and later he made it "cavort" in front of Becky's house. At his final departure the text has hitherto inexplicably read, "Finally he rode home reluctantly with his poor head full of visions.") Mr. Walters's speech in Sunday school has been improved by its reduction. A speech of Joe Harper's before the venture in piracy has been cleared of burlesque. Howells objects to "cussedness" as a Yankee expression and Mark makes it "Old Scratch." Howells checks Alfred Temple's "Aw—what a long tail our cat's got" (which Mark had already substituted for "Aw—go blow your nose") and it comes out "Aw—take a walk." Where Tom now says, in the next speech, that he will "bounce a rock off'n your head," Howells has objected, soundly, to "mash your mouth." There are perhaps a half-dozen further stylistic changes, as where Tom's "throes of bliss" on receiving the Barlow knife become a "convulsion of delight," and where his original intention to "gloom the air with a lurid lie" is altered to "take refuge in a lie." But more interesting and important are the mild "obscenities" that Mark mentions in his letter.

Howells cannot be charged with the change of "the devil" to "Satan" toward the end of the book nor (I think—the copy is not clear) with the softening of "foul slop" to "water" where the Thatcher's maid drenched the adoring Tom, whose "reeking" garments are then made merely "drenched." Mark had also softened Injun Joe's intentions towards the Widow Douglas. His original explanation that to get revenge on a woman "you cut her nose off— and her ears" had been altered to "you slit her nostrils—you notch her ears" when the amanuensis copy was made, and where Huck now tells the Welshman that he heard "the Spaniard swear he'd spile her looks" he originally added "and cut her ears off." Perhaps Olivia Clemens or Mark's children had shrunk from these expressions, though more likely it was Mark's own nerves that flinched. But Howells's nerves required further alterations.

The poodle which relieves the suffering of the congregation by sitting down on a pinchbug now goes "sailing up the aisle" and no more; but originally he sailed up that aisle "with his tail shut down like a hasp." Howells writes in the margin, "Awfully good but a little too dirty," and an amusing phrase goes out. Much more important, by far the most important change anywhere in the manuscript is the modification of Chapter XX. Here, in the margin opposite Becky Thatcher's stolen glimpse of "a human figure, stark naked" in Mr. Dobbins's textbook of anatomy, Howells writes, "I should be afraid of this picture incident," and so cancels one of the truest moments of childhood in the manuscript. Reproached by Becky for sneaking up on her, Tom had originally said, "How could *I* know it wasn't a nice book? I didn't know girls ever——." Becky's apprehension of being whipped carried a postscript, "But that isn't anything—it ain't *half*. You'll tell everybody about the picture, and O, O, *O!*" Meditating on what a curious kind of fool a girl is, Tom was originally permitted to think:

But that picture—is—well, now it ain't so curious she feels bad about that. No . . . [Mark's punctuation] No, I reckon it ain't. Suppose she was Mary and Alf Temple had caught her looking at such a picture as that and went around telling. She'd feel—well, I'd lick him. I bet I would. [Then, farther toward the end of the soliloquy] Then Dobbins will tell his wife about the picture. [Note the information that Dobbins is married.]

And Becky was originally permitted to think, "He'll tell the scholars about that hateful picture—maybe he's told some of them before now."

The omission of this, the single allusion to sex in the book (which, observe, had survived the scrutiny of Olivia Clemens), is very interesting. The omission is clearly chargeable to Howells, and yet I suspect that Mark himself would soon have felt uneasy and, in manuscript or in proof, would have deleted those sentences of his own initiative. We are told that his anecdotes and conversation could be plentifully obscene and there is the published *1601* as well as the unpublished speech to the Stomach Club, "Some Thoughts on the Science of Onanism," and several other fragments, as well as some savage satires written during his last years but not intended to be published. Nevertheless he was almost lustfully hypersensitive to sex in print; he was in fact, as a writer, rather more prudish than Howells. His timorous circumlocutions, published and unpublished are astonishing; he once argued that there could be no such thing as an age of consent, for all seduction was essentially rape; and, in an unpublished venture of Tom and Huck into the Indian country, he was as tremulous as a Bertha M. Clay when he had to suggest what might happen to a captured heroine. Of thirty-nine notebooks kept as banks of deposit for his books, only three contain any entries at all that deal with sex, and one of these does not contemplate its use for fiction. In *The Gilded Age* even a false marriage (whose daring presence in the book, besides, is probably due to Charles Dudley Warner) must be atoned for with a heroine's death—and, in short, of all Mark's published fiction only *Pudd'nhead Wilson* is aware of sexual desire as a human motive. Certainly childhood as he depicts it is naturally sexless—and he would probably have removed this blemish without Howells's warning.

Mark could not have written about boyhood as it appears in the works of Sigmund Freud even if he had thought of it in that way, but there is no evidence that he thought of it as otherwise than sexless. Boyhood existed forever in the idyll of Hannibal, and he remembered Hannibal as he was to make Eve remember Eden, as an eternal summer before the Fall. The published *Autobiography* makes this clear, and the Mark Twain Papers contain many unpublished manuscripts and groups of notes that embody his memories of Hannibal. One of these manuscripts, "Villagers of 1840-43," is specially pertinent here. In the course of discussing many of Mark's neighbors it notes that some of the Blankenship girls (they would be Huck Finn's sisters) were charged with prostitution but adds, "not proven." It chronicles one adultery, one crime of passion, and one free union. Then it summarizes the subject in a separate paragraph:

Chastity. There was the utmost liberty among young people—but no young girl was ever insulted, or seduced, or even scandalously gossiped about. Such things were not even dreamed of in that society, much less spoken of and referred to as possibilities.

Ever, not even dreamed of, possibilities! Those are emphatic words but Mark meant them. Whatever the defect of experience or recognition that made him thus libel a full-blooded folk, that is how he remembered Eden.

Before this essay no one, I think, had noticed the softening of Chapter XX, but Howells's remaining modification has become famous. Curiously enough, he missed the offense when he read the manuscript. He did encounter in Huck's passionate grievance against the Widow Douglas, "she'd gag when I spit," and that had to go, but he passed "they comb me all to hell" without questioning it. But Mark had already spent some concern on the phrase—writing "hell," then changing it to "thunder," and finally restoring the dreadful word—and demanded judgment from his arbiter. In the letter of January 18, 1876, already quoted he said:

There was one expression which perhaps you overlooked. When Huck is complaining to Tom of the rigorous system in vogue at the widow's, he says the servants harass him with all manner of compulsory decencies, and he winds up by saying: "and they comb me all to hell." (No exclamation point.) Long ago, when I read that to Mrs. Clemens, she made no comment; another time I created occasion to read that chapter to her aunt and her mother (both sensitive and loyal subjects of the kingdom of heaven, so to speak) and *they* let it pass. I was glad, for it was the most natural remark in the world for that boy to make (and he had been allowed few privileges of speech in the book); when I saw that you, too, had let it go without protest, I was glad, and afraid, too—afraid you hadn't observed it. Did you? And did you question the propriety of it? Since the book is now professedly and confessedly a boy's and girl's book, that darn word bothers me some, nights, but it never did until I had ceased to regard the volume as being for adults.

Howells wrote, the next day:

As to the point in your book: I'd have that swearing out in an instant. I suppose I didn't notice it because the locution was so familiar to my Western sense, and so exactly the thing that Huck would say. But it won't do for the children.

So the expletive joined the simile about the poodle's tail and Tom's meditations about a naked figure in a textbook.

Mark's own changes in the manuscript are usually stylistic and always for the best. It is interesting to discover that Injun Joe's companion in the grave-robbing was originally Old Man Finn. He became Muff Potter, no doubt, to prevent Huck's oath from putting his father's life in jeopardy. And there is one deletion which not only suggests that there was another intermediate stage of the book but also makes one thankful that, though Mark was tempted, he found grace to resist the kind of extravaganza that defaces the last quarter of *Huckleberry Finn*. At the end of Chapter III, Tom, saddened by Aunt Polly's cruelty, goes down to the river, where he sits on a raft in the darkness, takes out his wilted flower, and thinks of Becky with the melancholy that made Burton diagnose love as a neurosis. And "at last," the text says, "he rose up sighing and departed in the darkness." Until Mark crossed out the passage, the manuscript went on, "A dimly defined, stalwart figure emerged from behind a bundle of shingles upon the raft, muttering 'There's something desperate breeding here,' and then dropped stealthily into the boy's wake." There is no telling what wild notion was in Mark's mind but he was beginning to burlesque a passage already strained to the breaking-point and, remembering such passages elsewhere that he did not strike out, one is overjoyed to see heavy ink cancelling this one in time.

With *Adventures of Huckleberry Finn, Tom Sawyer* stands at the head of Mark Twain's work. Both are masterpieces, both transcend their own weaknesses, both belong to the exceedingly small number of American books that have permanently enriched world literature, both are among the common possessions of even unliterary readers everywhere, both have the simple but mysterious attribute of mythology that makes permanence sure, both are compacted of literary truth. This one is the lesser of the two, it is not so profound nor so fine a book as *Huckleberry Finn,* its plane of greatness is a lower plane. But it is true to itself and it has qualities that its more mature companion piece does not share.

Its limitations have already been suggested herein. The gravest of them is that the boys are of no particular age and therefore much that they do and feel is psychological anachronism. Howells's partly indecipherable comment on Chapter III, "Tom is either too old for that or too young for . . ." is true of the book as a whole. Precisely as the story takes place in a year that has no anchorage in time (well, if pedants must, it is not later than 1845—and therefore, since Mark was born in 1835, Tom has not yet reached his tenth birthday), so the emotions of boyhood swing through half a dozen ages. The sham battle, the forest outlawry, the mischief of the school scenes, the treasure-digging and the cure of warts are proper to the age of eight or nine. But Tom's adoration of Becky is nearer adolescence, and the boys who camp on Jackson's Island, shadow Injun Joe, want to take a drink when forbidden by the pledge, minister to Muff Potter in jail, and save the Widow Douglas are twelve or thirteen. Surely Tom can be no younger than that, may even be older, when he testifies in court and comforts Becky in the cave.

Throughout the book time curves back on itself and boyhood is something more than realism, it is a distillation, a generalization, a myth. It is not itself but its own essence and a wish for the merely statistical would be impertinent. Precisely as the voltage of Huck Finn makes ridiculous any mundane doubt of his ability to live forever on handouts and in hogsheads, so in the bared presence of what all boys wish and dread it is silly to ask how old Tom and Huck are when they crouch behind the elms that spread over Hoss Williams's grave.

Structurally *Tom Sawyer* is a better job than most of Mark's fiction. Only *The Prince and the Pauper,* whose form was determined by the simple contrast of its formula, moves so smoothly in its own medium. Nevertheless, one is sometimes troubled by Mark's lordly improvisations. When Injun Joe cherishes a five years' grudge against Dr. Robinson he is well within belief, for he is half Indian and half white—"two," so Eugene Rhodes says, "two bad breeds." But belief grows reluctant when this vindictive mind is found to be meditating a second revenge. The horsewhipping inflicted on him by the Widow Douglas's husband reduces him from truth to mere plot. In the same way, the boys are sick too much. Tom's earlier illnesses are acceptable but when anxiety inflicts on Huck Finn a fever not to be distinguished from any early Victorian heroine's and Tom also is overcome, the illusion weakens: this is a mere device, time must be found for Injun Joe to starve. And it would be comforting if the time scheme were less arbitrary. A Missouri summer may indeed begin in April but it cannot last so long as it is made to here. Art trespasses on relativity.

Finally, though the book is more profoundly true to the phantasies of boyhood than any other ever written, and to maturity's nostalgia for what it once was, though it has forged the symbols that seem likely to express boyhood more permanently than any other in literature, it cannot be thought of as comprehensive or profound realism. The term is dangerous; certainly the forged symbol transcends literalism and the truth of *Tom Sawyer* is the kind of truth that only symbols can express—like the symbols of *Antigone* or those of *Macbeth*. But you need only differentiate boyhood from its symbols to perceive how much of it Mark ignores. There is, we have seen, no sex—none of the curiosity, the shame, the torment, the compulsion of young ignorance groping in mystery. Becky and Tom in the empty schoolroom do not belong in the same world with any pair of ten-year-olds in a hayloft, and though Tom thinking of her by the dark river is profoundly true he never goes on to think of her as any boy must in the years when girls are last known to be females. "Such things were not even dreamed of in that society."

Furthermore, Tom's immortal daydreams never get much above the childish level. Piracy, highway robbery, the outlaws of the forest, the circus, the vagabondage of Jackson's Island—yes, thank God. But was there no glance forward as well, had he no nebulous, inarticulate vision of growing up, did he get no nearer than this to the threshold of ambition and desire, where boyhood darkly flowers in frustrated poetry? Has a boy no griefs and losses outside of phantasy, no satisfactions and no achievements more real than these? Is a boy's mind no wider and no deeper than Tom's? Where are the brutalities, the sternnesses, the strengths, the perceptions, and the failures that will eventually make a man? Well, in part Mark's will was to ignore such things, as when he denies us the entire struggle of fear, pity, and horror out of which Tom's decision to reveal what he had seen in the graveyard issues, in order to give us the simple melodrama of the revelation. And in part he was incapable of the analysis which the probing of motives and psychological intricacies requires: his understanding was intuitive and concrete and he was sure only of behavior, fumbling when he had to be introspective.

So with St. Petersburg, the society in which Tom's summer is played out. What is asserted of it is all memorably true but much has been left out. Mark was to go on and tell the rest in other books, but there the society was formed out of nostalgia and the book became a pastoral poem, an idyll of an America that had already vanished when it was written. And by now it must be clear that, though there is also a direct answer to the doubts we have expressed, this discussion has so far been conducted on false premises.

For the discussion leaves out what millions of readers have experienced in the sixty-six years since *Tom Sawyer* was published. No book can become world literature, as this one has become, unless it has authority over the imagination of mankind, and such authority makes merely idle the kind of doubt expressed here. It is a complex thing but the basis of it is that it embodies universal phantasies. When Tom triumphs in the whitewashing, enacts the death of Robin Hood, is punished for his beloved's fault, establishes his pirates' den on Jackson Island, and dramatically insures justice to Muff Potter, the dreams of all childhood everywhere are fulfilled in him. "I wish *I* had been on that island," Howells said and the same wish, known or only felt, has been wakened and gratified in everyone who ever read the book. It is a deep wish—for natural beauty and daring adventure, for dawn and midnight storm and flowing river, and underneath that for all the freedoms that the soul needs. It is at the very core of desire. But darker needs are also voiced and allayed. The book's enchantment is so strong that it beguiles one into forgetting how much of the spell issues from dread and horror. The story pivots on body-snatching, revenge, murder, robbery, drowning, starvation, and the fear of death. It exists in a medium darkened by witchcraft and demonology; ghosts are only an amulet's width away; the malevolence of the unseen world is everywhere a danger as tangible as Injun Joe. All these give it primary drama—but also they crystallize, more perfectly than anywhere else in literature, the terrors that are as indissolubly a part of boyhood as the reflex of freedom. If Mark could not analyze the ferments of the mind's dark side, he has given them enduring symbols. Tom writhing with guilt during a thunderstorm; Tom and Huck cowering behind the trees while murder is done and then, in darkness and moonlight, hearing Bull Harbison howl above Muff Potter who will surely die; Tom and Huck preserved from death only by the collapse of a stairway that Injun Joe is mounting; Tom and Becky wandering in the cave with dwindling candle and then awaiting death in darkness; the halfbreed chipping at the sill in the knowledge that he must die—these and many other images are an ecstasy from the soul's fear, and boyhood finds in them a richer, deeper expression than literature has elsewhere given it. The symbols speak for millions out of the shadow of unbodied dread.

In this way *Tom Sawyer* transcends realism, transcends its narrative, transcends its characters and becomes mythology. No actual boy ever filled his pockets with fees paid for the privilege of whitewashing a fence, or followed the pathway of terror from an opened grave to treasure buried under a cross. The way of fact is the curve of an arc; myth, like poetry, travels straight across, on the chord. Millions have assented as Tom Sawyer moves along the chord, and millions more will assent. He is a universal myth, a part of the small store of truth that American literature has added to the treasure of mankind.

And mythological truth has another facet. St. Petersburg, I have said, is an idyll, the enchanted village of Mark's remembrance. It has the quality of the phrase from an old song, "Over the hills and far away," which he could never think of without tears. This village, though violence underlies its tranquillity as it underlies most dreams of beauty, is withdrawn from the pettiness, the greed, the cruelty, the spiritual squalor, the human worthlessness that Huck Finn was to travel through ten years later, that are the fabric of Hadleyburg and Dawson's Landing. There is indeed no abdication of Mark's perceptions: for all the tenderness that draws the portrait of Aunt Polly she is clearly seen, and the trivial concerns of the village personages are rendered with calm finality. Minor realisms about provincial society are here engraved for all time. But in spite of them the village is really a part of Lyonnesse, sunk forever under waters more limpid than the Mississippi that flows beside it.

As such it perfectly preserves something of the American experience, more of American dreaming, and still more of the beauty that was our heritage and that still conditions both our national memory and our phantasy. On one side of it is Cardiff Hill, a remnant of the great forest, on the other side is the great river: both at the very base of our awareness. Between these beauties the village is sleepy, peaceful, and secure. The world invades it only as romance and adventure; the energies of the age are over the horizon. Time has stopped short; the frontier has passed by and the industrial revolution is not yet born. Life is confident and untroubled, moves serenely at an unhurried pace, fulfills itself in peace. Islanded in security, in natural beauty, St. Petersburg is an idyll of what we once were, of what it is now more than ever necessary to remember we once were. Here also the book captures and will keep secure forever a part of America—of America over the hills and far away.

1950

LIONEL TRILLING

WHEN AT LAST *Huckleberry Finn* was completed and ·published and widely loved, Mark Twain became somewhat aware of what he had accomplished with the book that had been begun as journeywork and depreciated, postponed, threatened with destruction. It is his masterpiece, and perhaps he learned to know that. But he could scarcely have estimated it for what it is, one of the world's great books and one of the central documents of American culture.

Wherein does its greatness lie? Primarily in its power of telling the truth. An awareness of this quality as it exists in *Tom Sawyer* once led Mark Twain to say of the earlier work that "it is *not* a boys' book at all. It will be read only by adults. It is written only for adults." But this was only a manner of speaking, Mark Twain's way of asserting, with a discernible touch of irritation, the degree of truth he had achieved. It does not represent his usual view either of boys' books or of boys. No one, as he well knew, sets a higher value on truth than a boy. Truth is the whole of a boy's conscious demand upon the world of adults. He is likely to believe that the adult world is in a conspiracy to lie to him, and it is. this belief, by no means unfounded, that arouses Tom and Huck and all boys to their moral sensitivity, their everlasting concern with justice, which they call fair-

---

"*Huckleberry Finn,*" *from* The Liberal Imagination: Essays on Literature and Society *(New York: Viking Press, 1950), pp. 104-17. ©1948 by Lionel Trilling and reprinted by permission of the Viking Press, Inc.*

ness. At the same time it often makes them skillful and profound liars in their own defense, yet they do not tell the ultimate lie of adults: they do not lie to themselves. That is why Mark Twain felt that it was impossible to carry Tom Sawyer beyond boyhood—in maturity "he would lie just like all the other one-horse men of literature and the reader would conceive a hearty contempt for him."

Certainly one element in the greatness of *Huckleberry Finn,* as also in the lesser greatness of *Tom Sawyer,* is that it succeeds first as a boys' book. One can read it at ten and then annually ever after, and each year find that it is as fresh as the year before, that it has changed only in becoming somewhat larger. To read it young is like planting a tree young—each year adds a new growth ring of meaning, and the book is as little likely as the tree to become dull. So, we may imagine, an Athenian boy grew up together with the *Odyssey.* There are few other books which we can know so young and love so long.

The truth of *Huckleberry Finn* is of a different kind from that of *Tom Sawyer.* It is a more intense truth, fiercer and more complex. *Tom Sawyer* has the truth of honesty—what it says about things and feelings is never false and always both adequate and beautiful. *Huckleberry Finn* has this kind of truth, too, but it has also the truth of moral passion; it deals directly with the virtue and depravity of man's heart.

Perhaps the best clue to the greatness of *Huckleberry Finn* has been given to us by a writer who is as different from Mark Twain as it is possible for one Missourian to be from another. T. S. Eliot's poem, "The Dry Salvages," the third of his *Four Quartets,* begins with a meditation on the Mississippi, which Mr. Eliot knew in his St. Louis boyhood:

> I do not know much about gods; but I think that the river
> Is a strong brown god . . .

And the meditation goes on to speak of the god as

> almost forgotten
> By the dwellers in cities—ever, however, implacable,
> Keeping his seasons and rages, destroyer, reminder of
> What men choose to forget. Unhonoured, unpropitiated
> By worshippers of the machine, but waiting, watching and waiting.

Huckleberry Finn is a great book because it is about a god—about, that is, a power which seems to have a mind and will of its own, and which to men of moral imagination appears to embody a great moral idea.

Huck himself is the servant of the river-god, and he comes very close to being aware of the divine nature of the being he serves. The world he inhabits is perfectly equipped to accommodate a deity, for it is full of presences and meanings which it conveys by natural signs and also by preternatural omens and taboos: to look at the moon over the left shoulder, to shake the tablecloth after sundown, to handle a snakeskin, are ways of offending the obscure and prevalent spirits. Huck is at odds, on moral and aesthetic grounds, with the only form of established religion he knows, and his very intense moral life may be said to derive almost wholly from his love of the river. He lives in a perpetual adoration of the Mississippi's power and charm. Huck, of course, always expresses himself better than he can know, but nothing draws upon his gift of speech like his response to his deity. After every sally into the social life of the shore, he returns to the river with relief and thanksgiving; and at each return, regular and explicit as a chorus in a Greek tragedy, there is a hymn of praise to the god's beauty, mystery, and strength, and to his noble grandeur in contrast with the pettiness of men.

Generally the god is benign, a being of long sunny days and spacious nights. But, like any god, he is also dangerous and deceptive. He generates fogs which bewilder, and contrives echoes and false distances which confuse. His sand bars can ground and his hidden snags can mortally wound a great steamboat. He can cut away the solid earth from under a man's feet and take his house with it. The sense of the danger of the river is what saves the book from any touch of the sentimentality and moral ineptitude of most works which contrast the life of nature with the life of society.

The river itself is only divine; it is not ethical and good. But its nature seems to foster the goodness of those who love it and try to fit themselves to its ways. And we must observe that we cannot make —that Mark Twain does not make—an absolute opposition between the river and human society. To Huck much of the charm of the river life is human: it is the raft and the wigwam and Jim. He has not run away from Miss Watson and the Widow Douglas and his brutal father to a completely individualistic liberty, for in Jim he finds his true father, very much as Stephen Dedalus in James Joyce's *Ulysses* finds his true father in Leopold Bloom. The boy and the Negro slave form a family, a primitive community—and it is a community of saints.

Huck's intense and even complex moral quality may possibly not appear on a first reading, for one may be caught and convinced by his own estimate of himself, by his brags about his lazy hedonism, his avowed preference for being alone, his dislike of civilization. The fact is, of course, that he is involved in civilization up to his ears. His escape from society is but his way of reaching what society ideally dreams of for itself. Responsibility is the very essence of his character, and it is perhaps to the point that the original of Huck, a boyhood companion of Mark Twain's named Tom Blenkenship, did, like Huck, "light out for the Territory," only to become a justice of the peace in Montana, "a good citizen and greatly respected."

Huck does indeed have all the capacities for simple happiness he says he has, but circumstances and his own moral nature make him the least carefree of boys—he is always "in a sweat" over the predicament of someone else. He has a great sense of the sadness of human life, and although he likes to be alone, the words "lonely" and "loneliness" are frequent with him. The note of his special sensibility is struck early in the story: "Well, when Tom and me got to the edge of the hilltop we looked away down into the village and could see three or four lights twinkling where there were sick folks, maybe; and the stars over us was sparkling ever so fine; and down by the village was the river, a whole mile broad, and awful still and grand." The identification of the lights as the lamps of sick-watches defines Huck's character.

His sympathy is quick and immediate. When the circus audience laughs at the supposedly drunken man who tries to ride the horse, Huck is only miserable: "It wasn't funny to me . . . ; I was all of a tremble to see his danger." When he imprisons the intending murderers on the wrecked steamboat, his first thought is of how to get someone to rescue them, for he considers "how dreadful it was, even for murderers, to be in such a fix. I says to myself, there ain't no telling but I might come to be a murderer myself yet, and then how would I like it." But his sympathy is never sentimental. When at last he knows that the murderers are beyond help, he has no inclination to false pathos. "I felt a little bit heavy-hearted about the gang, but not much, for I reckoned that if they could stand it I could." His will is genuinely good and he has no need to torture himself with guilty second thoughts.

Not the least remarkable thing about Huck's feeling for people is that his tenderness goes along with the assumption that his fellow men are likely to be dangerous and wicked. He travels incognito, never telling the truth about himself and never twice telling the same lie, for he trusts no one and the lie comforts him even when it is not necessary. He instinctively knows that the best way to keep a party of men away from Jim on the raft is to beg them to come aboard to help his family stricken with smallpox. And if he had not already had the knowledge of human weakness and stupidity and cowardice, he would soon have acquired it, for all his encounters forcibly teach it to him—the insensate feud of the Grangerfords and Shepherdsons, the invasion of the raft by the Duke and the King, the murder of Boggs, the lynching party, and the speech of Colonel Sherburn. Yet his profound and bitter knowledge of human depravity never prevents him from being a friend to man.

No personal pride interferes with his well-doing. He knows what status is and on the whole he respects it—he is really a very *respectable* person and inclines to like "quality folks"—but he himself is unaffected by it. He himself has never had status, he has always been the lowest of the low, and the considerable fortune he had acquired in *The Adventures of Tom Sawyer* is never real to him. When the Duke suggests that Huck and Jim render him the personal service that accords with his rank, Huck's only comment is, "Well, that was easy so we done it." He is injured in every possible way by the Duke and the King, used and exploited and manipulated, yet when he hears that they are in danger from a mob, his natural impulse is to warn them. And when he fails of his purpose and the two men are tarred and feathered and ridden on a rail, his only thought is, "Well, it made me sick to see it; and I was sorry for them poor pitiful rascals, it seemed like I couldn't ever feel any hardness against them any more in the world."

And if Huck and Jim on the raft do indeed make a community of saints, it is because they do not have an ounce of pride between them. Yet this is not perfectly true, for the one disagreement they ever have is over a matter of pride. It is on the occasion when Jim and Huck have been separated by the fog. Jim has mourned Huck as dead, and then, exhausted, has fallen asleep. When he awakes and finds that Huck has returned, he is overjoyed; but Huck convinces him that he has only dreamed the incident, that there has been no fog, no separation, no chase, no reunion, and then allows him to make an elaborate "interpretation" of the dream he now believes he has had. Then the joke is sprung, and in the growing light of the dawn Huck points to the debris of leaves on the raft and the broken oar.

> Jim looked at the trash, and then looked at me, and back at the trash again. He had got the dream fixed so strong in his head that he couldn't seem to shake it loose and get the facts back into its place again right away. But when he did get the thing straightened around he looked at me steady without ever smiling, and says:
>
> "What do dey stan' for? I'se gwyne to tell you. When I got all wore out wid work, en wid de callin' for you, en went to sleep, my heart wuz mos' broke bekase you wuz los', en I didn' k'yer no mo' what became er me en de raf'. En when I wake up en fine you back agin, all safe en soun', de tears come, en I could a got down on my knees en kiss yo' foot, I's so thankful. En all you wuz thinkin' 'bout wuz how you could make a fool uv ole Jim wid a lie. Dat truck dah is *trash;* en trash is what people is dat puts dirt on de head er dey fren's en makes 'em ashamed."
>
> Then he got up slow and walked to the wigwam, and went in there without saying anything but that.

The pride of human affection has been touched, one of the few prides that has any true dignity. And at its utterance, Huck's one last dim vestige of pride of status, his sense of his position as a white man, wholly vanishes: "It was fifteen minutes before I could work myself up to go and humble myself to a nigger; but I done it, and warn't sorry for it afterwards either."

This incident is the beginning of the moral testing and development which a character so morally sensitive as Huck's must inevitably undergo. And it becomes an heroic character when, on the urging of affection, Huck discards the moral code he has always taken for granted and resolves to help Jim in his escape from slavery. The intensity of his struggle over the act suggests how deeply he is involved in the society which he rejects. The satiric brilliance of the episode lies, of course, in Huck's solving his problem not by doing "right" but by doing "wrong." He has only to consult his conscience, the conscience of a Southern boy in the middle of the last century, to know that he ought to return Jim to slavery. And as soon as he makes the decision according to conscience and decides to inform on Jim, he has all the warmly gratifying emotions of conscious virtue. "Why, it was astonishing, the way I felt as light as a feather right straight off, and my troubles all gone. . . . I felt good and all washed clean of sin for the first time I had ever felt so in my life, and I knowed I could pray now." And when at last he finds that he cannot endure his decision but must sacrifice the comforts of the pure heart and help Jim in his escape, it is not because he has acquired any new ideas about slavery—he believes that he detests Abolitionists; he himself answers when he is asked if the explosion of a steamboat boiler had hurt anyone, "No'm, killed a nigger," and of course finds nothing wrong in the responsive comment, "Well, it's lucky because sometimes people do get hurt." Ideas and ideals can be of no help to him in his moral crisis. He no more condemns slavery than Tristram and Lancelot condemn marriage; he is as consciously *wicked* as any illicit lover of romance and he consents to be damned for a personal devotion, never questioning the justice of the punishment he has incurred.

Huckleberry Finn was once barred from certain libraries and schools for its alleged subversion of morality. The authorities had in mind the book's endemic lying, the petty thefts, the denigrations of respectability and religion, the bad language, and the bad grammar. We smile at that excessive care, yet in point of fact *Huckleberry Finn* is indeed a subversive book—no one who reads thoughtfully the dialectic of Huck's great moral crisis will ever again be wholly able to accept without some question and some irony the assumptions of the respectable morality by which he lives, nor will ever again be certain that what he considers the clear dictates of moral reason are not merely the engrained customary beliefs of his time and place.

1951

HENRY SEIDEL CANBY

IN USING GIBBON'S famous title I am giving to it a meaning much more limited than the crash of a civilization. It is the decline and fall of Mark Twain's creative power which is interesting for this book. His business failure was only a harsh incentive to his industrious pen, the death of his beloved Susy was a disaster from which emotionally he never recovered; but the last ten years of his life, to 1910, were triumphant, if by triumph one means world-wide acclaim and a long-sought-for financial security. Yet I agree with Mr. DeVoto that the *Yankee* in 1889 was the last display of his creative powers in full strength, adding that *Pudd'nhead Wilson* in 1894 and *Joan of Arc* in 1896 were steps in the decline of one of the most characteristic geniuses, while the brilliant *The Mysterious Stranger* left unpublished in probably 1905 gives some explanation of his fall. And yet these last three books are only a sparse salvage from a mass of writing, finished and unfinished, which belongs to this period. Something happened to Mark Twain in later middle age more serious for the creative writer than his bankruptcy or the death of a beloved daughter. . . .

. . . Mark, in this new and later mood, left unfinished or unpublished many manuscripts not only because some of them were weak, but also because others were or threatened to be too strong. To break down in the midst of a story was his characteristic in this period—

"Decline and Fall: Mark Twain," from Turn West, Turn East *(Boston: Houghton Mifflin Co., 1951), pp. 239-57. Reprinted by permission of the publishers.*

and that I shall take up later. But of the most promising of these later manuscripts which were finished, he seems to have been afraid. Like a moving-picture star he was morbidly afraid of failure. He was in no great danger of shocking his public by being "too coarse," or "too rough"—Olivia could take care of that. But to shock them morally, to disturb the religious-ethical code of America—the old-time religion in which he grew up with daily doses from his mother —was, to put it mildly, incompatible with popularity. Even the brilliant Ingersoll had to fight his way. The audience that Twain had gathered he was sure would not stand it—not for a single book.

And it is clear from numerous and often quoted references in later life that if he were to write from his heart, this was the kind of book he would have written—a book shocking in its ideas, not in any sense in its sexual morality. In that direction—in spite of the bawdy *1601,* privately circulated and offending none of its readers—he was not drawn. . . .

Something was wrong with Mark, and it is not enough to say that his shift from a confident optimism to bitter cynicism merely reflects a changed mood in his overconfident country. It is true that, superficially, he was as representative of that country as a tough, sweet maple tree whose sap flows from cold nights and sunny days, and whose roots are deep in the soil. Yet his responses are too violent to be satisfactorily explained by external history. What reversed his faith in human nature? What caused his still overflowing energy to beat and break against a wall when he tried to create? Why did his old vein of tender boyish imagination lead only to baleful fire and ashes? And why, in those remarkable frustrated fantasies which DeVoto in his *Mark Twain at Work* has published from his unfinished manuscripts, does the inner life depicted there explode into diatribe, or come near to insanity?

He had undoubtedly shifted with his times from the extravagant optimism of Walt Whitman and his own Colonel Sellers and Manifest Destiny to the social criticism of the eighties and nineties and the Henry and Brooks Adamses who, like Henry James, believed that America, having overrun a continent, had failed to make a civilization. Thoughtful Americans by the later decades of the century had come to believe that the American dream of a brotherhood of equality had been sold in the market place and was indeed only a dream. Yet

Walt Whitman (another printer's apprentice and journalist) who experienced at firsthand the debauching of the democratic processes, died in these same nineties still confident of the democratic program, still confident of the ultimate victory of a democracy based on faith in the common man. And Mark himself was too comfortably at home in the market place to be philosophical about its effects. He did not give up speculating because he thought it was wrong for the business of America to be business, but because he was a bad speculator and found someone wiser than himself to handle his profits for him. More than a change from a land of hope to a land (for the sensitive few) of disillusion is needed to explain the morbid pessimists of genius who have from time to time since the mid-century appeared in our literature. Mark, an *émigré* from optimism, in his last important book is as bitter as Swift, without the great Dean's evident reason for cynicism.

Something ailed Mark himself, and was more important than anything in current history. He had never been much concerned with current history. Looked at it, yes, the stupidities of Congress, the venalities of politicians, at stupidity anywhere. But when his imagination was warm he had always rejected the contemporary and gone back to the past, his own past, or much earlier centuries. He seems to have had from youth a horrid fascination, like a boy's for gangster pictures, for the depravities of early history. Suetonius was his bedside book, and he reveled in his debauched tyrants who stood for civilization in their day. See him in *The Innocents Abroad,* telling horror stories or examples of injustices to man at each old tomb or monument, explaining to his fellow Innocents the cruelty of man to man. But a faculty of self-protection kept all this from youth and his beloved country while his adolescence lasted. We were tough, but at least we were humanitarians at heart. It was in fact a boy's version of history that he made for himself while he expanded his idylls of the river and his adventures in the Middle Ages. Such history was uncomplicated by too much knowledge, which may have helped him in his youth from passing a judgment on humanity that has turned many an artist into a preacher. But when the creative memories of this youth dimmed and dulled, a brooding over a human race which simply did not, and would not, behave like a boy's dream but was stupid when it was not vicious, mean in its pretensions, hope-

less in its future, captured a mind which under its gay fictions must
have been sensitive to disillusion from the start. Mark grew up in a
young civilization, and stayed young himself when that society about
him was becoming adult. Only the vivid boy in him enabled him to
carry on with his nostalgic realism of youthful experience so long. But
he was born neurotic, which accounts for the brilliant sensitivity
which makes his two finest books masterpieces. Yet in the end neuroticism destroyed him as a creative artist.

In calling Mark a neurotic genius I am taking the simplest and
most indisputable meaning of a term which has been generalized into
vagueness. A neurotic is simply a mind of too great sensitivity, too
much sensibility as the eighteenth century would have called it. His
sensitiveness easily escapes controls. Hamlet of course was a neurotic
genius, and Horatio's chastening of his excesses is the best example
I know of intellectual neuroticism. "Alas," Hamlet says, "poor Yorick! . . . a fellow of infinite jest, of most excellent fancy"—whose
flashes of merriment were wont to set the table in a roar. And now
only a stinking skull—"To what base uses we may return, Horatio."
And Horatio replies, " 'Twere to consider too curiously, to consider so."

A certain neuroticism, of course, is invaluable, perhaps indispen-
sable to a writer, and in calling Twain a neurotic we are comparing
him with the curiously long list of great American writers who in the
most successful country of the nineteenth century have built triumph
as well as some failures upon their morbid excess of sensibility—
Hawthorne, Poe, Melville, Thoreau perhaps—and in our day Robinson Jeffers and William Faulkner. Neuroticism becomes dangerous
only when it defeats its own ends by an excess which denies the
validity of the creative artist's own genius. What had given Mark
such vivid delight, and led him to create with such sympathy a boy's
pageant of America in its youth, was followed by a disillusion almost
to be expected. He considered it "too curiously" in his maturity and
this very sensitivity betrayed him.

Even in his creative period of the Hartford-Quarry Farm days, I
am told by Dr. Booth of Elmira, who knew him, that he was subject
to depressions and wild outbursts against "the human race."

There is another aspect of neuroticism in Twain, which cannot
be charged to intensity of happy experience, and is more irrational

than a reaction from happiness. When Mark was twenty-two and a pilot on the river, his young brother died of his burns in the explosion of a steamship where Mark had got him a job. This job entailed no more dangers than thousands of travelers risked on the Mississippi, and were such as Mark never counted for himself. His brother's ship had an accident, his did not, that was the extent of his responsibility. But his letter home is of such self-torture and exaggerated remorse as can be interpreted only by saying that if he was not guilty of his brother's death, then he personally must be guilty of something else. And this neuroticism of considering too curiously runs as a guilt complex through his life. If his daughter dies of disease, he personally is guilty. Appearing in his letters, and with special reference to his beloved ones such as Olivia, one can see a coiling spring of remorse and guilt which apparently explains the final relief when after listening to Satan's nephew he decides first that an immoral God is to blame, and finally that all evil and good are no more than a thought.

Perhaps a psychiatrist will find some new explanation for such neuroticism as this. The present efforts of psychiatric critics to find a cause are not persuasive. He did not have an unhappy childhood, nor a brutal father, nor a dominating mother. That his mother jilted the man she said she wanted to marry, and took another (Mark's father) whom she respected but did not love, is scarcely material for a guilt complex. It is only fair to say that Mr. DeVoto's knowledge of psychiatric conditions, which is superior to mine, leads him to differ with me here. He feels that Sam's father exercised some compulsion upon him, especially in regard to women, which marked him for life. But at best this is not proven. The late Dixon Wecter also was without a final solution. If some secret sin was hidden in his past more serious than "cussing" and the kind of wild oats cultivated in mining camps, it had plenty of opportunities to reveal itself when Mark asked for an exposure of his sins and vices in his attempt to win Olivia honestly. His earlier life as a roving reporter was about as private as a traffic policeman's, and in any case Mark was never one to hide his light under a bushel, even if it were a red one. As for his family, his father's family and his own, he is always accusing himself of some injustice, some neglect, some failure of care, a concern almost unique in the none too good records of literary genius.

Neither Freud nor the behaviorists seem to help us here. I suggest a possible course in heredity, whatever else may have contributed to the result. The gnawing remorse from beginning to end of his personal confessions may be over trivial things, but the revelations of the subconscious in the fantasies published by Mr. DeVoto are not trivial. Indeed for every outburst against the damned human race in his later years you can find somewhere in his personal confessions a *mea culpa*. No, the *results* of this neurotic guilt and excessive sensitivity are easy to point out; the cause is not. Some later psychologists may discover a hitherto undetected paranoia, coming from a conformation of the brain, and pin it on Mark. I prefer to say that Mark's neurotic tendencies (for good as well as ill) were both due to oversensibility, and were congenital. The complex, if that is the right word, was born in him—a tendency like genius or meanness. . . .

Mark was an Innocent himself, born in a region and a time when everything, it seemed, could be explained by the future. He had been a boy then and happy, and had only to transfer his boy's sensitiveness to his imagination. When he brought his simple, but how vital, enthusiasm East, he kept his impressions fresh because they were already beyond comparison or competition with current living. They remained true and idyllic so long as he could reconstruct them in terms of a boy's imagination. He had been that boy. He was still a boy at his own creative depth. Even the Boss is still a boy proposing to overthrow superstition and economic slavery with the lightheartedness of a Tom Sawyer. But this feat of nostalgic realism was made possible by a memory so intense in its sensitivity as to threaten reaction. He had made a pattern for self-expression into which the modern world, which he now begins to experience violently, will not fit. It is viable neither for idyll nor for laughter except on the shallow upper levels. Once again he turns to the past, and at second hand this time, depicts a woman whom every evil smites. Yet she keeps her faith. These are the same old evils that he once shrugged off by laughter because he believed that the heart of the world was good. But they are beyond laughter now. And so the boys find it when Satan's nephew begins to speak for adult Mark.

And so one begins to see his vulnerability. The evil of the world strikes at him personally, as a man, not as a boy. Hitherto it has been struggle and adventure, now it is an assault by history. Pap Finn was a poor-white, but there was still an aura of the epic pioneer about him. Give him his rights and he could still, so he says, get to the top of the New World. But the wretched squatter left behind a half-century later in a lost valley of the Appalachians, living in squalor and decay, has no more hopes, nor dignity. Mark's reaction is very different, but his drop was great. He loses his fortune and most of his wife's, and goes bankrupt. He loses by a brain tumor his beloved Susy. All the intensity of his joy in living turns inward and finds nothing but disillusion. He must be guilty. The Lord giveth, and the Lord taketh away. Blessed be the name of the Lord. He will not accept the third proposition. The Lord is guilty, the human race is guilty for having believed in such a God. But this strikes at the foundations of his faith in life, and what was as serious for his creative powers, the confidence upon which his work was based. His New World faith is shattered, and with it faith in the people of his imagination. He cannot write any longer about the only thing that interested him, human personality in a world fit for it, because he no longer believes in personality. It is a scum of iridescence on a foul pool. By the stern necessity of a man writing who must always write because this is his condition, he drives on. He fails when he imitates his earlier self, succeeds only with trivia, and as his persistent neuroticism deepens, makes almost inarticulate symbolic pictures for himself of the distress of his uncontrolled imagination. Only once again does the artist take control, and then, with a boy as spokesman, he writes *The Mysterious Stranger,* where Tom and Huck grown up, are told that good and evil and happiness and misery are all illusions, the products of a cheating, vagrant thought, and so wiped out of literature.

1962

JOHN C. GERBER

MARK TWAIN'S range in point of view is readily apparent in those works in which he uses fictional narrators. To reassure oneself on this point it is necessary only to recall some of his more famous narrators: Thomas Jefferson Snodgrass, Huckleberry Finn, Hank Morgan, Sieur Louis de Conte, King Leopold, and Captain Ben Stormfield, not to mention Adam, Eve, a horse, and a dog. What is not so readily apparent, however, is that an analogous range in point of view exists in those works narrated not by personae but by "Mark Twain" — such works as the travel letters and books, "Old Times on the Mississippi," "The Private History of a Campaign That Failed," and the bulk of the short newspaper and magazine sketches.[1] In some of these Twain played it straight; that is, he employed in them a point of view that was essentially his own. In others he assumed a pose, a point of view other than his own. And in still others, especially in the longer works, he alternated between real and assumed points of view.[2] My concern in this essay is with the nature and range of these assumed points of view.

Fundamentally, there are two ways to confront life falsely. Either one can pretend that life is more agreeable to the spirit and more amenable to the will than it really is, or one can pretend that it is less so. One can exaggerate his superiority to human affairs or his inferiority to them. As the narrator "Mark Twain," Twain did both. He pretended undue superiority, for example, in posing as the Gentleman,

"Mark Twain's Use of the Comic Pose," from PMLA, *LXXVII (June, 1962), 297-304. Reprinted by permission of the Modern Language Association and the author.*

the Sentimentalist, the Instructor, and the Moralist; he assumed undue inferiority in posing as the Sufferer, the Simpleton, and the Tenderfoot. On examination, each of these poses proves to have identifiable characteristics and quite discernible effects on style.

The discussion that follows has three parts: a description of some of the more common comic poses of superiority, a description of some of the more common comic poses of inferiority, and certain general reflections upon Twain's use of the comic pose.

I

Among the poses of superiority, that of the Gentleman most clearly identifies Twain with the Southwestern humorist who preceded him. Like A. B. Longstreet, Johnson J. Hooper, T. B. Thorpe, and Joseph G. Baldwin, Twain endowed his Gentleman with social elevation, an air of condescension, and a language notable primarily for its formal elegance. Appropriately, this was the chief pose that Twain assumed in the first piece known to be signed "Mark Twain," a letter from Carson City that appeared in the Virginia City *Territorial Enterprise* in February of 1863. In this letter he pretends to view Clement T. Rice, a reporter for the rival *Daily Union,* with lofty disdain. Referring to Rice as "The Unreliable," Twain brings him on the scene in this way: "About nine o'clock the Unreliable came and asked Gov. Johnson to let him stand on the porch. That creature has got more impudence than any person I ever saw in my life. Well, he stood and flattened his nose against the parlor window, and looked hungry and vicious — he always looks that way — until Col. Musser arrived with some ladies, when he actually fell in their wake and came swaggering in, looking as if he thought he had been anxiously expected."[3] In this and in later *Enterprise* letters Twain as the Gentleman sniffs at the way Rice eats, drinks, sings, borrows money and clothes, carries on at concerts, and reports events in the *Union.* Once, when the Unreliable falls ill, the Gentleman as the true patron of the needy sends him a coffin.

When he left Virginia City in May 1864, Twain carried the pose of the Gentleman along with him as an important part of his arsenal of comic devices. In the San Francisco years just following, he used it most successfully in the piece that not only boosted his reputation in the West but started it in the East, "The Notorious Jumping Frog of Calaveras County." The patronizing attitude and the formal narrative style of the Gentleman narrator in "The Jumping Frog" are almost too familiar to need repetition: "I have a lurking suspicion that *Leonidas W.* Smiley is a myth; that my friend never knew such a personage; and that he only conjectured that if I asked Old Wheeler about him, it would remind him of his infamous *Jim* Smiley, and he would go to work and bore me to death with some exasperating reminiscence of him as long and as tedious as it should be useless to me."[4]

In subsequent travel letters to the Sacramento *Union* from Hawaii, and to the *Alta California* from Nicaragua, New York, Europe, and the Holy Land, Twain made the role even sillier. Possibly in imitation of currently popular English as well as American travel-burlesques, he posed in these letters as the Gentleman chiefly when reporting his altercations with Mr. Brown, his fictional companion.[5] Having made Brown a thorough vulgarian, Twain extracted as much comic contrast as he could from the scenes with Brown by making himself a thorough stuffed shirt. In one letter from Hawaii, for instance, Brown suggests a change in what "Mark Twain" is writing and is rebuked thus: "Brown, that is the first charitable sentiment I have ever heard you utter. At a proper moment I will confer upon you a fitting reward for it. But for the present, good-night, son. Go, now. Go to your innocent slumbers. And wash your feet, Brown — or perhaps it is your teeth — at any rate you are unusually offensive this evening. Remedy the matter. Never mind explaining — good-night."[6] In other letters Twain as the Gentleman patronizes Brown for his inability to stay on a donkey, for becoming seasick, for substituting "pheasant" for "peasant," and for mistaking water-closet signs for signs designating the names of French railway stations. When Twain dropped Brown in revising the *Alta* letters for *Innocents Abroad,* he dropped the pose of the Gentleman, and seldom used it thereafter. It was the kind of pose that lent itself to buffoonery but not to more subtle comic effects.

Another pose of superiority confined largely to the early work was that of the Sentimentalist. In this pose Twain pretended to a sensitivity, often an elation, denied to more cloddish mortals. As the Sentimentalist he viewed life as a sequence of such exquisitely moving experiences that it could be communicated only in the most rhapsodical terms. The comic possibilities of acting in such fashion seem to have occurred to

Twain most forcefully after he created Mr. Brown, for it was not until he did so that he began to exploit the role extensively. Usually he assumed the pose in order to give Brown a chance to demolish it. Thus when Twain as Sentimentalist grows lyrical about the sights and sounds of Honolulu, Brown reminds him of its scorpions and "santipedes" and mosquitoes.[7] When in a fine poetic frenzy he reads his own version of "Polonius' Advice to His Son," Brown vomits.[8] And when he waxes ecstatic over Nicaraguan girls ("such liquid, languishing eyes! such pouting lips! such glossy, luxuriant hair! such ravishing, incendiary expression!") Brown brings him to earth with, "But you just prospect one of them heifers with a fine-tooth"—[9]

Interestingly, the exclusion of Brown from *Innocents Abroad* did not eliminate the pose of the Sentimentalist as it did the pose of the Gentleman. On the contrary, there is more of the Sentimentalist in the book than in the original letters. The most frequently quoted example, possibly, occurs where Twain adopts the pose of the Sentimentalist to lampoon the mawkish treatment of the Holy Land to be found in other travel books. At the tomb of Adam his filial affection is "stirred to its profoundest depths." He leans upon an altar and bursts into tears. "I deem it no shame to have wept over the grave of my poor dead relative. Let him who would sneer at my emotion close this volume here, for he will find little to his taste in my journeyings through Holy Land. Noble old man — he did not live to see me — he did not live to see his child. And I — I — alas, I did live to see *him*" (*Works*, II, 307). Toned down somewhat, the pose of the Sentimentalist is observable in *Roughing It* where Twain's eyes secrete "generous moisture" for Mormon women, and in later works such as "A Burlesque Biography" and "A Wonderful Pair of Slippers." But in these the sentimentality is not pushed so close to lunacy. It was only during the eighteen-sixties that Twain substantially exploited the giddier possibilities of the role.

A pose of superiority that Twain never completely discarded was that of the Instructor, the experienced person anxious to be of help to his less knowing readers. The motive of the Instructor Twain himself sets forth at the beginning of his little essay on "Curing a Cold":

It is a good thing, perhaps, to write for the amusement of the public, but it is a far higher and nobler thing to write for their instruction, their profit, their actual and tangible benefit. The latter is the sole object of this article.

If it prove the means of restoring to health one solitary sufferer among my race, of lighting up once more the fire of hope and joy in his faded eyes, or bringing back to his dead heart again the quick, generous impulses of other days, I shall be amply rewarded for my labor; my soul will be permeated with the sacred delight a Christian feels when he has done a good, unselfish deed. (*Works*, VII, 363)

With similar high resolve Twain informed his readers about the habits of the Siamese twins (aged fifty-one and fifty-three), provided them with hints about the raising of poultry, and showed them (with illustrations) how through practicing from three to seven hours a day any one of them could become as fine an artist as he. Twain soon discovered that the Instructor was a "natural" for his travel accounts with the result that no travel book is without several instances of the pose. Sometimes the explanation of the Instructor appears as a set-piece, such as the retelling of a European legend or the disquisition at the end of *A Tramp Abroad* on "The Awful German Language." More frequently it is simply a paragraph or two slipped without warning into the middle of a passage of straight travel reporting. The lead-in may be perfectly sensible: "It may interest the reader to know how they 'put horses to' on the continent" (*Works*, X, 19). But the explanations themselves show a wild over-eagerness to be helpful. The details become absurd, the time sequence confused, and the language vague or inappropriate. Later humorists like Benchley and Perelman may have exploited the role of the Instructor more fully than Twain, but none of them has extracted from it such boisterous idiocy.

Of all of Twain's poses of superiority, that of the Moralist is the most common — and the most complicated. Twain's pose of moralism may be distinguished from his sincere expression of moral indignation by the contrived details, the exaggeration or falsification of feeling, the inappropriateness of tone. What is especially interesting about this pose, however, is that Twain uses it for such variant purposes and with such diverse effects. Sometimes, for instance, he adopts the pose simply to appear coy; he pretends to be shocked when he is not really shocked at all. There is little reason to suppose that he did not enjoy girlie shows as much as the bulk of his male readers did. Yet in his letters to the Sacramento *Union* and to the *Alta* he pretends like a prim Victorian to be repelled by such goings-on as the Hawaiian hula and the lavish New York production of "The Black Crook." In *Inno-*

cents Abroad he reports that at a performance of the can-can in the Paris suburb of Asnières he placed his hands before his eyes "for very shame." But then, giving the game away, he adds that he looked through his fingers (*Works,* I, 130). In somewhat more serious vein he uses the pose of the Moralist to make fun of such things as moralism itself. The very titles indicate this intent in "Advice to Little Girls" and "Some Learned Fables, For Good Old Boys and Girls" (*Works,* XXIV, 305-306; VII, 137-167). Loftily in "Aurelia's Unfortunate Young Man" he advises Aurelia Maria to marry her intended, even though the lad had successively lost his smooth complexion, one leg, both arms, an eye, the other leg, and his scalp. "We must," Twain abjures her, "do the best we can under the circumstances" (*Works,* VII, 309). Much more seriously — and somewhat more grotesquely — he uses the silly pose of the Moralist to mount an attack on such serious evils as the treatment of the Chinese in San Francisco, the insanity plea in murder charges, and the lynching of Negroes in the South. In "The United States of Lyncherdom," for example, with shock tactics worthy of Swift he implores the American missionaries to come home and go to work in the South, asking them whether they have anything so appetizing in China as a Texas lynching. "O kind missionary," he pleads, "O compassionate missionary, leave China! come home and convert these Christians!" (*Works,* XXIX, 249). In such a passage Twain uses the pose to mask outrage instead of delight, and the pose becomes the instrument of satire instead of farce. But it is the pose of the Moralist nonetheless, and the style of writing exhibits the same exclamatory and histrionic quality it possesses in the description of the can-can.

II

Although there are humor and variety in Twain's poses of superiority he never manages to achieve with them the sharply conceived characterizations he creates with his poses of inferiority. Like so many humorists, he is at his best when portraying himself as the butt, the person of inexperience in an alien and malevolent world. As the butt, his three most common poses are those of the Sufferer, the Simpleton, and the Tenderfoot. Of these, the pose of the Sufferer is easily the most farcical.

Unlike Benchley and Thurber in their roles of the little man in an alien world, Twain as Sufferer endures travail that is more the result of the machinations of others than of his own confusion or ineptness. Then, too, his woes are more physical than psychological. Most of the situations he gets into are the hackneyed ones: riding a bony mule, bathing without soap, eating nauseating native food, being cheated by clever merchants, falling over chairs in the dark, having to listen to amateur musicians, being victimized by heartless chambermaids. Some of the situations, however, are more novel. At Steamboat Springs, Nevada, Twain is given a "Wake-up Jake" which has him retching and bleeding at the nose for forty-eight hours; at Niagara he is thrown over the Falls by a band of resentful Irish Indians and almost drowns because the only person in a position to rescue him is unhappily the local coroner on the prowl for business; in Tennessee as a new writer for the *Morning Glory and Johnson County War Whoop* he is stoned, shot, cow-hided, thrown out of the window, and scalped.[10]

When set upon, Twain's Sufferer usually reacts in one of two dramatically different ways. Either he becomes paranoid or he becomes unbelievably stoical. When paranoid, he is sure that he is being deliberately tortured or swindled. The torturers become "imposters" or "villains" or "assassins," and the Sufferer longs to get even. Sometimes he does, too, as in the instance of the seventh incompetent watchmaker to whom Twain in "My Watch" takes his timepiece for repairs. This one, a former steamboat engineer, advises Twain that his watch "makes too much steam — you want to hang the monkey-wrench on the safety-valve!" This is too much for the Sufferer. He brains the watchmaker on the spot, and has him buried at his own expense (*Works,* VII, 5). On other occasions, however, the Sufferer reacts with almost formal dignity. In *Innocents Abroad,* for instance, he remains calm and composed even while being vilely "polished" by the attendant in a Turkish bath. "I soon saw that he was reducing my size. He bore hard on his mitten, and from under it rolled little cylinders, like macaroni. It could not be dirt, for it was too white. He pared me down in this way for a long time. Finally I said: 'It is a tedious process. It will take hours to trim me to the size you want me; I will wait; go and borrow a jack-plane'" (*Works,* II, 90-91).

The Sufferer is easily the most farcical of Twain's comic roles. The results of the pose can be seen in the ludicrous situations, the wildly exaggerated imagery, the disproportionate reactions of the narrator, the tone of grossly injured innocence, and the gaudily pictorial style. In no other role did Twain so fully exploit the Western penchant for exaggeration. It is not surprising, therefore, to discover that he employed the pose most frequently during his Western years and the decade and a half just following. In all its pristine rowdiness the Sufferer appeared as late as 1879 in *A Tramp Abroad*. Thereafter, however, Twain turned to the role less and less frequently though he never finally rejected it.

In the Simpleton Twain created a role in which his main trouble was mental rather than physical. As Simpleton he pretends to believe the impossible — or at least the outrageously improbable. What is more, he pretends to be anxious that his readers believe it too. The result is an earnest and solemn style quite in conflict with the silly evidence and the absurd logic. Probably the most famous example of Twain as Simpleton is in *Innocents Abroad* where he tells about visiting the tomb of Adam and the column there marking the center of the earth. It *is* the center of the earth, the Simpleton solemnly assures us, because among other reasons it was from under this very column that the dust was taken from which Adam was made. "This can surely be regarded in the light of a settler. It is not likely that the original first man would have been made from an inferior quality of earth when it was entirely convenient to get first quality from the world's center. This will strike any reflecting mind forcibly. That Adam was formed of dirt procured in this very spot is amply proven by the fact that in six thousand years no man has ever been able to prove that the dirt was *not* procured here whereof he was made" (*Works*, II, 306). In the same straight-faced fashion the Simpleton in *Roughing It* passes along various whoppers about Brigham Young, such as the one that for reason of economy he had to sell seventy-two bedsteads for his wives at a loss and substitute a communal contraption seven feet long and ninety-six feet wide. At other points in the book he tells of a Mr. Harris riding by "with a polite nod, homeward bound, with a bullet through one of his lungs, and several through his hips"; of Washoe winds that blow the hair off of the heads of Carson residents while they are looking skyward for their hats; of a former high chief of Honaunau who was fourteen or fifteen feet tall and who carried a coffin-shaped stone weighing several thousand pounds a considerable distance because he wanted to use it for a lounge.[11]

Despite the appealing idiocy of the Simpleton, it was with the Tenderfoot that Twain created his most effective and most memorable comic pose. The Simpleton is a manufacture: an adult imbecile created for the purpose of comedy and satire. The Tenderfoot comes more out of real experience. As Twain develops the point of view, it is that of the greenest of greenhorns, a youth certainly more stupid that Twain actually was, and probably more lovable. Eventually, of course, the pose of the Tenderfoot is the one that gets transmuted into the greatest of his narrative personae, Huck Finn. But as a pose its most interesting treatment can be found in *Roughing It,* the cub pilot chapters in *Life on the Mississippi,* and in "A Private History of a Campaign That Failed."

In the travel letters and in *Innocents Abroad,* the Tenderfoot, like his other poses, is a pretense Twain adopts for the single incident and then quickly discards for his real viewpoint or another pose. In the first half of *Roughing It,* however, Twain uses the Tenderfoot pose consistently enough to make it a controlling element in the movement of the story. Although the pose is never a firm one, since it frequently slides off into another pose or into the point of view of the thirty-five year old author, it is nevertheless sustained well enough in the early parts of the book that, as Henry Nash Smith has already pointed out, a basic movement is perceptible from the point of view of the Tenderfoot to that of a knowing old-timer. "The narrative is not everywhere controlled by this theme, but the pattern of initiation is sufficiently clear in the first half of the book, to constitute an expressive structure."[12] Unfortunately for the total unity of *Roughing It,* this pattern disappears in the second half of the book, where in rewriting the Sandwich Island letters Twain once more becomes the quick-change artist, playing a whole repertoire of roles.

It is in "Old Times on the Mississippi" that Twain manipulates and sustains the role of the Tenderfoot successfully enough to make it a consistent and appealing characterization. Even here, though, the pose is not a firmly held one. Typically, what Twain does is to introduce each incident from his own viewpoint as an adult of about forty, then slide into the pose of the Tenderfoot in narrating an incident, and finally return to the viewpoint of the adult for comment on the incident. The pose, therefore, is not maintained throughout the work but is assumed and discarded so adroitly that one is hardly conscious of the change. Furthermore, its effects are not dissipated by resort to other and more raucous roles. As a matter of record, Twain was almost twenty-two when he apprenticed himself to Horace Bixby to learn the river from St. Louis to New Orleans, and he undoubtedly knew as much about the river as most beginning pilots. But he pretends in "Old Times" that he was not more than sixteen and that he was so green he did not know he had to stand a regular watch or memorize landmarks. From the beginning it is obvious that the pretense is one that Twain found congenial. When writing as the Tenderfoot he is at great pains to see his material as the greenhorn might. The results appear especially in the sharply pictorial detailing, the colorful rendering of river talk, and the combination of wonderment and anxiety — sometimes fear — in the Tenderfoot's attitude toward the river. Except for Huck Finn, no other point of view excites his sensibilities so richly.

I even got to "setting" her and letting the wheel go entirely, while I vaingloriously turned my back and inspected the stern marks and hummed a tune, a sort of easy indifference which I had prodigiously admired in Bixby and other great pilots. Once I inspected rather long, and when I faced to the front again my heart flew into my mouth so suddenly that if I hadn't clapped my teeth together I should have lost it. One of those frightful bluff reefs was stretching its deadly length right across our bows! My head was gone in a moment; I did not know which end I stood on; I gasped and could not get my breath; I spun the wheel down with such rapidity that it wove itself together like a spider's web; the boat answered and turned square away from the reef, but the reef followed her! I fled, but still it followed, still it kept — right across my bows! I never looked to see where I was going, I only fled. The awful crash was imminent. Why didn't that villain come? If I committed the crime of ringing a bell I might get thrown overboard. But better that than kill the boat. So in blind desperation, I started such a rattling "shivaree" down below as never had astounded an engineer in this world before, I fancy. Amidst the frenzy of the bells the engines began to back and fill in a curious way, and my reason forsook its throne — we were about to crash into the woods on the other side of the river. Just then Mr. Bixby stepped calmly into view on the hurricane-deck. My soul went out to him in gratitude. My distress vanished; I would have felt safe on the brink of Niagara with Mr. Bixby on the hurricane-deck.[13]

Whereas Twain adopted the pose of the Tenderfoot in these cub pilot sketches primarily for comic effect, it seems clear that something deeper motivated its use in "The Private History of the Campaign That Failed." Twain could hardly have been unaware of the criticism levelled at him by fellow Missourians for his failure to fight for the Confederacy. Certainly he could not have been unaware of it in the winter of 1884-85 when he visited St. Louis, Hannibal, and Keokuk, Iowa, on a lecture tour with George Washington Cable. Indeed an anonymous account of his war "experience" appeared in the Keokuk *Gate City* either while he was in Keokuk, or just after. Published in the *Century Magazine* of December 1885 "The Private History" therefore may properly be considered a reply to his critics and something of an apology. Ultimately his defense rests on the contention that he was young, green, and, in short, a Tenderfoot.

For his purposes, Twain's strategy in "A Private History" was extraordinarily astute. He could not have fully submitted to the pose of the Tenderfoot without making the sketch a farce; on the other hand, he could not have used only his adult point of view and gain the sympathy for his actions that he coveted. So he wisely combined the two points of view. On the surface, the "Private History" is the reminiscence of a fifty-year old man who is looking back upon experiences he had when he was presumably about sixteen (he was actually twenty-five). He calls himself and his companions in the Marion Rangers "boys" and he recalls indulgently how they played games, showed off, and scrapped among themselves. Yet as he maintains this adult point of view on the surface, he adds to it the point of view of the Tenderfoot by confronting the important material as the boy might. The sense of excitement is the Tenderfoot's; so are the resentment at the discipline, the increasing discouragement, and finally the the panic when it becomes known that Union troops are approaching. Almost irresistibly, as Twain merges his mature point of view with that of the innocent Tenderfoot, the reader does so too — and finds himself empathizing with the boy and excusing him for all that he does. His antics become the buffoonery of a youngster rather than the irresponsibility of a grown man. The major struggle becomes not one of the Confederacy and the Union, but of boys pitted against men. When Twain as the Tenderfoot kills a stranger supposed to be a Union soldier (a piece of pure fiction) and subsequently retires from soldiership to save his self-respect, the "retirement" seems somehow admirable. A sensitive and idealistic boy is simply pulling out of a malignant conflict in which he does not belong. Huck Finn is once more "lighting out."

The Tenderfoot of "The Private History" is, in short, one of Twain's most subtle poses. He adopts it while seeming not to do so; he employs it for serious purpose while seeming to extract from it only the usual comedy. Without doubt, it is one of the best demonstrations of his dexterity in handling point of view.

III

Even so brief a sampling of Twain's poses suggests several conclusions. The first is that the pose offered him the kind of psychic support that he wanted and needed. Since he slips into a pose at least once in almost every "Mark Twain" work, it is clear that the pose was a device that Twain found agreeable. If it did nothing else, it gave him a chance to extend into his writing his penchant for acting. One suspects, however, that he found the pose agreeable for more profound reasons. Ridden by anxieties, Twain undoubtedly welcomed the pose because its restricted point of view simplified life and made it more tolerable. From the maze of conflicting ways of seeing and judging experience the pose isolated one. Even when he did not fully submit to its demands, the mask still tended to effect a point of view less complicated than his own. Furthermore, it pushed life to a distance and made it less disturbing. Without the pose, Twain had to confront the human scene immediately and directly. And being the kind of man he was, his emotions almost inevitably became excessively engaged. What he found to his liking he sentimentalized about; what frustrated him he raged at. With the pose inserted between himself and the human scene, however, Twain could be more equable, for in effect his position became that of a spectator rather than that of a participant. In addition, since his poses were chiefly comic ones, the scene itself became not only more distant but less ominous. How profoundly the pose served Twain as a psychic prop is, of course, a matter of speculation. But one cannot help observing that for a person of Twain's temperament, it seemed to offer the ideal therapy: simplification, detachment, minimization.

Whatever question there may be about the pose's psychic aid to Twain, there can be little or none about its aesthetic usefulness. While tending to set bounds for the operation of his imagination, the pose stimulated its operation within those bounds. It is the nature of the pose to break up old habits of perception by introducing fresh or at least different ones. What results is not a new vision but a dual vision. In effect, two consciousnesses are at work, that of the pose and that of the author. The pose consciousness disciplines the imagination; the interplay between the pose consciousness and the author consciousness energizes it. When Twain contemplated Mississippi valley life simply as the adult author, as he did in much of the latter part of *Life on the Mississippi,* he wrote in what can only be called a pedestrian fashion. But when he imposed upon this adult point of view the consciousness of a sixteen-year-old boy, as he did in writing the cub pilot chapters, the perceptions became more acute, the situations more ingeniously contrived, and the style more richly dramatic. One is tempted to go further, especially with the travel accounts, and assert as a general truth that Twain's "posed" writing, taken as a whole, shows greater ingenuity and often greater sensibility than his straight writing.

The principal effects of the pose on Twain's humor are apparent in the humor's variety, continuousness, and economy. The variety is self-evident. When added to his narrative personae like Huck Finn and Hank Morgan, his repertoire of poses gives him a range in comic viewpoint that few other humorists — if any — have enjoyed. In the individual work, the pose, so long as he was willing to hold it, enabled him to sustain his humor by providing a second self-consistent system of thought continuously juxtaposed and at odds with the normal. So long as Twain poses as the Simpleton, for example, the thought processes and values of the Simpleton are in continuing though implicit conflict with the more sophisticated processes and values of Twain himself — and of the reader. Instead of the final and all-destroying flash that comes with the capper on a joke, the pose results in a persisting sense of incongruity. The joke, so to speak, never ends so long as the pose is retained. Furthermore, since the pose creates this conflict in thought processes and values implicitly, it encourages economy in statement. By the rules of the game, the pose barred Twain — or at least discouraged him — from injecting the personal interpretation and fulmination that so often made his "unposed" writing tedious. Instead, he was encouraged by the pose to concentrate upon his narrative. One of the reasons why "The Jumping Frog" is a superior work is that, controlled by the pose, Twain forgot himself and focused steadily upon the comic possibilities of his material. Every statement is a rendering of one of these possibilities. There is no waste, no gratuitous authorial underlining.

Similarly, the pose encouraged Twain to make his satire implicit and hence more economical in statement. Confronting his targets directly, Twain tended to belabor them unnecessarily, often resorting to a heated sarcasm that called more attention to itself than its subject. But with the pose he could point up the foibles and evils that offended him simply by observing them through the eyes of one of his comic constructs. As reported by the gullible Simpleton, for example, the cupidity of those in charge of the Church of the Holy Sepulchre becomes humorously and yet depressingly apparent in *Innocents Aboard* without any editorial comment from Twain.

Yet for all that Twain achieved with the comic pose, it cannot be said that he substantially exploited its finest aesthetic possibilities. For one thing, he did not consistently take advantage of its capacity, just described, for sustaining the humor or satire and for achieving economy of statement. Too often his adoption of a pose was so casual and so brief that it exerted almost no control over the narration. For another thing, Twain used the pose principally for broad rather than subtle effects. The roles he played with most gusto were those of the Sufferer and the Enthusiast, and in them he developed only the most raucous kind of farce. If somewhat less wildly idiotic in concept, the poses of the Instructor, the Simpleton, and the Gentleman still resulted in farcical situations and absurdly manipulated styles. As the Moralist Twain ran a gamut of effects from coyness to grotesque horror. Only in a role like that of the Tenderfoot did he manage to infuse his comedy with poignancy — and profundity as well.

If he seldom used the comic pose for subtlety of effect, Twain with almost equal rarity used it to give a work tonal and structural unity. Exceptions have already been noted: the use of the Gentleman to provide a structural casing for the "tedious" recollections of Simon Wheeler; the use of the Tenderfoot to create movement in the first half of *Roughing It;* the use, again, of the Tenderfoot to establish tonal harmony in "Old Times on the Mississippi." But these are exceptional cases. Ordinarily in the short pieces and certainly in the longer works Twain did not hold a pose long enough for it to operate as a unifying device. On the contrary, in alternating poses and straight writing he converted the pose into a disruptive device that more frequently than not undermined the structure and annihilated tonal unity. There is no denying Twain's range and dexterity in manipulating the comic pose. But there is some question about the effects he thereby achieved. It seems not unfair, in summation, to say that though Twain's manipulation of the pose resulted in a truly extraordinary output of high-spirited and cleverly staged short comic acts, it too seldom resulted in sustained and compelling comic drama.

1. The implication here that "Mark Twain" is not a persona for Samuel L. Clemens is intentional. Except in a few short works like "The Jumping Frog of Calaveras County" the pseudonym fails to operate with anything like the aesthetic force and consistency expected of a persona. It does not exert substantial control over the point of view, the material, the style, or the literal values. The most that can be said for Clemens' famous pseudonym in this regard, it seems to me, is that it serves as a sign of a comic sensibility at work. To insist on more than this is to indulge in oversimplification that obscures the intricate and successful uses Twain *does* make of the comic pose or mask while narrating as "Mark Twain." I take issue, therefore, with a scholar like Kenneth S. Lynn, who in parts of his *Mark Twain and Southwestern Humor* (Boston, 1959) tries to treat "Mark Twain" as a stable and self-consistent character.

2. In his *Horse Sense in American Humor* (Chicago, 1942), Walter Blair was the first to show substantially how in a work like *Innocents Abroad* Twain is for several paragraphs the silly ass, then for several paragraphs the serious commentator, and so on (pp. 195-202). More recently, Franklin R. Rogers has called this alternation of the humorous and the serious one of Twain's three "major and distinctive structural devices." *Mark Twain's Burlesque Patterns* (Dallas, Texas, 1960), p. 26.

3. *Mark Twain of the Enterprise*, ed. Henry Nash Smith (Berkeley, Calif., 1957), p. 50.

4. *The Works of Mark Twain*, Definitive Edition (New York, 1922), VII, 17. Hereafter this edition will be indicated simply as *Works*.

5. For the influence of other travel-burlesques on Twain's travel letters and books, see Franklin R. Rogers, op. cit., especially pp. 30–36.

6. Walter F. Frear, *Mark Twain and Hawaii* (Chicago, 1947), p. 355.

7. Frear, pp. 277–278.

8. Frear, pp. 367–368.

9. *Mark Twain's Travels with Mr. Brown*, eds. Franklin Walker and G. Ezra Dane (New York, 1940), p. 41.

10. *Mark Twain of the Enterprise*, pp. 73–75; *Works*, VII, 63–67, 35–43.

11. *Works*, III, 108, 146, 147; IV, 261.

12. Henry Nash Smith, "Mark Twain as an Interpreter of the Far West: The Structure of *Roughing It*," *The Frontier in Perspective* (Madison, Wis., 1957), p. 214. Professor Smith feels that the old-timer as well as the tenderfoot is an assumed point of view. While agreeing with Professor Smith's major argument about the movement in *Roughing It*, I am inclined to feel that the point of view of the old-timer is not an assumed one but the point of view of the real S. L. Clemens as he wrote the book.

13. *Works*, XII, 74–75. In the treatments here of "Old Times" and "The Private History" I am drawing somewhat on more detailed discussions I attempted in "The Relation between Point of View and Style in the Works of Mark Twain," *Style in Prose Fiction: English Institute Essays, 1958* (New York, 1959), and "Mark Twain's 'Private Campaign,'" *Civil War History*, I, (March 1955), pp. 37–45.

1963

HAMLIN HILL

KENNETH ANDREWS HAS NOTED THAT "Every book [Mark Twain] ever wrote, except *The Prince and the Pauper* and *Joan of Arc,* was constructed with its prospective sale as the important condition of its composition."[1] Most Twain students, aware of the gleeful reports of money earned and copies of books sold that are sprinkled throughout Twain's letters, would not disagree with this statement; but very little has been said about the ways that Twain, with deliberate calculation, went about constructing his books so that they would appeal to their prospective customers. Usually, critics and biographers have conceded that since his books were sold "by subscription only," and since subscription books had to be 600 to 700 pages long, Mark Twain desperately dragged into his own books anything he could use as "padding."

Thus the exigencies of subscription publication have been blamed for the long excerpts Twain "borrowed" from other authors in *Innocents Abroad, A Tramp Abroad,* and most notably in the last parts of *Life on the Mississippi.* But there is more to the story; those three words "by subscription only" hold the key, I believe, to more than the mere bulk of Twain's major travel books. They prompted several of the humorist's most familiar literary devices and techniques. The author who was overwhelmingly concerned with sales and who was a subscription-book publisher himself could not have been ignorant of the tastes of the special audience to whom subscription books — mid-nineteenth-century American style — made their appeal.

"Mark Twain: Audience and Artistry," from the American Quarterly, *XV (Spring, 1963), 25-40. Reprinted by permission of the* American Quarterly *and the author.*

The post-Civil War period saw the rise of this phenomenal Hartford-centered business: from 1861 to 1868, for example, one contemporary source calculated that Hartford subscription houses alone had made $5,000,000 by selling 1,426,000 copies of only 30 different titles.[2] Obviously, the literary-minded were not the market for these books; publication by subscription no longer meant the subsidization of works of literature like *Paradise Lost,* or of scholarship like Johnson's *Dictionary.*

Instead of the urban, literate reader, the subscription book aimed at enticing the common man, the masses, the rural, semiliterate, usually Midwestern customer who had rarely bought a book before. A deluge of book-agents (one contemporary account estimated the number at 50,000 annually),[3] the forefathers of today's encyclopedia salesmen, swarmed through the small towns and the rural areas of the country with a prospectus — a hundred or so sample pages from the work offered, with strips of the various bindings available pasted inside the cover, and with blank pages in the back on which customers wrote their orders. Agents were forbidden to sell to bookstores; and by 1897, A. D. Worthington & Co., publishers of Mary A. Livermore's *The Story of My Life,* cited in the prospectus two U. S. Circuit Court decisions in Ohio and Pennsylvania which gave subscription publishers the right to sue booksellers who offered subscription works "in the trade."[4] Because of the animosity of the regular trade, a war of words took place in the 1870s that helps to pinpoint the aims of the subscription publishers and to characterize the audience of the subscription book.[5]

The Trade Circular Annual for 1871 pointed out that subscription books "are often absolutely worthless, and this is not only true with regard to the nature of their contents. . . . Beyond their title, there is nothing attractive about them." In 1872, *Publishers Weekly* moaned that one of these ugly ducklings sold for "five dollars, when the reading matter it contains, if worth anything would make about a dollar-and-a-half book in the regular trade."[6] More superciliously, the *Literary World* announced in August 1874 that "subscription books cannot possibly circulate among the better class of readers, owing to the general and not unfounded prejudice against them. . . . An author . . . who resorts to the subscription plan . . . descends to a constituency of a lower grade and inevitably loses caste."[7] (The author, in other words, had a choice that Charles Dudley Warner aptly summarized in an 1874 letter to Helen Hunt Jackson: "I think if you were to see your dainty literature in such ill-conditioned volumes, you would just die. There is no doubt, however, that 'by subscription' is the only way for the author to make any money.")[8]

In their defense, the subscription houses insisted that they were not damaging the regular trade because they were not selling to its customers. Elisha Bliss of the American Publishing Company proclaimed that "in the little towns where there are no book stores the book agent induces people to buy. . . . In that way, a nucleus is formed for hundreds of thousands of little libraries throughout the country, which would never have existed except for the book agent. . . . There is a large field covered with people that have no opportunity to buy books except in the way we sell them."[9] A Rev. John Todd was delighted in 1872 because he found subscription books supplied to "mechanics and farmers. . . in places wholly unexpected, and where, a few years ago, a new book would very seldom be found."[10] James S. Barcus eulogized "the rank and file of book salesmen that go up and down the highways and byways carrying good tidings of knowledge and erudition to the masses."[11] And finally, F. E. Compton has recently observed that this special audience was "far removed from bookstores, physically or spiritually, and most of them would never have bought a book if the subscription business had not 'sold' them the idea and brought the book to them."[12]

It is fairly easy to tell what these "mechanics and farmers" wanted in their books, or more to the point, what the subscription publishers thought they wanted. Size was an important factor; the book had to contain what Bret Harte called "the intrinsic worth of bigness . . . which commends itself to the rural economist, who likes to get a material return for his money."[13] Or as a writer for *The Nation* put it, "The rural-district reader likes to see that he has got his money's worth even more than he likes wood engravings. At least, such is the faith in Hartford; and no man ever saw a book agent with a small volume in his hand."[14] Almost always, the prospectuses played up the number of pages by using bold-face type or italics or capital letters to announce the size of the book: the prospectus for *The Curse of Drink or, Stories of Hell's Commerce,* edited by Elton R. Shaw, even increased its size by comparison. "THE COMPLETE BOOK," it advertised, "CON-

TAINS OVER 550 LARGE PAGES (equal to 800 pages of the usual sized book)."[15]

And the subscription reader, unmindful of literary frills, wanted fact, not fiction. He bought autobiographies and biographies and travel narratives, legal and medical do-it-yourself books, family Bibles and religious commentary — but few novels. In a list of books which the American Publishing Company offered for sale in 1885, for example, there were 32 works of nonfiction and only 17 of fiction, including children's books and the humorous works in which the company specialized.[16] The proportion generally was even more strongly balanced in favor of factual writing. "Mighty few books that come strictly under the head of *literature* will sell by subscription,"[17] Mark Twain once told Joel Chandler Harris; so nonfictional narrative was of primary interest.

Usually, the subscription-book reader wanted topical material, and subscription-book publishers exploited his interest. They were guilty, one of their number admitted, of "flooding the country with flashy books produced overnight on some spectacular event."[18] Right after the Civil War, dozens of books like *The American Conflict, The Great Rebellion, Four Years in Secessia, The Secret Service, Underground,* the *Pictorial Field History of the Civil War, The Spy of the Rebellion* and *A Personal History of Ulysses S. Grant* rolled off the presses. When Mormonism became a popular topic, *The Exposé, or Mormons and Mormonism, The Mormon Wife, The Past, Present and Future of Mormonism, "Tell It All:" The Story of a Life's Experience in Mormonism* and *Lament of a Mormon Wife* promptly appeared. Between the time of Stanley's commission to find Livingstone in 1869 and the first few years of the 1870s appeared *The Last Journals of David Livingstone, Africa and Its Explorers, or Livingstone Lost and Found* and *Livingstone's Life Work.* In the midst of the Nares, Nordenskiöld, *Polaris* and *Jeannette* polar expeditions of the early 1870's, subscription houses published *Our Lost Explorers, The Frozen Zone and Its Explorers* and a reprint of Kane's *Arctic Exploration.* Even as late as 1901, subscription publishers dashed off "memorial" volumes at the deaths of McKinley and Victoria.

Finally, the subscription-book reader apparently expected an odd mixture of sensationalism and moralizing that could both shock and elevate readers who were not very different from the Grangerfords and Shepherdsons interrupting their feud to listen to a sermon on brotherhood. Beginning with the *Life* magazine review of *Huck Finn* many critics have commented on the murders, lynchings and blood baths that take place in Twain's supposedly "humorous" books; but it was a quality of many subscription volumes. Scalpings, massacres, amputations and beheadings, gruesomely illustrated by cheap artists, sprinkled the pages of Richardson's *Beyond the Mississippi*. Those "memorial" volumes to McKinley, which were to contain complete biographies of the President, had prospectus material chosen almost completely from chapters dealing with the assassination: pictures of the fatal shots, very approximate likenesses of Emma Goldman and Czolgosz, medical diagrams showing where the two bullets penetrated McKinley's body. Although Mary Livermore's *The Story of My Life* contained very few chapters concerned with her schoolteaching activities on a Southern plantation, over half of the prospectus pages were chosen from these chapters, which depicted the brutality of the overseer and included a full-page illustration of a slave being whipped to death. Twain himself calculated that the banning of *Huckleberry Finn* by the Concord Public Library would double its sales. But there were, paradoxically, proprieties — hypocritical though they might have been — that the reader expected to be followed. The most sanguine book might be justified on the grounds that it was "Historical," "Accurate," "Realistic" or "Edifying." Thus the cover of the prospectus for Buffalo Bill's *Story of the Wild West* (1888) might picture the scalping of Yellow Hair (in three colors, including red for blood) as long as it insisted on its historical importance. George Bidwell's *Forging His Chains. . . With the Story of . . . the So-called £1,000,000 Forgery on the Bank of England and a Complete Account of His Arrest, Trial, Conviction, and Confinement for Fourteen Years in English Prisons* (1888) was a very "moral" book, its publisher insisted in the prospectus, because it taught the evils of the life the autobiography related. The average nineteenth-century American's taste allowed him, along the same lines, to read every last detail of Mrs. Stowe's account of Byron's incest as long as he canceled his subscription to the *Atlantic Monthly* immediately afterward; he could wallow in all the lurid details of the Beecher-Tilton affair as long as he maintained a pious air himself. And the instruments of popular culture, including the subscription-book publisher, allowed him to titillate his urge for sensationalism and provided him at the same time with a self-righteous excuse.

Twain's reaction to these subscription requirements was in part probably innate; he, too, like his audience, was small-town Midwestern in his upbringing, originally Calvinistic in his religion (though he confessed once that *Fanny Hill* "charmed" him), and he professed a natural preference for history and biography over fiction. As a copywriter for *Following the Equator* phrased it, "the medium he employs oftenest is the simplest — a plain American-English. He sees like an American, thinks like an American, feels like an American, reasons like an American, is American, blood and bone, heart and head, and this is the secret of [his] great success."[19] Or, as the Syracuse *Daily Standard* put it, "The eyes with which he sees are our eyes as well as his. . . . And thus the book becomes a transcript of our own sentiments."[20]

But, more important, there is strong evidence that he constructed his subscription books consciously to appeal to the tastes of a reader much like himself.

Certainly it is true that Twain was constantly aware of the size of the ideal subscription book. All that he needed to do was to remind himself to read his contracts, most of which called for enough manuscript to make a 600- to 700-page book. Through the 1870s and 1880s, Twain snatched up material from other authors, from his own earlier published works, from notes and suggestions in his notebooks. By the time he began his third travel book, *A Tramp Abroad,* he had wrestled with the problem of size and length so much that he actually began composing that book not according to a formal narrative arrangement but rather by assembling anecdotal, episodic material which could later be placed upon a narrative thread. He reported to his publisher that he had written about 50,000 words, "but it is in disconnected form," he explained, "and cannot be used until joined together by the writing of at least a dozen intermediate chapters."[21] To Howells, at about the same time, he wrote a revealing letter about two articles he thought were lost in the mails: "When a body is yoked down to the grinding out of a 600-page 8vo. book, to lose a chapter is like losing a child. I was not at all sure that I should use both of those chapters in my book, but to *have them around,* in case of need, would give that added comfort which comes of having a life-preserver handy in a ship which *might* go down."[22]

In recent years, Twain critics have spent considerable time pointing out and analyzing the ways that the humorist's writings followed an anecdotal, almost picaresque pattern. They have noted that he once mentioned to his wife a formula for speech-making which alternated humor with seriousness;[23] they have proposed its source in a technique of burlesque;[24] and they have argued that its apparent haphazardness reflects the "divine Amateur."[25] But the suggestions in these quotations about the composition of *A Tramp Abroad* indicate that one of the most typical of Twain's literary techniques was a structure to which subscription publication contributed enormously; it was the method whereby an epistolary journalist solved the problem of writing subscription-length books.

Even further, though, the way Twain worked statistical, expository and humorous material together was probably a result of his desire for audience appeal. Remember, the subscription-book readers wanted knowledge and information; they were not likely to make a pleasure excursion to Europe themselves, so the statistics and the descriptive material in the travel books satisfied their curiosity and gave them the vicarious thrills of looking down from the cathedral at Milan, of contemplating the Sphinx or of climbing the Matterhorn. (Even *Pudd'nhead Wilson,* its publishers insisted, was valuable because it "depicted the character of that period [the ante-bellum South] in such a realistic manner.")[26] These were experiences outside the realm of the popular reader, and by skillfully alternating description and statistics with humorous passages Twain gave them information in doses small enough to satisfy without becoming boring.

Twain's publishers exploited these values: *Roughing It* was advertised as "Designed to Amuse and Instruct";[27] a squib advertising *Innocents Abroad* announced that, "while running over with wit and humor. . . . it still teems with glowing descriptions, and with elegant and classical allusions." *A Tramp Abroad,* it was claimed, "will be found not only exceedingly amusing, but like its predecessors, brimfull [*sic*] of valuable information."[28]

Newspapers, too, called attention to this alternation of humorous and informative writing when they reviewed his travel books. Of *Innocents Abroad,* the Newark *Register* commented, "It is a rare and wonderful combination. The humor is natural, never forced; the narrative is instructive . . ."; the New York *Express* noted, "truth is told to us in such winsome form, that we cannot but listen to it with agreeable sensations"; the Trenton *True American* summed it up with, "The work abounds in historical facts, descriptions of different countries and important personages, scenes and incidents, so bound together by wit, pleasantry and flashes of grotesque humor, as to make it one of the most readable and amusing books of the period." For *A Tramp Abroad,* it was the same. The Scranton *Free Press* mused, "People do not like to read a volume of travels because it is dry and prosy, but when all this knowledge is combined with sparkling wit the reading becomes a pleasure instead of a task"; the Cleveland *Herald* noted, "Mark Twain has the happy faculty of combining much valuable information with most amusing stories"; and the *Tolland County Leader* said that factual material "which if given by other writers would be dry and uninteresting is here fairly 'sugar-coated,' as none but Clemens know how to do."[29]

Twain himself pointed out the formula when he wrote a letter in 1876 to Dan DeQuille, who was planning to write a subscription book about the Comstock Lode. DeQuille also had some humorous newspaper sketches he proposed printing separately. Twain told his friend to work both batches into the same manuscript: "I'll show you how to make a man read every one of those sketches, under the stupid impression that they are mere accidental incidents that have dropped in on you unawares in the course of your novel." In the same letter he advised DeQuille, "Bring along *lots* of *dry statistics* — it's the very best sauce a humorous book can have. Ingeniously used, they just make a reader smack his chops in gratitude. We must have *all* the Bonanza statistics you can rake and scrape."[30] Both these injunctions have as their explicit bases not a natural predilection on Twain's part for a literary form that imitates the rambling, associational order of the spoken language, but, instead, the man who is going to read the book. Statistics and sketches; exposition and humor; narrative and "accidental incidents"; it is exactly the formula that DeVoto said was "best adapted to his [Twain's] mind . . . a loosely flowing narrative, actually or fictitiously autobiographical — a current interrupted for the presentation of episodes, for, merely, the telling of stories."[31] But, according to these suggestions to DeQuille, it was a narrative pattern

that, because it balanced informal, reminiscent, autobiographical anecdotes with dry statistics, made Twain's travel books palatable to his
readers.

DeVoto also pointed out (pp. 245-46) that there was a form of
development in the technique:

> [*Innocents Abroad's*] steady progress is accomplished by means of stories.
> Some of them are brief, unelaborated anecdotes, in no way different from the
> type out of which they proceed, but others already show Mark's perception
> that this form can be utilized for more intricate effects. . . .
> This same framework produces "Roughing It," "A Tramp Abroad," "Life
> on the Mississippi," and "Following the Equator." The narrative interlude is
> organically developed in these later books; possibilities are more thoroughly
> realized. . . . Sometimes the intent is a mere mechanical joke . . . sometimes
> . . . it is a means for presenting in silhouette a lifetime or a civilization.

Improvement in the discrete anecdote was obviously more erratic
than DeVoto suggested: the "Skeleton of a Black Forest Novel" and
some of the Rhine legends in *A Tramp Abroad* were inferior to much
of the anecdotal material in *Roughing It*. But nothing in *Innocents
Abroad* equals some half-dozen yarns in *Roughing It,* and Twain never
wrote better sketches than the "Blue Jay Yarn" and "Nicodemus
Dodge." His craftsmanship in handling episodic material reached its
highest point when he called upon reminiscences from his own youth
and Western years, but refinement of the technique went beyond the
increased exploitation of autobiographical materials.

Formal arrangement in each of the first three travel books was
largely dictated by the material available to Twain beforehand. In
Innocents Abroad, with a sustaining narrative available from start
to finish, the stress of adding to the original material was least evident. In *Roughing It,* where travel narrative dwindled to the anticlimactic statistics on Virginia City mining and the factual reporting
of the Sandwich Islands letters, and in *A Tramp Abroad,* where he
wrote the mass of anecdotal material before thinking of a structural
pattern for the book, the rigors of composition were more apparent.
In order, *Roughing It, A Tramp Abroad* and *Life on the Mississippi*
(after the "Old Times on the Mississippi" segment) were looser,
more autobiographical, less unified than *Innocents Abroad,* simply
because they depended less and less on a preconceived "narrative
plank." But at the same time, the anecdotal material became more

and more successfully integrated into the narrative movement, at
least through *A Tramp Abroad.* In *Innocents,* most of the anecdotes
were on an associational level, tied onto the narrative thread by only
the most mechanical means. Thus Twain introduced the account
of himself in his father's office with the corpse by the sentence, "It is
hard to forget repulsive things. I remember yet. . . ." The "Benton
House" passage followed the statement, "We are stopping at Shep-
herd's [*sic*] Hotel, which is the worst on earth except the one I
stopped at once in a small town in the United States." The story of
the avalanche on Holliday's Hill proceeded from a description of the
Great Pyramid to a brief mention of a bluff on the Mississippi above
Selma, Missouri, to the sentence, "In still earlier years, than those I
have been recalling, Holliday's Hill, in our town, was to me the noblest
work of God." In a large share of *Roughing It,* as Professor Henry
Nash Smith has shown, most of the anecdotes related in some way to the
narrative pattern describing "the process by which the tenderfoot
narrator is transformed into the old timer, the vernacular character."
Only the story of the camel who ate the manuscript in Syria was of
the artificial, associational sort. And in *A Tramp Abroad,* too, most
of the anecdotes contributed to the burlesque. Even the "Blue Jay
Yarn" and the "Nicodemus Dodge" story exploited the distinction
between appearance and reality that underscored the spoofing of
a "walking tour" by two inspired idiots incapable of realizing that
they were not walking at all. *A Tramp Abroad* would have been a
much better book if Twain had only written more anecdotes, had
possessed a larger stock of "chapters" to thread onto the narrative
plank.

So the process worked both ways: although successive travel
volumes increasingly lost cohesiveness and unity as Twain concen-
trated on smaller units of composition, those units—sketches, tales,
yarns and anecdotes—improved both intrinsically and in the ways
Twain blended them into the books. Though the patchwork arrangement may have had the oral tale and Twain's newspaper apprentice
work as its origin, it was the subscription-length book which forced
its refinement and adaptation to sustained works.

Twain was aware, too, of the topical interests of the subscription
audience, and his choice of subject matter was frequently dependent
on the timeliness of his material. In a letter of July 22, 1869, to Elisha

Bliss, Twain complained about delays in the printing of *Innocents Abroad* which he felt would damage the value of the book: "I have ceased to expect a large sale from a book whose success depended in a great measure upon its publication while the public were as yet interested in its subject."[32]

Roughing It, which Henry Nash Smith notes "Twain conceived of writing . . . in the first place because he believed his experience of the mining boom provided him with a subject that would interest his readers,"[33] was published during a vogue of Western Books, including Bret Harte's, John Hay's, Joaquin Miller's, Clarence King's, and among subscription volumes, Richardson's *Beyond the Mississippi,* Mrs. Frances Victor's *The River of the West,* Mrs. Fanny Kelly's *Narrative of My Captivity Among the Sioux Indians* and Stephen Powers' *Afoot and Alone.* Indeed, there were so many books dealing with Western travel and adventure between 1869 and 1872 that Twain feared the sales of *Roughing It* would be damaged because its material was "too hackneyed."[34]

This same desire for topicality influenced the humorist's fiction. In *The Gilded Age,* his use of graft and corruption was, Albert Kitzhaber has suggested, "no more than an attempt—and a successful one—to get a good sale by capitalizing on current news."[35] The Pomeroy scandal, Tweed's conviction, the Credit Mobilier, the failure of Jay Cooke, all were current events that would stimulate interest in Warner's and Twain's novel. In the Preface to the London edition, Twain felt the necessity of pointing out to his English audience that the book dealt with the current American problem of the "shameful corruption which has lately crept into our politics, and in a handful of years has spread until the pollution has affected some portion of every State and Territory in the Union."

Tom Sawyer, too, was written, as Walter Blair has indicated, in the wake of a number of books "satirizing some of the excesses of Sunday School fiction,"[36] by such writers as Thomas Bailey Aldrich, C. B. Lewis, James M. Bailey and Robert Burdette. "Old Times on the Mississippi" appeared in concert with many articles and books exploring the South and the Mississippi Valley. Parts of *Huckleberry Finn* were written during the "bloody shirt" campaign of 1880 and exploited the lynchings, murders and other Southern pastimes that, in Blair's words, "Northern newspapers, predominantly Republican, somehow found . . . newsworthy."[37] Consistently, then, Twain was aware of and adapted to his purposes themes and topics that, although they were not of literary interest to most of the major writers of his generation, had captured the popular imagination.

Mark Twain's strange mixture of sensationalism and moralizing is one of his most singular — and most puzzling — characteristics. The peculiar juxtaposition of grisly humor, using death, mutilation and putrefaction for its source, and highly respectable (and often maudlin) bursts of moral propriety constitutes one of the most incongruous aspects of Twain's writing. The problem of explaining the writing of *1601* and "Some Thoughts on the Science of Onanism," on the one hand, and the moral indignation of the outburst against Titian's "Venus" in the last chapters of *A Tramp Abroad,* on the other, will certainly not find a pat solution in an examination of Twain's subscription audience; nevertheless, there are some interesting correlations.

The fact that physical violence can, and in American literature frequently does, act as a sublimation for sexual violence is a common enough idea; so is D. H. Lawrence's belief that Victorian literature "tickled the dirty little secret" of pruriency. At any event, the public — and especially the subscription-book reader — liked sensationalism. It even made best-sellers out of many sensational (and sensual) books that were wise enough to "point a moral" at the conclusion.[38] In other words, there was a time-tested formula that allowed the writer for a popular audience to include the morbid, the gruesome, even (though not in Twain's case) the lascivious in his writing as long as he also insisted on the didactic function of his material.

From the story of the corpse in his father's office from *The Innocents Abroad,* through the tales of Slade in *Roughing It,* the account of the glacier yielding up frozen bits and pieces of the members of an early climbing expedition in *A Tramp Abroad,* to the wholesale carnage of *The Prince and the Pauper, Huckleberry Finn* and *The Connecticut Yankee,* Twain manifested an almost adolescent curiosity for the macabre, the grotesque and the morbid. Even as late as *Following the Equator,* he quoted gory descriptions of native home-remedies (including self-amputation by fire) and his publisher devoted a full-page illustration to a kangaroo decapitating a man. The illustrations and contents chosen to go into Twain's prospectuses reinforce the idea that both author and publisher expected physical violence to appeal to an audience perhaps not too far removed from the one that viewed the death of Boggs in *Huck Finn* by "squirming and scrouging and pushing and shoving to get at the window and have a look." Whatever theory one might advance to explain the psychological basis of Twain's fascination, the subscription publication of his books could only reinforce the idea that it made good, marketable copy.

It is important, too, that Twain almost never publicly sermonized against his popular audience. The persona of Mark Twain preferred Tahoe to Como, chromos to the Old Masters, and rural American food to European cuisine; he railed against all the values Henry James became aware of in Paris, and — with only a few exceptions — wrote satire that intended, in Dixon Wecter's words, "to captivate the groundlings."[39] Twain, it is true, was a "groundling" himself, from Missouri both by birth and by temperament; and Fred L. Pattee correctly suggested once that Twain "measured not by appearance or by tradition, but by intrinsic worth."[40] Even if he did so from the innate bases of his own mind, he was a groundling with some literary aspirations that his fulminations against appearances and tradition seriously undercut. Consider in close contexts two of Twain's most famous statements concerning his own art: "Humor must not professedly teach, and it must not professedly preach, but it must do both if it would live forever. . . . I have always preached. . . . If the humor came of its own accord and uninvited, I have allowed it a place in my sermon, but I was not writing the sermon for the sake of the humor. I should have written the sermon just the same, whether any humor applied for admission or not."[41] The other statement is his famous letter of 1889 to Andrew Lang:

The thin top crust of humanity — the cultivated — are worth pacifying, worth pleasing, worth coddling, worth nourishing and preserving with dainties and delicacies, it is true; but to be caterer to that little faction is no very dignified or valuable occupation, it seems to me; it is merely feeding the over-fed, and there must be small satisfaction in that. . . .

Indeed I have been misjudged, from the very first. I have never tried in even one single instance, to help cultivate the cultivated classes. I was not equipped for it, either by native gifts or training. And I never had any ambition in that direction, but always hunted for bigger game — the masses.[42]

Though this statement is defensive, having been prompted by the hostile English reception of *A Connecticut Yankee*, the two remarks together nevertheless suggest that Twain was able to objectify his attitude into a tenet of audience-appeal. It was a quality, too, which publishers and newspapers called attention to. *Innocents Abroad* and *Roughing It* were both advertised as "Particularly adapted to Family Reading," therefore presumably implying, as the New Jersey *National Standard* claimed for *Innocents,* "its morals are of a high tone." Or, as the *New Jersey Journal* unctuously phrased it, *Innocents Abroad* was "pure in morals, and just the thing for fire-side reading."

Thus strange mixtures in tone constantly crop up in Twain's subscription books, mixtures that run all the way from the starkest bloodletting to downright prudery. However difficult this anomalous combination becomes to the critic or the psychoanalyst, it played upon two of the expectations of the subscription audience.

Other forces pulled Twain in the opposite direction; the desire for literary as well as popular acclaim made the humorist "feel the aspirations of an artist, to crave deeper approval than had come to the crackerbox humorists like Sam Slick or Jack Downing."[43] His strivings for narrative unity and structure, for example, might be attributed to the tug the other way. When Howells advised Twain during the writing of *Tom Sawyer,* "Don't hurry the writing for the sake of making a book,"[44] he was pointing up the conflict between literary and subscription standards. Twain was too sensitive about his own reputation not to be aware that the animosity of the regular trade was as strong toward a subscription-book author as it was toward the book itself. In the 1880s Twain was to receive several personal attacks on this very score: The Chicago *Tribune* pointed out that *The Stolen White Elephant* had been "placed in the hands of a respectable publisher instead of offering booksellers a premium on dishonesty in order to obtain for their shelves copies of a book 'sold only by subscription' "; when Twain made fun of the banning of *Huck Finn* by the Concord Public Library, the Boston *Advertiser* raised questions as to whether "his impudent intimation that a larger sale and larger profits are a satisfactory recompense to him for the unfavorable judgment of honest critics, is a true indication of the standard by which he measures success in literature;"[45] and in 1886, John Wanamaker printed an advertisement in the Philadelphia *Press* commenting on Twain's sale of Grant's *Memoirs.* The "unfortunate manner of publication," Wanamaker claimed, had made the family of Grant, the book-buying public and the bookstores all "losers." "And who are the gainers? Book-pedlers and book-pedler publishers; nobody else."[46] Even earlier, though, Twain couldn't have ignored the subscription-trade book war of the 1870s, and he certainly would not have failed to notice that Howells, his literary court of last resort, had turned down the idea of publishing his campaign biography of Hayes with the American Publishing Company.[47] As he depended more and more on Howells' pronouncements about him in the *Atlantic* book reviews, Twain was obviously yearning for the critical approval of those "honest critics."

So even though Twain could announce significantly in 1887 that James R. Osgood (a trade publisher then) was "the best publisher who ever breathed, and that [Osgood] could have every thing he owned," he also told Howells two years later, after six years of relative literary failures, "I want to make a book which people will *read*."[48] It wasn't just the problem of income, either; Twain was aware of the two distinct audiences, one of whom he had not reached, even with Howells' help, and the other which he reached all too well by painting himself striped and turning cartwheels. But he loved that audience, too, and needed its approval just as much as he did the approval of those "honest critics." The letter to Andrew Lang followed by over a decade a comment Twain made to Howells about the public reception of his drama, *Ah Sin*: "Nearly every time the audience roared," he moaned, "I knew it was over something that would be condemned in the morning (justly, too) but must be left in — for low comedies are written for the drawing-room, the kitchen & the stable, & if you cut out the kitchen & the stable the drawing-room can't support the play by itself."[49] Even though Osgood might be the best publisher in the country, he did not sell books by the fifty-thousands and he did not sell books for the kitchen and the stable. Most frequently Twain chose the course calculated to market his books to the widest audience, and among all the factors that shaped his art, the implications of those words on the title pages of his major works — "Sold by Subscription Only" — played a major part.

1. *Nook Farm: Mark Twain's Hartford Circle* (Cambridge, 1950), pp. 156-57.
2. "Subscription Books," *Trade Circular Annual for 1871* (New York, 1871), p. 110.
3. "Subscription Books," New York *Herald-Tribune*, October 28, 1874, p. 8.
4. Prospectus for Mary A. Livermore, *The Story of My Life or The Sunshine and Shadow of Seventy Years* (1897), in the Coe Library, University of Wyoming.

5. In addition to articles cited in footnotes herein, the subscription-regular trade war was carried on in the following: "Subscription Books," *Publishers Weekly,* III (March 1, 1873), 217-18; "Subscription Books Again," *ibid.* (March 15, 1873), pp. 262-63; "Letter to the Editor: Subscription Books," *ibid.,* pp. 263-64; "Subscription Books in the Regular Trade," *ibid.,* IV (September 6, 1873), 239; "The Trade and Subscription Books," *ibid.,* XVII (April 24, 1880), 425; "Subscription Books," *ibid.,* XIX (May 7, 1881), 510; " 'Sold Only by Subscription,' " *ibid.* (May 21, 1881), 548-49; "Two Views of Book Canvassing," *Critic,* XXV (July 21, 1894), 44. A. L. Vogelback, "The Publication and Reception of *Huckleberry Finn* in America," *American Literature,* XI (1939), 266-67, cites two articles on the subject in the Chicago *Tribune,* June 10, 1882, and July 16, 1882, p. 5.

6. "The Subscription Book Trade," *Publishers Weekly,* II (July 25, 1872), 94.

7. S. R. Crocker, "Subscription Books," *Literary World,* V (August 1874), 40.

8. Andrews, p. 122.

9. "Subscription Books," New York *Herald-Tribune,* October 28, 1874, p. 8.

10. "Book Publishing and Book Selling," *The American Publisher,* I (January 1872), 4.

11. James S. Barcus, *The Science of Selling . . .* (New York, 1917), p. 7.

12. F. E. Compton, *Subscription Books* (New York, 1939), p. 36.

13. "Review of *Innocents Abroad,*" *Overland Monthly,* IV (January 1870), 100.

14. "Review of *Innocents Abroad,*" *The Nation,* IX (September 2, 1869), 194-95.

15. In the Coe Library, University of Wyoming, in a collection of thirty-seven prospectuses which I have examined.

16. In the prospectus for Albert D. Richardson's *Personal History of U. S. Grant* (1885) in the Coe Library, University of Wyoming.

17. *Mark Twain's Letters,* ed. Albert B. Paine (New York, 1917), I, 402. The reviewer for *Old and New,* IX (March 1874), 386, pointed out that *The Gilded Age* was "the first instance, so far as we know, of a story-book issued 'by subscription.' "

18. Compton, p. 37.

19. Prospectus for *Following the Equator* in the American Literature Collections, Yale University Library.

20. Quoted in the 1872 prospectus for *The Innocents Abroad,* in possession of the present writer. This salesman's dummy contains eight pages of contemporary newspaper estimates of Twain, and .all further uncited newspaper quotations are taken from it.

21. Clemens to Frank Bliss, Heidelberg, July 13, 1878, quoted in Walter Blair, *Mark Twain & Huck Finn* (Berkeley, 1960), p. 164.

22. *Mark Twain-Howells Letters,* eds. Henry Nash Smith and William M. Gibson (Cambridge, 1960), I, 248. The "chapters" were "The Great Revolution in Pitcairn" and "The Recent Great French Duel."

23. *The Love Letters of Mark Twain,* ed. Dixon Wecter (New York, 1949), pp. 165-66.

24. Franklin R. Rogers, *Mark Twain's Burlesque Patterns* (Dallas, 1960), pp. 26-27.

25. The phrase, originally Arnold Bennett's, has been quoted to the point of triteness.

26. Prospectus for *Pudd'nhead Wilson* in the American Literature Collections, Yale University Library.

27. Prospectus for *Roughing It,* in the possession of the present writer.

28. Prospectus for *A Tramp Abroad* (1879) in the possession of Franklin Meine, Chicago.

29. *Ibid.*

30. *The Big Bonanza,* ed. Oscar Lewis (New York, 1947), pp. xviii-xix.

31. Bernard DeVoto, *Mark Twain's America* (Boston, 1932), p. 245.

32. Clemens to Elisha Bliss, Elmira, July 22, 1869, typescript in the Mark Twain Papers, General Library, University of California, Berkeley; copyright © 1963, the Mark Twain Company.

33. "Introduction," *Roughing It* (New York, 1959), pp. xi-xii.

34. *The Love Letters of Mark Twain,* p. 166.

35. "Mark Twain's Use of the Pomeroy Case in *The Gilded Age,*" *Modern Language Quarterly,* XV (March 1954), 56. Though Twain's and Warner's novel and Henry Adams' *Democracy* were the major attempts to utilize the topic in fiction, it was constantly before the public in newspapers, magazines and nonfictional prose. See Lisle A. Rose, "A Bibliographical Survey of Economic and Political Writings, 1865-1900," *American Literature,* XV (1944), 381-410.

36. "On the Structure of *Tom Sawyer,*" *Modern Philology,* XXXVII (August 1939), 79.

37. *Mark Twain & Huck Finn,* p. 224. Louis J. Budd, "The Southward Currents Under Huck Finn's Raft," *Mississippi Valley Historical Review,* XLVI (September 1959), 222-37, uncovers much material in books and magazines of the late 1870s and early 1880s on topics relating to the Redeemed South (see especially p. 226, n. 13). Even as late as *Pudd'nhead Wilson* (1894) Twain was insisting that the material about fingerprinting was "absolutely fresh, and mighty curious and interesting to everybody" (*Mark Twain's Letters,* II, 591).

38. See, for example, the chapter "Sentiment and Sensation in the Sixties and Seventies" in Frank Luther Mott's *Golden Multitudes* (New York, 1947) pp. 143-48.

39. "Mark Twain" in Spiller *et al.*, *Literary History of the United States* (New York, 1953), p. 922.

40. *A History of American Literature Since 1870* (New York, 1915), p. 56.

41. *Mark Twain in Eruption*, ed. Bernard DeVoto (New York, 1940), pp. 202-3.

42. *Mark Twain's Letters*, II, 527.

43. Dixon Wecter, "Mark Twain," *Literary History of the United States*, p. 922. As early as 1865, he was calling the profession of humorist an "unworthy & evanescent" one. See *My Dear Bro, A Letter from Samuel Clemens to his Brother Orion* (Berkeley, 1961), p. 8.

44. *Mark Twain-Howells Letters*, I, 90.

45. Vogelback, pp. 265-67.

46. Herbert Feinstein, "Mark Twain & The Pirates," *Harvard Law School Bulletin*, XIII (April 1962), 11.

47. See *Mark Twain-Howells Letters*, I, 145.

48. *Ibid.*, pp. 208, 250.

49. *Ibid.*, I, 193. Twain discussed the same sort of audience with the same perspective in his later years when he mused about what he called "submerged renown." See *Mark Twain's Autobiography*, ed. Albert B. Paine (New York, 1924), I, 248-50.

NOTES ON THE CRITICS

CHARLES HENRY WEBB (1834-1905): American publisher, inventor, playwright, columnist, broker, humorist, whaler, founder and editor of the *Californian* in 1864; early friend of Mark Twain and Bret Harte.

BRET HARTE (1836-1902): Extremely popular American humorist, editor, poet, short story writer, dramatist, novelist; early friend and late enemy of Mark Twain.

GEORGE T. FERRIS (1840-?): American author, traveler, historian, biographer, music scholar; books include a long history of the Johnstown flood, *Great German Composers* (1878), *Great Leaders: Historic Portraits* (1889).

JOHN NICHOL (1833-94): Scottish poet, lecturer, critic, biographer, professor at Glasgow University; fiery and independent thinker; author of article on American literature in 1882 *Encyclopaedia Britannica*.

H. R. HAWEIS (1838-1901): English clergyman, traveler, critic, author of *Music and Morals* (1871), *American Humorists* (1882), *Travel and Talk* (1896).

OLIVER WENDELL HOLMES (1809-94): A leading New England Brahmin and popular poet, essayist, novelist, biographer, lecturer, wit; physician and Dean of Harvard Medical School.

ANDREW LANG (1844-1912): Distinguished Scottish poet, biographer, classicist, translator, critic, essayist, historian, editor (Poe, Scott, Burns, Dickens), folklorist; prolific and erudite in many different fields.

FRANK R. STOCKTON (1834-1902): American magazine editor, popular novelist and short story writer — greatly admired for ingenuity and humor.

HENRY C. VEDDER (1853-1935): American clergyman, journalist, church historian, literary critic; on editorial staff of Baptist newspaper, then professor in theological seminary.

CHARLES MINER THOMPSON (1864-1941): American author, critic, literary editor of *Boston Advertiser,* for many years editor of *Youth's Companion*.

WILLIAM DEAN HOWELLS (1837-1920):Prolific American author of novels, plays, poems, travel books, short stories, influential criticism;

editor of *Atlantic Monthly* and later of "Easy Chair" department in *Harper's Magazine;* champion of early realists and friend of many — especially Mark Twain.

WILLIAM LYON PHELPS (1865-1943): Famed professor of English at Yale for forty-one years, popular essayist, lecturer, critic, syndicated columnist; conducted "As I Like It" department for *Scribner's Magazine;* when a boy was neighbor of Mark Twain.

CHARLES WHIBLEY (1859-1930): English scholar and critic, connected with *Scots Observer,* instituted the Tudor Translations, contributed to *Spectator, Daily Mail,* and monthly for thirty years to *Blackwood's,* where he was noted for his violent attacks on many popular opinions.

ARCHIBALD HENDERSON (1877-1963): American professor of mathematics, studied under Einstein in Germany; biographer (Shaw's "American Boswell"), essayist, historian. "He's the only man in the world," said W. L. Phelps, "who can talk professionally on equal terms with Einstein and Shaw."

G. K. CHESTERTON (1874-1936): Popular English poet, novelist, critic, journalist, historian, short story writer; wrote books on Browning, Dickens, Blake, Shaw, St. Francis of Assisi; also created Father Brown, the priest-detective.

STUART P. SHERMAN (1881-1926): American professor, New Humanist, critic, carried on lively warfare with H. L. Mencken, edited book section of *New York Herald Tribune.*

HENRY VAN DYKE (1852-1933): American professor, poet, essayist, dramatist, diplomat, translator, author, lecturer, Presbyterian clergyman; devoted his life to fusing religion with the enjoyment of everyday life.

JOHN MACY (1877-1932): American critic, historian, editor, whose radical social views influenced his judgment of authors (especially revered literary figures); urged use of regional materials in fiction; husband of Anne Sullivan Macy, who was tutor of Helen Keller.

WALDO FRANK (1889-): American newspaperman, editor, novelist, translator, critic; specializes in interpreting modern culture (especially of Latin America); author of books also on Spain, Russia, Israel, Cuba.

VAN WYCK BROOKS (1886-1963): A leading American critic, essayist, biographer, literary historian; his "Finders and Makers" series of books reviews U.S. literary and cultural history in a carefully re-searched yet popular fashion.

BRANDER MATTHEWS (1852-1929): Professor at Columbia University, critic, essayist, editor, short story writer, dramatist; prolific writer on French and English drama; president of Modern Language Association 1910; friend of Mark Twain, who teased him about his sinister name.

GAMALIEL BRADFORD (1863-1932): American biographer, poet (2,000 poems), dramatist (15 plays: one printed, none produced); wealthy invalid; major work was series of 114 "psychographs" — character sketches of well-known figures.

VERNON LOUIS PARRINGTON (1871-1929): American professor, literary historian, biographer, critic, Pulitzer Prize winner; opposed belletristic approach to literature and focused on writers close to the economic, political, and social thought of their day.

CONSTANCE ROURKE (1885-1941): American teacher, biographer (Davy Crockett, Audubon, *et al.*); specialized in American humor and folklore; sought to relate arts (in broadest sense) to U.S. culture; admired for the originality of her research.

V. F. CALVERTON (1900-1940): American critic and editor; founded *Modern Quarterly* (left-wing organ); his books interpreted U.S. from Marxist point of view, but opposed Stalinism; wrote one novel and one book of short stories.

GRANVILLE HICKS (1901-): American professor, literary critic, novelist, radio broadcaster, editor, lecturer; once on staff of *New Masses,* but a strong anticommunist since 1939; currently writes "Literary Horizons" page in *Saturday Review.*

WALTER BLAIR (1900-): Professor at University of Chicago, where he has taught and inspired more Twainians than has anyone else; has written widely on American humor and folk themes, sometimes in collaboration with Franklin J. Meine; author of the invaluable *Mark Twain & Huck Finn* (1960).

DE LANCEY FERGUSON (1888-1966): Professor at Brooklyn College; critic of the short story; editor of poems and letters of Burns; author of biography of Burns and of excellent *Mark Twain: Man and Legend* (1943).

BERNARD DE VOTO (1897-1955): Harvard professor, critic, historian, voluminous writer with wide interests, lecturer, occupant of

Harper's Magazine's "Easy Chair" 1935-55; author of *Mark Twain's America* (1932), *Mark Twain at Work* (1942); literary executor of Mark Twain Estate 1937-46.

LIONEL TRILLING (1905-): Professor at Columbia University, critic, essayist, biographer, novelist, editorial adviser for several periodicals; books include *Matthew Arnold* (1937), *The Liberal Imagination* (1950), *Freud and the Crisis of Our Culture* (1955).

HENRY SEIDEL CANBY (1878-1961): American professor, critic, biographer, editor; cofounder and first editor of *Saturday Review of Literature* (1924); first chairman of editorial board of Book-of-the-Month Club (from 1926, for twenty-eight years); books on Thoreau and Whitman; called by Allan Nevins "the most constructive single figure on the literary scene."

JOHN C. GERBER (1908-): American professor, critic, lecturer, editor; author of Mark Twain chapter in annual *American Literary Scholarship*; chairman of editorial board of forthcoming authoritative edition of Mark Twain's works; past president of National Council of Teachers of English and Midwest Modern Language Association.

HAMLIN HILL (1931-): American professor, critic, editor; author of *Mark Twain and Elisha Bliss* (1964), and of forthcoming *Mark Twain's Letters to His Publishers;* edited with introductions *Huckleberry Finn* (1962), *A Connecticut Yankee* (1963), *The Gilded Age* for forthcoming authoritative (Gerber) edition of Mark Twain's works.